Historical Problems:
Studies and Documents

Edited by

PROFESSOR G. R. ELTON
University of Cambridge

24

THE COMING OF THE FRIARS

THE COMING
OF THE FRIARS

Rosalind B. Brooke

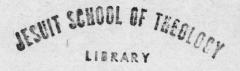
LONDON: GEORGE ALLEN & UNWIN LTD
NEW YORK: BARNES & NOBLE BOOKS
(A division of Harper & Row Publishers, Inc.)

British ISBN 0 04 942045 3
American ISBN 0-06-490700-7

Published in the U.S.A., 1975 by
HARPER & ROW PUBLISHERS, INC.
BARNES & NOBLE IMPORT DIVISION

Printed in Great Britain
in 10 point Plantin type
at the Alden Press, Oxford

AUTHOR'S NOTE

' "How did they come here?" . . . "In the Usual Way, if you know what I mean, Pooh", and Pooh, who didn't, said "Oh!" Then he nodded his head twice and said, "In the Usual Way. Ah!" '

Historically the phrase 'the coming of the friars' seems to have been coined by or for the English chronicler Thomas of Eccleston who in the mid-thirteenth century described the arrival of the Franciscans in England, and the establishment, organisation and progress of their province there. In this book my aim has been to seek the mainsprings of the two great acts of creation which produced the Franciscan and Dominican Orders in the first quarter of the thirteenth century. This means that there can be little space for Eccleston's theme – their spread and growth after the founders' deaths – still less for the development of that ambiguous reputation which led, for example, to bitter conflicts in the University of Paris in the mid-thirteenth century and inspired Chaucer to his portrait of the wanton, grasping friar of his Prologue in the late fourteenth. I cannot attempt to sketch the other Orders, neither the tiny groups which disappeared, nor the two Orders of Carmelite Friars and Austin Friars which survived. This means that my book is incomplete; and in legend the Carmelites, who claimed a link with Elijah's stay on Mount Carmel, and the Austin Friars who in more modest fact sprang partly from hermit groups formed in the twelfth century, perhaps have a right to be considered older than the Orders with which I deal. Yet, to explain the friars as an historical phenomenon, the essential task seems to me to compare the aims of the two founder saints with those of their predecessors and rivals of earlier generations, to explain what was old and what was new. Strict adherence to chronology would make such a comparison difficult to follow; and for this reason I have sandwiched 'The Preparation' between chapters on Francis and Dominic.

R.B.B.

ACKNOWLEDGEMENTS

It is a pleasure to acknowledge the generous help I have received: and I warmly thank the General Editor, Professor Geoffrey Elton; the staff of Messrs George Allen and Unwin Ltd; Dr J. V. Fearns, to whom I owe much in the section on Peter of Bruis and in the choice of documents, as references to his work, to his Thesis (to which he kindly allows me to refer) and to his own very useful selection of documents in Latin, *Ketzer und Ketzerbekämpfung im Hochmittelalter* (Göttingen, 1968), will show; and the many others who have helped and encouraged me, particularly Miss Brenda Bolton, Dr Christopher Holdsworth and, most especially, Professor Robert Markus, for kindly reading the book in draft, and my husband, Professor Christopher Brooke, for his constant, unstinted collaboration.

Most of the translations of documents are my own, though I have often benefited from the interpretations of others. Document 11 is from Dr Marjorie Chibnall's edition and translation of John of Salisbury's *Historia Pontificalis*, and I am very grateful to her and to Messrs Thomas Nelson and Sons for permission to use it; also hers are the quotations from *The Ecclesiastical History of Orderic Vitalis* on pp. 44–5, 49, 55, for which too she generously gave permission, as did the Delegates of the Oxford University Press, who have also allowed me to use my own version of *Scripta Leonis, Rufini et Angeli* . . . in Document 6. I thank the Honorary Secretary of the Honourable Society of Cymmrodorion for permission to use the late M. R. James's translation of Walter Map, *De nugis curialium*, on pp. 46–8, 60, 151–2, and for Document 13. Document 26, Matthew Paris, is based on the translation of J. A. Giles, which I have adapted.

ABBREVIATIONS

Abbreviations	*Full Title*
1, 2 Cel.	Thomas of Celano, *Vita Prima* (First Life) and *Vita Secunda* (Second Life), in *Analecta Franciscana*, Vol. X (Quaracchi, 1926–41), pp. 1–117, 127–268.
EFG	R. B. Brooke, *Early Franciscan Government, Elias to Bonaventure* (Cambridge, 1959).
Eubel	*See below*, under Sbaralea.
Fearns	*Ketzer und Ketzerbekämpfung im Hochmittelalter* (selected Latin texts), ed. J. V. Fearns (Göttingen, 1968).
Grundmann	H. Grundmann, *Religiöse Bewegungen im Mittelalter* (Hildesheim, 1961), 2nd edn.
Maisonneuve	H. Maisonneuve, *Études sur les origines de l'Inquisition* (Paris, 1960), 2nd edn.
Mandonnet-Vicaire	P. Mandonnet and M.-H. Vicaire, *Saint Dominique, l'idée, l'homme et l'oeuvre* (Paris, 1937), 2 vols.
MGH SS	*Monumenta Germaniae Historica, Scriptores.*
MOPH	*Monumenta Ordinis Fratrum Praedicatorum Historica.*
Opuscula	*Opuscula sancti patris Francisci* (Bibliotheca Franciscana Ascetica Medii Aevi, Vol. I), (Quaracchi, 1941), 2nd edn.
PL	*Patrologiae Cursus Completus, series Latina*, ed. J. P. Migne (Paris, 1844–64), 221 vols.
Sabatier	P. Sabatier, *Vie de S. François d'Assise* (Paris, 1894 (1893)), Eng. trans. by L. S. Houghton (edn of London–New York, 1922).
Sbaralea	*Bullarium Franciscanum*, Vol. I, ed. J. H. Sbaralea (Rome, 1759); reference is also given to Eubel, i.e. C. Eubel, *Bullarii Franciscani Epitome* (Quaracchi, 1908).
Sherley-Price	L. Sherley-Price, *S. Francis of Assisi* (London, 1959), with translations of *The Mirror of Perfection* and St Francis's writings.
SL	*Scripta Leonis, Rufini et Angeli sociorum S.*

	Francisci: the Writings of Leo, Rufino and Angelo, Companions of St Francis, ed. and trans. R. B. Brooke (Oxford Medieval Texts, 1970).
Testimonia Minora	*Testimonia Minora saeculi XIII de S. Francisco Assisiensi*, ed. L. Lemmens (Quaracchi, 1926).
Thouzellier	C. Thouzellier, *Catharisme et Valdéisme en Languedoc à la fin du XIIe et au début du XIIIe siècle* (Louvain–Paris, 1969), 2nd edn.
Vicaire (1964)	M.-H. Vicaire, *Histoire de S. Dominique* (Paris, 1957), 2 vols; cited from English translation by K. Pond (London, 1964).
Vicaire (1965)	M.-H. Vicaire, *Saint Dominique: la vie apostolique* (Paris, 1965).
Vicaire (1967)	M.-H. Vicaire, *Saint Dominique et ses frères: évangile ou croisade?* (Paris, 1967).

CONTENTS

DOCUMENTS

INTRODUCTION

Prologue

The wider the variety of sources we can study the fuller and deeper our understanding of a historical problem is likely to be. These sources include not only documents but paintings and buildings and other physical remains. The medieval Orders of friars have left physical traces: churches, conventual buildings, place and street names. They have been painted in frescoes, altar pieces, crosses. Anyone who goes to Albi, or to Caleruega, or to Assisi, can discover, from the buildings and localities connected with the saints, and from the countryside itself and its inhabitants, an imaginative insight into the life and work of St Dominic or St Francis. If we cannot travel, photographs are helpful. Excellent pictorial biographies, with photographs especially taken by von Matt provide a vivid and evocative introduction.[1]

The Franciscans and Dominicans have continued in existence, and so there is also here a living witness. The passage of time has brought substantial changes. Only perhaps the Carthusians among medieval religious orders have succeeded in maintaining a mode of life virtually unchanged throughout their history. Yet the friars continue to profess the Rules sanctioned for them by Pope Honorius III early in the thirteenth century and many of the essential elements of their original apostolate can be seen still at work today.

This book sets out to explore and to illustrate what we may learn from another category of sources, which normally provides the bulk of the historian's raw material – the written documents left by the people or institutions we are studying.

To be fully useful to the historian, source material, of whatever kind, has to be properly understood and analysed. If I were to take a spade to the top of the Wrekin and start to dig, I might find a piece of old iron, but I would discover for myself nothing of moment about the

---

[1] L. von Matt and W. Hauser, *St Francis of Assisi*; L. von Matt and M.-H. Vicaire, *St Dominic* (Eng. trans., London, 1956–7); see also photographs of Assisi by Wim Swaan in C. Brooke and Wim Swaan, *The Monastic World 1000–1300* (London, 1974).

prehistoric community that made its home there. Worse, my untutored exertions might actually destroy evidence that an archaeologist could have used and made revealing. Scientific excavations need experienced guidance both in their execution and in the interpretation of what is found. The historian is dependent upon the techniques and expertise of a whole variety of disciplines – not only archaeology, but, for example, air photography, statistics, languages, dead and living, palaeography and diplomatic, which enable him to read and to determine the provenance and date of manuscripts. Skills such as these, whether he acquires them himself or benefits from their application by others, render his material intelligible and usable. The documents offered here have been processed – collected, deciphered, translated, selected. The student of medieval history is fortunate that his sources are finite. In the modern world the bulk of documentation can become unmanageable. Records deposited at the Public Record Office have doubled in bulk in the last forty years and are currently accumulating at the rate of more than a mile a year. For the early Middle Ages the problem is to find and interpret the scanty remains of the small deposit which is all that there ever was. By the thirteenth century more people and greater prosperity have left many more traces, so that even on a limited theme it is not possible to include anything like all the important, let alone all the relevant, documents. The documents and excerpts of documents included here have been chosen because they yield a cross-section of the types of source that can be used. It is a personal selection, intended not only to try to reveal from many different angles the significance and interest of the Orders of friars but also to illustrate how twelfth- and thirteenth-century sources can be critically but sympathetically handled and interpreted. An example will show what this can mean.

'When St Francis was at St Mary of the Portiuncula for the General Chapter which was called the Chapter of Mats, where five thousand friars were present, a number of wise and well-educated friars said to the cardinal who was later Pope Gregory, who was present at the Chapter, that he should persuade St Francis to follow the advice of wise friars like themselves and allow himself to be sometimes guided by them. They cited the Rule of St Benedict, of St Augustine and of St Bernard which teach how to live thus, and thus, methodically. When he had listened to the cardinal's advocacy on this, St Francis took him by the hand and led him to the friars assembled in chapter and addressed them thus: "My brothers! My brothers! God has called me by the way of simplicity and shown me the way of simplicity. I do not want you to name any Rule to me, not St Augustine's, nor St Bernard's, nor St Benedict's. The Lord said to me that he wished that I should be a new-born simpleton in the world. God did not want to lead us by another way than by this kind of learning, but God will confound you through your learning and your wisdom. I have faith in God's constables, that through them he will punish you and you will return to your condition to your shame, whether you like it or not." The cardinal was flabbergasted and said nothing, and all the friars were afraid.'[1]

This story provides a convenient starting-point and exposes a vital problem. In a dramatic form it introduces the main protagonists and it is itself one of our sources. It comes from a small collection of stories known as the *Verba Sancti Francisci*, which circulated in the early fourteenth century – a century after St Francis that is – and in Spiritual circles, who used it as propaganda in their bitter quarrel with the Conventuals over the Order's fidelity to its founder. Should it then be dismissed as a late and tendentious tract? The leaders of the Spirituals claimed that the *Verba* was written by a first-rate authority, by brother Leo, St Francis's confessor and his close companion in his later years. This attribution, and the date at which the tract was written, have posed most complicated and technical problems: problems of manuscript tradition and authority, of style and content and credibility. I have argued in detail elsewhere the grounds for believing that the *Verba* was written in the mid-thirteenth century, and by brother Leo.[2]

The story concentrates as in a nutshell issues with which this book will attempt to deal. The old and the new are sharply juxtaposed. St Francis restated for his own time the Pauline paradox that a Christian must become a fool to gain true wisdom (1 Cor., 3:18). His message was evidently popular – even if we discount the figure of five thousand, the Order was growing rapidly. But certain of his educated followers were not happy about it and thought they knew better. They enlisted a future Pope, patron of both Orders of friars, who on this occasion ranged himself on the side of the conservatives. St Francis repudiated their attempt to impose the pattern of the old monastic Orders, emphatically and with success.

What was the significance of this? How new were the friars?

[1] *SL*, No. 114.
[2] *SL*, pp. 57–66.

St Francis[1]

St Francis called himself and his followers Friars Minor. It was a new name, to signify, he once said, a company of people differing in humility and in poverty from all who had gone before, and content to possess Christ alone. He coined it in 1210 when, twelve in number like the apostles, they went at his instigation to Rome where he persuaded the Pope, Innocent III, to approve for them a simple Rule based on the Gospel. Though, as we shall see, he had precursors, advisers and helpers, St Francis was the originator of friars as distinct from other religious, and was himself in this sense the first friar. If we want to know what a friar essentially is, we cannot do better than begin with him.

[1] On the sources, see Docs 1–7, 23–6 below; J. R. H. Moorman, *Sources for the Life of St Francis of Assisi* (Manchester, 1940); Brooke, in *Latin Biography*, ed. T. A. Dorey (London, 1967), pp. 177–98; Brooke, *Early Franciscan Government* (Cambridge, 1959), Chap. 1; and *SL*, introduction. But the two classic studies are still well worth reading: P. Sabatier, *Vie de S. François d'Assise* (Paris, 1893/4) Eng. trans. by L. S. Houghton (London, edn of 1926), pp. 347–432, and F. C. Burkitt, in *St Francis of Assisi: Essays in Commemoration* (London, 1926), pp. 15–61. The writings of Francis are edited in *Opuscula* (Quaracchi, 1941), 2nd edn, and translated by L. Sherley-Price, *St Francis of Assisi* (London, 1959); Thomas of Celano's *Lives* and others, including Bonaventure's, were edited in *Analecta Franciscana*, Vol. X (Quaracchi, 1926–41), and translated by A. G. Ferrers Howell (London, 1908); St Bonaventure's, with the *Mirror of Perfection*, is in the Everyman *Little Flowers* (i.e. *Fioretti*) (London, 1910); the writings of the companions are in *SL*. I do not discuss here the date and status of the so-called *Legend of the Three Companions*, on which see Moorman (op. cit.) and Brooke in *Latin Biography*, pp. 188f.

On Francis, Sabatier is still the most remarkable (see C. Brooke, *Medieval Church and Society* (London, 1971), Chap. 10); correctives in Fr Cuthbert, *Life of St Francis of Assisi* (London, 1912), and numerous others. On the Order, D. Knowles, *Religious Orders in England* (Cambridge, 1948–59), 3 vols; J. R. H. Moorman, *A History of the Franciscan Order* [to 1517] (Oxford, 1968); P. Gratien, *Histoire de la Fondation et de l'évolution de l'ordre des Frères Mineurs au xiiie siècle* (Paris-Gembloux, 1928); for early chronicles, see below Chap. 7 and Doc. 25.

His Life

St Francis was born c. 1181. He was the son of a wealthy cloth merchant and as a young man had ambitions to become a knight and do deeds of chivalry. But he became dissastisfied with the gay and extravagant mode of life possible to himself and his friends, and increasingly conscious of the contrast between his own good fortune and the misery, poverty and sickness he saw around him. He had a particular horror of leprosy, but one day when he met a leper he forced himself not only to give him alms but to kiss him. The experience was climacteric. The normally accepted values and attitudes to which he had hitherto conformed underwent a profound reversal. From now on he rejected wealth and honour and comfort, all the material advantages that are normally desired, and positively sought poverty and suffering. He describes his conversion in his Testament: 'The Lord granted me, brother Francis, to begin to do penance in this way, that, when I was in sin, it seemed to me very horrible to see lepers, and the Lord himself led me among them and I helped them. And when I left them that which had before seemed to me horrible was transformed into sweetness of body and soul. After that I remained only a little time before I left the world' (Doc. 1).

One day he was praying in a little church just outside the walls of Assisi, the church of San Damiano, when he thought the painted crucifix above the altar spoke to him: 'Francis, go and repair my house, which you see is in ruins.'[1] This was to be interpreted later as signifying the revival that Francis was to bring about in the church, a revival which many believed actually saved it from being engulfed by heresy or split by a premature reformation. But Francis understood it, as he was to understand the Gospel calling, quite literally. He went through the streets begging for stones. Many thought him mad and his father was furious. Francis had taken some of his father's cloth to market and sold it, intending to use the money to help rebuild the church, but his father, when he found he could not compel his son to return home and take what he considered his proper place in the family business, demanded the money back. Francis returned it to him, in public, in the square in front of the bishop's palace, and not only the money. He took off his clothes and gave them back too, saying: 'Now I will say freely: "Our Father who art in heaven, not father Peter Bernardone"; for I now surrender to him not only his money, but all my clothes. Naked I will go to the Lord.'[2] Thus dramatically and symbolically Francis renounced his family and all it stood for. He could not have made a

---

[1] Thomas of Celano, *Vita Secunda* (2 Cel.), c. 10; cf. von Matt and W. Hauser, *St Francis of Assisi*, pl. 26 (the crucifix).

[2] 2 Cel., c. 12.

more effective protest. His extraordinary success as a teacher was partly due to his readiness to exaggerate and to dramatise, capturing the imagination of his audience.

After about two years devoted to solitary prayer, the care of lepers and the repair of dilapidated churches, Francis's vocation took final shape. He heard a priest read from the Gospel Jesus's instructions to his disciples when he sent them out to preach: 'As you go proclaim the message: "the kingdom of heaven is upon you".... Provide no gold, silver or copper to fill your purse, no pack for the road, no second coat, no shoes, no stick; the worker earns his keep' (Matt., 10:7-10). Francis took this to heart as a personal command and acted on it immediately. He kicked off his shoes and, dressed only in the simple grey tunic tied with a cord that became the habit of his Order, set out to preach. He lived as he understood the apostles had lived, obeying the Gospel himself and calling on others to do the same.

His Order began very simply. When a citizen of Assisi, called Bernard, asked to join him they opened the Gospel together for guidance on how to proceed, and the first words they read were: 'if you wish to be perfect, go, sell your possessions, and give to the poor, and then you will have riches in heaven; and come, follow me' (Matt., 19:21). So Bernard distributed all his wealth to the poor. Others quickly followed his example. Almost immediately, when they were only eight in number, Francis sent them out as missionaries, as Christ had sent out his apostles. His instructions to them, as reported by his first biographer, Thomas of Celano, were a conflation of excerpts from the Gospels, the Acts of the Apostles and the Epistles.[1] 'Go, in pairs', he said, 'through the different parts of the world, proclaiming peace to men, and repentance for the remission of sins. Be patient in trouble, confident that God will keep his promise. Reply humbly to questions, bless your persecutors, give thanks to those who injure and slander you, since on their account the kingdom of heaven is prepared for us.'

The early Friars Minor did indeed suffer abuse and maltreatment, as well as privation, in the course of their missions. Since they had chosen to go about as ragged, barefoot, dirty, vagabond beggars, it is not surprising that their reception was not always friendly. They were taken for thieves, for heretics, for scroungers. Yet they made progress. In 1210 Innocent III gave them his blessing and authorised their penitential preaching. For a few years slowly and then with ever increasing rapidity their numbers grew, and their influence extended. Soon they felt they needed, and acquired, organisation and its attendant administrators. Institutionalisation set in. They became an Order of Friars Minor, owing its origin, its life, its inspiration to St Francis, yet distinct

[1] I Cel., c. 29; see notes to Quaracchi edition.

from him with its own corporate identity, its own problems, its own history. St Francis was averse to exercising management control. He entrusted the running and disciplining of the Order to others, confining himself on the whole to giving a living example to his followers. He died in 1226, in his early forties, worn out, blind, suffering from painful illnesses brought on by the life he had chosen. But he welcomed death with a song.

The Interpretation of Francis – Materials and Approach

What had he achieved? Judged by ordinary worldly standards his folly turned out to be spectacularly successful. He died head of a new religious Order that was eclipsing the older in popularity and papal favour. His followers numbered thousands and were spread all over Europe and beyond. He bore on his body the marks of the wounds of the Crucifixion – he is the first person known ever to have done so – and was already regarded and venerated as a saint. If we want to pursue the question and to understand what he did and why, the sources are unusually numerous and varied. The most important for this purpose can be classified as biographies, collections of stories that circulated in written form and orally, and his own writings. The biographies and the collections of stories were written after his death, but facts about him, anecdotes, reminiscences began to be recorded very soon after his death and by people who knew him. The earliest biography, the *First Life* (*Vita Prima*) of Thomas of Celano, commissioned by Pope Gregory IX, was written as early as 1228–9 and provided 'an elegant, brief, authentic and yet edifying statement of Francis's life, personality and sanctity'.[1] In 1246 in response to an appeal for further information to be gathered and recorded while there were friars still living who had known St Francis, three of his close companions, Leo, Rufino and Angelo, sent in a collection of stories. 'We who, though unworthy, lived long in his company thought it right to send in ... – with strict attention to truth – a few accounts of his many acts, which we ourselves have seen, or could discover from other holy friars. ... We were not content simply to narrate miracles, which do not create, but only demonstrate holiness; we wished to make known striking examples of his discourse and his holy will and pleasure. ... We have picked as it were from a field of flowers those we thought the more fair. ...' These stories were utilised by Celano in his *Second Life* (*Vita Secunda*), produced in 1247, and were disseminated in a variety of tracts and compilations, especially in the early fourteenth century, when they formed the basis of the *Mirror of Perfection*.[2]

[1] Brooke in *Latin Biography*, ed. T. A. Dorey (London, 1967), p. 186; the quotation which follows is in *SL*, pp. 87, 89.   [2] See *SL*, and below, Doc 6.

Biographies, anthologies, mentions in chronicles and the like reveal St Francis's life and aims as seen by others. What have we of his own? Not all he wrote has survived, but there remains a fair sample: letters, admonitions, prayers and praises, including the Canticle of Brother Sun, unlike the rest composed not in Latin but in Italian, the earliest recorded Italian song, two versions of his Rule, and the Testament. From these we should gain an impression of what St Francis thought important and what he was trying to do. We will begin with the last, his Testament, written not long before his death (Doc. 1).

The Testament

This is hardly a will in the ordinary sense. Francis refused to possess anything. He lived without settled home, a beggar in borrowed clothes. He had nothing material to leave. But he had caused others to profess the Rule God had inspired him to write and he was acutely conscious of the imperative need to be himself, in his own life, a model and example to all his friars. What he did want to hand on was the witness of his life for their encouragement and guidance. The Testament is his autobiography. It is short, but it contains, clearly stated, the points he considered fundamental. Francis described himself as ignorant and claimed to write simply and purely. Yet he was articulate, and in this case, or so it seems to me, the simple words had been very carefully thought out. What emerges from the Testament? Something very different from the sentimental picture of the romantic enthusiast who married Lady Poverty and preached to the birds. Three things are emphasised: faith, the apostolic life, and obedience. After recording how in his own experience contact with lepers, the afflicted, sick, poor, hopeless, shunned outcasts of society, transformed his understanding of values, Francis at the outset affirmed his faith in churches and in priests. Priests he reverenced for the sake of their office, regardless of their individual personal fitness, because they and they alone are privileged to consecrate and administer the sacrament. His reverence for the word of God was all-embracing, from its simplest manifestations, pieces of paper with writing on them, to the teaching of the theologians. Next he testified to the personal call he had received to model his life on the Gospel and he briefly characterised the apostolic life, as he had had it written in the Rule which the Pope had confirmed. He reminds his brothers of how he and his followers had lived and that he wished them all to work, to be content with such clothing as the apostles had worn and with humble lodgings, consistent with the poverty and defencelessness incumbent on them. Wishes and exhortation escalate into commands. They are firmly ordered on obedience not to seek any privileges or concessions, however good the cause, to obey their own officers, to say the office according to the rite of the Roman Church, to apprehend any of their members who are not catholic and bring them before the Cardinal Protector. Finally they are to read the Testament together with the Rule and observe them both literally. Not even the Minister General is to have the authority to add or subtract from these documents, or gloss them. Thus, in the Testament, St Francis was trying to bind his successors. Such attempts, even if well-intentioned, are neither proper nor practical; he was not successful.

Later Interpretation of the Testament

Within four years the Order wanted the Testament abrogated and the Pope agreed – the Friars Minor were not legally bound by the Testament, Gregory IX declared in the bull *Quo elongati*, 'though you should conform in all things to Francis's just prayers and holy desires'.[1] The rather strange medley of conflicting good intentions, which runs right through the papal pronouncement, reflects a corresponding unease and conflict of aspirations among the friars, which is perhaps one reason why a solution that was neither consistent nor in much of its detail acceptable was made the foundation of what was to be an abiding compromise. Although the Pope told them they were not under obligation to obey the Testament, they did not cease to reverence Francis's wishes. The great majority did not remain content with what was compulsory; some went so far as to make fidelity to Francis's wishes an absolute priority, regarding any deviation as a betrayal of his ideal. It was even claimed that the Testament had greater moral authority than the Rule because St Francis had written it after the imprint of the stigmata. Disagreement polarised into bitter controversy between conventual and spiritual parties within the Order, and because this happened the Testament has been seen and interpreted in the context of conflict. Angelo Clareno, a leader of the Spirituals in the early fourteenth century, wrote: 'Francis promises obedience . . . to the Pope and his successors – who neither can nor ought to command anything which is contrary to conscience and the Rule.' And Paul Sabatier, who quotes this passage in his great life of St Francis, published in 1893–4, says this of the Testament:

'it is to these pages that we must go to find the true note for a sketch of the life of its author, and an idea of the Order as it was in his dreams. . . . The individual conscience here proclaims its sovereign authority. "No one showed me what I ought to do, but the Most High himself revealed to me that I ought to live conformably to his holy Gospel." When a man has once spoken thus, submission to the

[1] Sbaralea, pp. 68–70 (Greg. IX, No. 56); Eubel, *Supplementum*, No. IV.

Church has been singularly encroached upon. We may love her, harken to her, venerate her, but we feel ourselves, perhaps without daring to avow it, superior to her. Let a critical hour come, and one finds oneself a heretic without knowing it or wishing it.'[1]

Sabatier tried to think himself into the past, to give himself, as he said, 'a heart of the thirteenth century', but here the fact that he was a Protestant pastor has undoubtedly coloured his appreciation of what St Francis wrote. His subjective approach gave him a rare imaginative insight, but he saw most clearly what most attracted him, and an incomplete portrait can be partial and misleading. A. G. Little assessed Sabatier's achievements thus:

'Sabatier was . . . the first to recognise the paramount importance of St Francis's own writings as authorities for his life and thought, and the first to use them effectively as a touchstone of the authenticity of other sources. . . . But I, for one, certainly did not realise from the *Vie de S. François d'Assise* the undoubted fact that the central subject of all the general letters of St Francis was the sacrament of the Body and Blood of Christ.'[2]

As a result of criticism Sabatier developed and deepened his understanding. The originality of St Francis, he announced, in an inspired essay, was in his catholicism. This might not seem very surprising: thousands of others were catholic. But Francis's catholicism was exceptional, not, he now emphasised, in being individualistic or verging towards schism or heresy, but quite simply because Francis had advanced so far along the road that others have difficulty in following him even with their eyes. Francis's faith was so profound and so natural that all his spiritual progress was made instinctively as a son of the Church – a son not a slave. He was profoundly submissive and he was perfectly free.[3]

Obedience in the Testament, Salutatio Virtutum *and the Admonitions*
Aided by the Testament itself and the light thrown on it by scholars, we can perhaps go on to examine further Francis's attitude to obedience, central to an understanding of his position and his achievement, and a

[1] Sabatier, Eng. trans., p. 334 (slightly adapted), citing a letter by Clareno, ed. F. Ehrle in *Archiv für Litteratur- und Kirchengeschichte . . .*, Vol. I (Berlin, 1885), p. 563.
[2] A. G. Little, *Franciscan Papers, Lists and Documents* (Manchester, 1943), p. 182.
[3] P. Sabatier, 'L'originalité de Saint François d'Assise', in *Franciscan Essays* (British Soc. of Franciscan Studies, 1912), pp. 1–17, especially pp. 3–4, 7–9.

characteristically complex, paradoxical problem posed by this avowedly simple man. There are several different layers of obedience within the Testament itself. Francis evidently saw no incongruity in firmly resolving to obey the Minister General and then as firmly ordering him about. As founder he felt answerable for the souls of all who followed him – there are many stories illustrating his concern always to set a good example lest any should be scandalised or discouraged or harmed through failure on his part – but he also felt that his responsibility ended with teaching. His authority was spiritual and had no sanctions other than conscience. As an individual, he wished to coerce or punish no one, and to submit his personal will. The most arresting statement of his concept of obedience comes in his Salutation of the Virtues (*Salutatio Virtutum*), a personal selection which he groups in pairs: wisdom and simplicity, poverty and humility, love and obedience. They are heroic virtues, and before he can possess one a man must be born again. 'Holy obedience confounds all bodily and worldly desires and holds the mortified body obedient to the spirit and obedient to his fellow. It makes a man subject to all the men in the world and not only to men but even to animals and beasts that they may do with him what they will, so far as is given to them by the Lord from on high.' His thought is expressed in more practical idiom in one of his admonitions, on perfect and imperfect obedience.[1]

'Our Lord says in the Gospel: "None of you can be a disciple of mine without parting with all his possessions" (Luke, 14:33). And "whoever cares for his own safety is lost" (Matt., 16:25). That man parts with all his possessions and loses his body and soul who gives himself totally to obedience in the hands of his superior. Whatever he does or says, knowing it is not against the other's will, provided it is good, is true obedience. If ever the subject sees something that would be better and more useful to his soul than what his superior has ordered him, he shall sacrifice his will to God; he should take every care to put into effect what the superior has proposed. That which contents God and one's neighbour is true and loving obedience.

'If a superior should order a subject to do anything against his conscience, although he is not to obey yet he is not to renounce him, and if on this account others persecute him he is to love them the more for God's sake. He who prefers to suffer persecution than to separate himself from his brothers truly lives in perfect obedience, because "he lays down his life" (cf. John, 15:13) for his brothers. There are many religious who, on the pretext of seeing a better course than their superiors command, look back (cf. Luke, 9:62) and return

[1] *Opuscula*, pp. 20–1, 6–7.

to the vomit (cf. Prov., 26:11) of their own will. Such men are homicides; by their bad example many souls are lost.'

These are strong words. They make it clear that Francis was emphatic on the positive value to the individual of voluntary obedience – the third of the traditional monastic vows, poverty, chastity and obedience, which amounted to a triple renunciation of self, the giving up of material possessions, of the joys of marriage and of family, and of one's own desires and will. The obedience he envisaged was not blind – commands to do wrong were to be disobeyed, and punishment accepted for this disobedience – and it could be positive and total because it should be the response to an exercise of office in harmony with itself. His next admonition shows this side of the coin: if a man was given authority over others he should react in precisely the same way as if he were assigned the task of washing their feet (Admonition 4). His concept of office as service, conferring not importance or privilege but responsibility and obligations, and of obedience as life saving, was simply a restatement of Christ's teaching in the Gospel.

This is true in a very precise sense, for most of the admonitions open with a text or two from the Gospels, which Francis then expands into a little homily on the life of the friars. The Rule in its final form contains only about twelve quotations or substantial echoes, seven of them from the Gospels of Matthew and Luke; but in its earlier form (the *Regula Prima*) there are over a hundred biblical reminiscences of which well over eighty are from the Gospels, again preponderantly from Matthew and Luke. In spite of these figures, some passages from the Epistles also deeply influenced his thought, and occasionally he built an admonition round a saying of St Paul; the seventh (Doc. 3) is a good example.

Francis's Obedience in Practice

Actual translation of theory into practice was not easy for Francis. Though we need not doubt his conviction of his own readiness to obey a novice of an hour's standing,[1] many of the brothers stood in great awe of him. When he had a mind to do something they did not dare to cross him. His difficulty, and theirs, is caught in flashes of recorded conversation. Francis thought he had spoken inconsiderately about a leper, and therefore said to Peter Cathanii, whom he had appointed Minister, General and was fully resolved to obey in all things: 'I am going to tell you the penance that I wish to do . . . so that you can confirm it for me, and not contradict me at all.'[2] It would seem too that Francis was an early exponent of Rousseau's theory of the 'real' will. Time and

[1] *SL*, pp. 274–5.   [2] *SL*, p. 127.

again, he proposed to do something eccentric, which others initially disapproved, confident that he had only to explain his reason for them to concede; and usually they did. This applied even to cardinals. When Francis was staying with Hugolino, Bishop of Ostia and Cardinal Protector of the Order, he went out begging as usual although the cardinal was giving a dinner party. He came to table late and proceeded to distribute among the guests the stale, coarse scraps he had collected, to the embarrassment of his host. When Hugolino remonstrated privately with him afterwards he explained:

'No, my lord, I showed you great honour, since when a subordinate exercises and fulfils his office and obedience to his lord . . . he does honour to his lord. . . . It is necessary for me to be the model and example of your poor people . . . to teach those who are and will be in the Order how to act. . . . Certainly when I am staying with you, who are our lord and pope, or with great men, rich in worldly things . . . I do not want to be ashamed to go for alms; on the contrary I want to hold and keep it before God as a very regal and noble dignity and honour of the great king, who, although he is lord of all, wished for our sake to become the servant of all, and although he might be rich and glorious in his majesty, came to us poor and despised in our humanity. Therefore I want the friars who are and will be to know that I hold it a greater consolation of mind and body when I sit at the friars' poor board and see before me the poor alms which they have acquired from door to door for the love of the lord God, than when I sit at your board or that of other great men, abundantly provided with all foods, even though they are offered to me with great devotion. For the bread of alms is holy bread, which the praise and love of God sanctifies. . . .'

The cardinal could only reply: 'My son, do what is good in your eyes, since God is with you, and you with him.'[1]

Francis and the Community

The Francis depicted in the biographies, which rely chiefly on the externals, and the Francis of the writings are complementary, and support each other's evidence. He aimed to appear to others as he was. 'I want to live before God in hermitages and other places in the same way that men know and see me in public. For if they believe me to be a holy man and I do not live the life which befits holy men, I would be a hypocrite.' If food was specially prepared for him when he was ill, he took care that this should be well known. His first words in one sermon

[1] *SL*, No. 61.

to a great crowd of people were: 'You have come to me with great devotion, and believe me to be a holy man, but I confess to God and to you that in this time of fasting . . . I have eaten food cooked with lard.'[1] So we may turn from the salient features he himself emphasised in the Testament to the principles and attitudes revealed by a combination of all types of evidence.

He preached repentance and peace in an Italy in which strife was endemic. Assisi was intermittently involved in the struggle between Empire and Papacy, when imperial armies marched in the valley of Spoleto, and more frequently in local conflicts, notably with Perugia. The two cities stand on their hills within sight of each other, and their rivalry was of long standing: Perugia was Etruscan, Assisi Umbrian in origin. When Francis was a young man he took part in one of these neighbourly wars, was captured and spent a year in a Perugian prison. As a religious leader he made peace a keynote of his mission, and one of the stories told by his companions describes his righteous anger at being interrupted by tilting knights when he was preaching in the piazza at Perugia. 'We used to say a greeting which the Lord revealed to me: "The Lord give you peace" ', he says in his Testament (Doc. 1.) One of the companions described how this was received. 'In the early days of the movement, when St Francis was travelling with a friar who was one of the first twelve, this friar accordingly greeted men and women on the road, and those who were in the fields, saying: "The Lord give you peace." Since people had never before heard such a greeting given by religious, they were very much surprised and some almost indignant. "What do you mean by such a greeting?" they would say. So the friar began to feel very ashamed and said to St Francis: "Let us use another greeting, brother." St Francis said to him: "Let them talk on, because they do not perceive what things are of God." '[2]

His attitude to the different elements in the society of his day, as revealed in these documents, is of particular significance. He admitted into his own brotherhood, the Order of Friars Minor, manual labourers, brigands, knights, clerics, university doctors, anyone at all, provided he wanted to join, was orthodox, and was willing to give up all his possessions to the poor. Francis actually felt more confident of the vocation of ordinary simple people, regarding learning as an impediment which made it more difficult for a man to live as a fool for God's sake. 'When he was shaved', wrote Thomas of Celano in his *Second Life*, 'St Francis often said to the barber: "See that you do not give me a large tonsure. I want my simple brothers to have their portion of my head." For he wanted the Order to belong as well to the poor and the illiterate, not only to the rich and learned. "God has no favourites" (Romans,

[1] *SL*, No. 40.   [2] *SL*, No. 67.

2:11), he said, "and the Holy Spirit, Minister General of the Order, rests equally upon the poor and simple." [1]

Only men were eligible. Francis provided an Order for women, the Poor Ladies, or Clares, after St Clare, the first woman to answer Francis's call to a life of absolute poverty; she came to him in 1212, a young girl full of enthusiasm, devotion and fortitude, but she was not allowed to enter completely into the new life. Francis was pioneering for men; he was not able or willing to emancipate women, and Clare and her companions were presently confined in an enclosure in the traditional mode.

For the majority of people, especially for the married, a step so drastic as entry into a religious Order was not feasible; and for these he provided guiding rules they could follow in their own homes. The Order of Penitence, or Third Order, had antecedents in the monastic confraternities, of people linked to a particular monastery by the monks' prayers. There were also pious confraternities of men of like mind or interest, of city clergy, of weavers, of neighbours. These were often dedicated to helping their members in sickness or emergency, or to the promotion of some project, as, in London, to propping up St Paul's or building London Bridge. Such aspirations and examples fused with Francis's call to all men and women of this world to create a large-scale, orthodox and influential penitential movement.

Orthodox, for Francis was very emphatic in his loyalty to, and respect for, the clergy and the hierarchy of the Church. Some of the friars in the early days made their confession to a priest of notoriously ill repute because they refused to believe ill of him. Their trust may have been naïve, but it was in conformity with Francis's wishes. It was easy to criticise. Parish priests were all too often ignorant and poor and unimpressive. Scorn for priests who lived less well and honourably than members of their congregation alienated many pious laymen, and many so alienated joined groups of penitents more or less heretical.

Francis clearly wished to avoid this danger. He insisted that parish priests were to be honoured, and treated with respect and submission, on account of their office. He brushed aside as irrelevant the quality of their private lives, their qualifications or lack of them. They and they alone were empowered to consecrate and administer the sacrament; and his reverence for the sacrament and the words of God is a constant theme reiterated in his admonitions, his letters and his Testament (Doc. 1, 4). As the priests themselves were not always mindful of their office, he did his best to remedy their deficiencies. In his early preaching tours around Assisi he found so many dirty churches that he took to carrying a broom with him. Having swept the church he lectured the

[1] 2 Cel., c. 193.

incumbent in private, so that laymen should not hear and lose their respect for the clergy. Francis himself was ordained deacon but never aspired to priest's orders.

Greater still was his deference to bishops, cardinals and Popes; yet with them he was persistent too and generally ended up by getting his own way. In the *Second Life* Thomas of Celano told how

'On one occasion St Francis came to Imola, a city of the Romagna, and presented himself to the bishop, requesting his licence to preach. The bishop said to him: "Brother, it is sufficient that I myself preach to my people." Bowing his head Francis humbly withdrew and after a short time came in again. The bishop asked him: "What do you want, brother? What is it now?" St Francis said: "My lord, if a father repulses his son through one door he must come back by another." Won over by his humility the bishop embraced him cheerfully and said: "You and all your brothers from now on have my general licence to preach in my diocese, as such holy humility deserves." '[1]

This was a successful instance of the way Francis chose to act, but such a method was not invariably successful; and some of the friars pointed out that much time might be saved if they by-passed the bishops and acquired a papal privilege authorising them to preach; and they could use the time to good advantage (cf. Doc. 1). Francis opposed this on principle, but here, as in much else, the arguments of common sense presently overrode his call to put into practice the foolishness of the Gospel.

Francis and the Papal Curia

The Gospel was the book on which Francis modelled his conduct and his Order, and the Pope was the authority in the world under and through whom he operated. Yet it was not until 1223 that Innocent III's successor, Honorius III (1216–27), finally enshrined the Rule in its revised form in the bull which may still be seen in the Treasury of the Basilica of St Francis at Assisi. The steps leading to the *Regula Bullata* (Doc. 2) are vividly described in the Chronicle of Jordan of Giano (Doc. 25), which I use as an excellent example of how Francis appeared to others of his day. In 1219 Francis went to Egypt, hoping to convert the Sultan by his preaching; presently news reached him of troubles and difficulties in Italy: his own dislike of formal organisation and clear-cut administration had reaped its reward. He hastened back to

[1] 2 Cel., c. 147.

Italy and to the Pope, and was allowed to choose Hugolino, cardinal-bishop of Ostia, later Pope Gregory IX, as Cardinal Protector of the Order, and with Hugolino's help to clear up the difficulties and check the brothers who had been receiving encouragement from the Curia to act against Francis's wishes. This proved the first step towards the final revision of the Rule and its confirmation in 1223.

The Pope was the successor of St Peter, the rock on whom Christ built his Church, and obedience to him was fully accepted by Francis as rooted in the Gospels. He established and maintained on his own initiative a close link with the Papacy. The relationship was ambivalent; Francis was totally obedient, but also totally convinced that as his life was based on the Gospel the Pope was bound to approve. The double foundation on which he built is clearly stated at the outset of the Rule (Doc. 2). 'The Rule and life of the Friars Minor is this, to observe the holy Gospel of Our Lord Jesus Christ by living in obedience, without property and in chastity. Brother Francis promises obedience and reverence to the lord Pope Honorius and his successors lawfully succeeding and to the Roman Church. And the other brothers are held to obey brother Francis and his successors.' And again at the end: 'I order the ministers on obedience to seek from the lord Pope one of the cardinals of the Holy Roman Church, who may be governor, protector and corrector of this brotherhood, to the end that we be always submissive and subject to the Holy Roman Church, firm in the Catholic faith, and always observe poverty, humility and the holy Gospel of Our Lord Jesus Christ, as we have firmly promised.'

The Rule of St Francis (Doc. 2)

A striking feature of medieval religious history is the emergence and popularity of religious Rules. Why were these Rules ever written? The early Christians were not monks. They had no Rule beyond the writings of the New Testament. Here they could read about Christ's life on earth and his teaching, but although the Gospels provide guiding principles for someone wishing to live a Christian life, they do not provide a detailed code of day-to-day conduct. Christ said, 'Go and do thou likewise' – not 'Go and do this and then this and then the other.' Many men would have preferred it if he had handed them an explicit legal code, and it is this desire to know exactly what is expected of one that lay behind the writing of monastic Rules and their wide-spread acceptance. During the Middle Ages, for the most part, men who wished to pattern their lives closely on that of Jesus joined a religious order. Such a man was called quite simply a religious and it was taken for granted that life in a cloister or in a hermitage was Christian. To help them on their way to salvation the religious had a

Rule. The most famous of these was the Rule of St Benedict, written in the sixth century for Benedict's own community.[1]

St Benedict intended his Rule as introductory to the full Christian life. He described it as 'a little Rule for beginners' which could train and equip his monks to press on beyond the Rule itself towards perfection of life. And some, a very few, have treated it as such. But for lesser men the Rule of St Benedict provided 'a school of divine service', in which they could live protected, occupied and restrained. The Rule consists of seventy-three chapters and it contains regulations bearing on every aspect of monastic life – what the monks should do at each hour of the day, how they should conduct divine service, what they should eat, what they should wear, what they should wear in bed, when they should speak, the kind of things they should think about. The life of the Rule was supposed to be closely modelled on the Gospel; and yet the life of a Benedictine monk and the life of an apostle, shall we say, were obviously very different. The freedom and discretion allowed to the apostles has been replaced by a host of external regulations. Some of these indeed seem actually to contradict the Gospels. Christ said to the apostles, 'Eat what is set before you', yet the monk must observe a whole series of fasts; the apostles travelled widely, yet the monk must never leave his monastery; and so on. Detailed practical guidance on the right course from day to day, such as is found in St Benedict's Rule, can safeguard a high standard of conduct and give a feeling of security, but it provides but limited opportunities for moral growth. St Benedict performed a great service to the Church, but it seems (I think) to many people, looking back on it now, that the Benedictine interpretation of the Christian life, as it was lived by most monks, lacked some of the elements we would consider essential to Christian living.

St Francis refused to base his order on any of the existing Rules. His followers were to be called Friars Minor, and he wrote a special Rule for them. The novelty of their Rule was not automatically a source of pride to the brothers. On the contrary it was rather an embarrassment. It laid them open to a criticism which touched at least some upon a sensitive spot. It was commonly supposed at the time that only the old and traditional was securely respectable. Innovation was presumptuous, an unwarranted slight on older Orders and their approved Rules. St Francis's refusal to compromise or to accept the counsels of experience

[1] On its place in the history of Rules, see D. Knowles, *From Pachomius to Ignatius* (Oxford, 1966). The fullest modern study and best edition is by A. de Vogüé, in Sources Chrétiennes (Paris, 1964–73); excellent translations in O. Chadwick, *Western Asceticism* (London, 1958), pp. 291ff., and in the parallel text and translation (ed. J. McCann, 1952).

and scholarship sprang from the strength of his inner conviction that
the way to which God had called him was new, and for its success and
truth must surrender nothing of its novelty. After the manner of St
Paul in the Epistle to the Galatians he claimed in his Testament (Doc.
1) that the Gospel he preached he had received not of man but by the
direct revelation of God. 'After the Lord gave me brothers, no one
showed me what I ought to do, but the Most High himself revealed to
me that I ought to live according to the pattern of the holy Gospel.'
And yet, of course, the Rule was not, indeed could not be, entirely new.
St Francis's first biographer, Thomas of Celano, said of the *Regula
Primitiva* of 1210 that St Francis wrote it simply and in few words,
using in the main the language of the Gospel but inserting some few
things that necessarily pertained to the religious life.[1] In the twelve
chapters of the *Regula Bullata* the balance is reversed. Here both the
content and the style reflect rich and varied sources. There are seventeen
quotations from the Bible; there are also quotations from the fathers,
from customs of religious houses and fraternities of the remote and of
the recent past, reflections and practical suggestions, passages from
canon and civil law, and from the Rule of St Benedict.

The wealth of this literary and historical inheritance is not surprising
or inconsistent. Francis could not go back to the Gospel as if the inter-
vening Christian centuries had never been; he could not, even if he
had wished, have rid his mind of certain general principles and pre-
suppositions regarding religious conduct and discipline which had
become so familiar to his age as to be part of that mental equipment
that is received and assimilated at a deeper level than conscious thought.
E. Gilson went so far as to say: 'To set out to live to the end the Rule
of St. Benedict, even as to set out to live the Rule of St Francis, is to
set out to live to the end the life of the Gospel.'[2] St Benedict does
indeed remind us often of the Gospel, but reading the Gospel does not
make us think immediately of St Benedict. St Francis followed much
more nearly the tone and manner of the Gospel and this was, paradoxi-
cally and tragically enough, the very reason why many were to find his
Rule at once insufficient and too exacting. When he had presented the
first draft of his Rule to Innocent III, the immediate reaction of some
of the cardinals had been disbelief – the thing was impossible, no man
could keep it up. Cardinal John of St Paul, already won over to Francis's
side, pointed out that this attitude came dangerously near to heresy –
to implying a denial of Christ's humanity – and by his acute and timely
argument induced the Pope to consider the petition with favour. 'If we

[1] 1 Cel., c. 32.
[2] E. Gilson, *The Mystical Theology of St Bernard*, Eng. trans. A. H. C.
Downes (London, 1940), p. 32.

refuse the request of this poor man', he said, 'as a thing too hard, and untried, when his petition is that the pattern of the Gospel life may be confirmed to him, let us beware lest we stumble at the Gospel of Christ. For if any man says that in the observance of Gospel perfection, and the vowing thereof, there is contained aught that is untried, or contrary to reason, or impossible to observe, he is clearly seen to blaspheme against Christ, the author of the Gospel.'[1] The Friars Minor were soon themselves to stumble. The deputation sent to Gregory IX in 1230 asked whether the obligation to observe the Gospel, with which the Rule began and ended, meant that the Order was bound by the many counsels of perfection that were not expressly quoted in the Rule, 'for they had not intended to bind themselves to these others, and scarcely or never could all of them be obeyed to the letter'.[2]

Christ did not come to make the way easier or even to make it plain. He provided no large-scale chart mapping the whole road which his followers would consult and use to find out exactly where they were. Instead he put up a few signposts to indicate the direction at certain points, particular examples by which we can recognise the good life, the life of the kingdom of God. This life can be lived: it cannot be stated in terms of abstract principles. Courage and obedience are not enough. There must be discernment also. The answers to the problems of life are not in the book and the application of even such apparently simple teaching as the Sermon on the Mount to a given situation is by no means always self-evident. We are left to work it out for ourselves, to try to understand the mind of Christ, to imagine what he himself would have done. Francis approached our life in the spirit of a true disciple. He too turned naturally to parables to strike home his meaning – at once more vivid, more memorable and more instructive than a direct answer – though his parables were more often acted than narrated. On the solemn occasion when he was permitted to preach before the Pope and cardinals he could not find words to tell his joy in Christ but conveyed it unforgettably by dancing. To a novice who asked his leave to have a psalter he replied: 'After you have a psalter you will want and hanker for a breviary; after you have a breviary, you will sit in an armchair like a great prelate, saying to your brother: "Bring me the breviary." And saying this, with great fervour of spirit he took a handful of ashes and rubbed them into his head as if washing it, all the time exclaiming: "I a breviary, I a breviary." '[3] Another time, wishing to test the vocation of two postulants, he told them to help him plant out some young cabbages and to be sure to do exactly as he did. He

---

[1] St Bonaventure, *Legenda Maior S. Francisci*, Bk. iii, c. 9, in *Analecta Franciscana*, Vol. X, p. 570.
[2] *Quo elongati*, see p. 25, n.1.
[3] *SL*, c. 73.

set to work purposefully, pressing the green leaves into the earth and leaving the roots sticking up. One unquestioningly copied him. The other remonstrated: 'This isn't the way cabbages are planted, father, but the other way up.'[1] He was told to do as he had been shown, and as he still could not bring himself to waste good effort and cabbages he was refused admission. A brother who picked up a coin was sternly ordered to carry it outside in his mouth and lay it in some ass's dung, so that money might revolt his senses.[2]

These are true parables, the natural expression of a mind that sees truth in concrete pictures, not (like allegories) pictorial representations of abstract thoughts. His use of them cannot be put down to conscious imitation of Christ. They were the result of a deeper affinity, for when Francis tried to teach in spoken parables he produced not parable but allegory: for example, the tale of the poor woman who bore a king splendid sons, or the little black hen who had more chicks than she could gather under her wing. His treatment here was the normal medieval one. A few of Jesus' parables were given an allegorical meaning in the Gospels themselves, and this kind of interpretation was generally believed to be Christ's own until modern criticism challenged the assumption and suggested that the evangelists were responsible for these passages. Christ's words were homely and direct, creating a concrete picture or scene in preference to stating an abstract truth, but the habit of subjecting them to allegorical interpretation, so early introduced, was capable of vast extension and elaboration. St Augustine's treatment of the parable of the Good Samaritan, where almost every word is made to stand for something else and the whole becomes a message in code to be deciphered by the elect, provides an excellent example.[3]

The contrast helps us to illustrate another difficulty in the Rule. Closely though he followed his master, Francis's understanding of the Gospel was naturally personal and imperfect, coloured by his own predilections and prejudices, and where his teaching differed it was not on the side of being more practicable. The poverty he envisaged was more extreme and dire than that of the apostles. They had shared their goods in common, distributing to each as he had need: Francis would have his brothers not merely poor but destitute, renouncing corporate as well as private ownership of property. The apostles had lacked

---

[1] This story, it must be admitted, comes from a late source, Bartholomew of Pisa, *Analecta Franciscana*, Vol. V, p. 141; full translation in J. R. H. Moorman, *A New Fioretti* (London, 1946), pp. 33–4.

[2] 2 Cel., c. 65.

[3] C. H. Dodd, *The Parables of the Kingdom* (London, 1935), pp. 11ff., a book to which these pages owe much.

nothing necessary, for, we are told, as many as were possessors of houses or land sold them and brought the money and laid it at their feet. Francis abhorred money, thought it intrinsically evil, and absolutely prohibited its use; the friars might receive it neither as payment for their labour, nor as alms, nor for the relief of others. Such a distinction between money and other commodities is not found in the Gospels any more than in the Acts.

Francis's repudiation and execration of money – in part his own response to the rapidly developing monetary economy of the Italy of his day – caused his Order serious embarrassment. It aggravated the practical difficulties. He wished his brothers to be principally dependent upon alms, and the ideal he set before them was so much in harmony with the aspirations of the age that men responded to his call in astonishing numbers. It could not in any case be easy for so great a community to be supported by the rest of the population. In country districts gifts in kind were less of a problem, but in towns, where large convents were soon established, money was more convenient and available, and collection from door to door and day by day of sufficient actual commodities for their support imposed in effect a burden not only on them but on their well-wishers, debarred from the simplest and quickest way of making them a gift. Consequently this prohibition suffered the common fate of too stringent legislation and defeated more than itself. Legal evasions were resorted to to get round it, which besides their immediate effect helped to undermine the authority of the Rule as a whole.[1] Nor was this all. Based upon a questionable interpretation of Gospel poverty, to which the Order was vowed, it gave rise to bitter controversy, persecution and schism, in which, by the turn of the thirteenth and fourteenth centuries, the Conventual, who wished to have freer use of goods and money, faced the Spiritual, who claimed to stand for the primitive purity and individualism of the Rule.[2]

Unlike St Benedict, who had a valuable grasp and appreciation of Roman Law, Francis was no legislator: he preferred to teach by example rather than by precept, but he was perhaps not entirely guiltless of isolating from the Gospel passages that were capable of being taken legally. Words addressed by Christ to a particular audience and for a particular occasion took on the aspect of fundamental law to be rigidly adhered to, and though he himself could soften this rigidity with a founder's licence it created a dilemma for those who lacked his sureness of touch and right to expound. It is small wonder then that some of his followers lacked confidence and trust in the liberty he gave them,

[1] See especially M. D. Lambert, *Franciscan Poverty* (London, 1961).

[2] See ibid., Chap. 7; J. R. H. Moorman, *A History of the Franciscan Order* (Oxford, 1968), Chap. 17; Gratien, op. cit., Chaps 13ff.

and felt that they ought to have external rules to safeguard their way of life, state their principles and define their commitments. While the Rule was in the process of being formulated some suggested that much could be learned from the older Orders whose foundations had stood the test of time; a little later they admired the procedure of the Dominicans; but excellences in others might not have tempted them had they not felt a lack in their own.

3

The Preparation[1]

Why was it not until the thirteenth century that Orders of Friars were founded? Why did their way of life become so popular then, and not earlier? Why, in particular, did such a type of religious not emerge during the twelfth century?

In the art of the twelfth century, in manuscript illuminations, in stained-glass windows, in the sculptured figures of tympana and capitals, Christ and the apostles are frequently represented as bearded and barefoot. This image is historical in concept; contemporary churchmen are not depicted in this guise. For some time other qualities, other characteristics, had in practice been favoured in followers of Christ. Wandering preaching had given place to a life of prayer and worship inside the cloister – St Benedict had thought the *gyrovagi* the worst kind of monks.[2] Monks became respectably dressed, shod and shaved; parish priests had settled homes and jobs. There were some who chose to live rough for Christ's sake; and occasionally their lives were recorded.

Heimrad of Hasungen[3]

One such was a Swabian serf called Heimrad, who was born in the

[1] For the general setting of Chapters 3–5, see R. W. Southern, *Western Society and the Church in the Middle Ages* (Harmondsworth, 1970), especially Chaps 6–7; *The Christian Centuries*, Vol. II, *The Middle Ages*, by D. Knowles and D. Obolensky (London, 1969). The fundamental study is Herbert Grundmann, *Religiöse Bewegungen im Mittelalter* (1st edn, 1935; 2nd edn, Hildesheim, 1961), with additional chapter, pp. 487–538, on new literature; see especially pp. 13ff. on apostolic life and poverty. *Studies in Church History*, Vol. 8, ed. G. J. Cuming and D. Baker (Cambridge, 1972), has a valuable collection of studies of *Popular Belief and Practice*, some on this period.

[2] *Rule of St Benedict*, c. 1.

[3] What follows is based on the lives of Heimrad of Hasungen and Meinwerk, bishop of Paderborn: *Vita S. Haimeradi*, ed. R. Köpke, *MGH SS*, Vol. X (1852), pp. 598–607; *Vita Meinwerci*, ed. G. H. Pertz, *MGH SS*, Vol. XI (1854), pp. 104–61 – the passage on Heimrad is on pp. 113–14 (cf. p. 145). The life of Heimrad was written down about sixty years after his death, and some of the details may be legendary.

tenth century and died in 1019. He was a peasant priest, such as one meets in many pages of Domesday Book, and such as must commonly have staffed the early parish or proprietary churches – the *Eigenkirchen* – of Imperial Germany. The lady he served had another priest besides Heimrad, and so Heimrad asked for and was granted his freedom. He promptly left and went to Hesse. His way of life was different from other people's and provoked mistrust and contumely, and so he had a hard and difficult time. As his biographer explains, people were unaccustomed to his kind of sanctity. He once went on pilgrimage, first to Rome and then to Jerusalem, where he retraced Christ's path to Calvary, himself carrying a cross. While he visited the holy places, climbed the Mount of Olives and went to Bethlehem he lived off alms. If he received more than he immediately needed he distributed it to other poor, taking no thought for the morrow. When his companion asked him: 'What shall we eat today, as there is nothing left in our purses and we ought to fast tomorrow?' he used to reply: 'Then let us fast today and we may eat tomorrow.'

When he returned to Germany an attempt was made to direct him into a traditional monastic cloister. At the monastery of Memleben he met Arnold, abbot of Hersfeld, who wanted to clothe him immediately in the monastic habit. Heimrad would not consent to this, but he did begin to live the regular life there, though he did not take the vows. One day in chapter, however, he prostrated himself before the unsuspecting abbot and monks and begged leave to depart. Asked why, he replied that he could not save his soul there. This provoked the abbot who, in anger, kicked him and ordered him to be turned out. As he waited at the door of the guest room for a horse, Heimrad voiced a complaint that he had not been treated properly, nor as honourably as his birth required, for he was brother to the emperor. His words were greeted with derision and he was brought once more before the abbot who ordered him to be tied to a fence and cruelly beaten. The threat of a flogging did not cause him to withdraw his claim. Conscious of his innocence he asserted that, whether slave or free, all are one in Christ, and that Christ himself told us we all have one Father in heaven, and called us all his brothers. His punishment was inflicted by Anzo, a monk 'so religious and of such gravity of manners as might extort faith even from infidels'.[1] While he was being flogged he recited the fifteenth Psalm 'Lord, have mercy . . .' but was unable to finish, so savagely was he beaten. Slung out in this state, he was taken into her cottage by a poor woman who wept for pity. But he said to her: 'Cease, woman, to grieve at my misfortune. Weep rather over your own sins, they concern you more.'

[1] *Vita S. Haimeradi*, c. 7, p. 601.

He found it difficult, however, to find a place where he could live unmolested. He stayed for a time at Kirchberg, until he was accused of breaking into a chapel and committing sacrilege. As he would neither confess nor purge himself he was driven out by the local inhabitants. At Kirch-Detmold he was, to begin with, more fortunate. Here there was an old, neglected church, in addition to the parish church, and at his request the parish priest allowed him to use this for celebrating his office. His mode of life acquired for him a reputation for sanctity, and men and women soon chose to go to him rather than to their parish priest. They brought their offerings with them, with the result that the priest felt both neglected and impoverished. Heimrad exacerbated his sense of grievance by tactlessly refusing a gift from the priest's wife, telling her to mend her ways. This provoked the priest so much that he set his dogs on him and drove him out.

This chosen life of poverty and privation, and the injuries done to him by the hostile and the uncomprehending, left their mark upon Heimrad whose appearance was unprepossessing, even alarming. His face and body, gaunt and sallow from repeated fasting, and his wretched clothing together produced an impression even of deformity. When Meinwerk, bishop of Paderborn, encountered him in the city he was so struck by this apparition that he asked him if he was the devil come forth. Heimrad humbly replied that he was not the devil. The bishop interrogated him further, and as he said he was a priest, heard him celebrate and then demanded to see the books he used. Finding them in a rough and poor condition he ordered them to be thrown at once into the fire; presumably he feared that Heimrad might be or become a heretic. Heimrad was again flogged; the Empress Cunegund, who was in Paderborn at the time with her husband Henry II and who evidently shared the bishop's revulsion, adding her commands for a flogging to his.

Heimrad bore all the blows and the insults patiently for the love of God. But he decided on a quieter existence and left the towns to live on a mountainside as a hermit. On Mount Hasungen he devoted himself to prayer and reading, fasting and vigils. The local people accepted him and attended his services. It was his custom, after he had celebrated mass, to preach to them, exhorting them on their return home to give all that they had in alms. When they laughingly replied – how then would they be able to meet future expenses ? – he assured them they would have treasure in heaven and that God would provide for them. He set them an example, often giving away his own clothes in alms. His reputation grew throughout the district; people of all classes and fortune venerated him, men and women, rich and poor, servile and noble. But the good opinion in which he was held by the laity was not yet shared by the clergy. The bishop of Paderborn was still prejudiced against him. One year, on the eve of the feast of St Andrew, a local count invited Bishop Meinwerk to dinner. He also invited Heimrad, whom he told to sit opposite him at the table. The bishop took this as a personal insult, indignantly abusing Heimrad, calling him a madman and an apostate. The count, who held Heimrad in great veneration, said he did not know that anyone held anything against him, and tried both to appease the bishop and apologise to Heimrad. The bishop swore that as he was thought holy by men he ought to sing the Alleluia at mass the next day: that would show his holiness! – and he promptly and in front of everyone ordered him to do this or he would have him flogged. When the count interceded he obtained no remission but rather poured oil on the flames. So the next morning he went secretly to Heimrad and begged him not to shirk his trial but rather to begin in the name of the Trinity and leave the rest to God. Heimrad was very reluctant, earnestly desiring to return home, but the count pleaded until he agreed. When the hour came, as the bishop still refused to remit his sentence, he came forward and solemnly and joyfully sang the Alleluia right through to the end. The count's chaplain testified that everyone marvelled, for they had never heard a sweeter intonation from the mouth of any man. When mass was ended the bishop took Heimrad aside privately and apologised, and after that was always his friend.

Thus vividly his biographer and Meinwerk's tell the dramatic incidents of Heimrad's life. After his death a chapel was erected on the site of his hermitage. Miracles multiplied, and some fifty years later a community of canons was installed at Hasungen, presently replaced by monks from Hirsau. It was their abbot, Hartwig, who commissioned the Life of the local saint, which was written by one of his monks, Ekkebert, between 1074 and 1088. Heimrad's is an isolated case. There may have been others like him, but they will have been few. His chief interest for us lies in his independence of spirit. He would not conform. He would lead the religious life, but not in the accepted, and acceptable, traditional fashion. He could not save his soul in a monastery, he said. It may not have been the stability of the cloister he found intolerable, for he was not a wandering preacher by vocation. He seems only to have moved from one place to another when he was forcibly expelled. He preached, but his audiences came spontaneously to him. His sermons were delivered after he had celebrated mass to any who cared to attend. He seems to have sought to establish himself somewhere, anywhere, with the facilities he needed as a priest. He begged the use of the neglected chapel at Kirch-Detmold, and the incident at Kirchberg suggests that he made an unauthorised entry into the chapel in order to celebrate. His refusal to purge himself of the resulting charge of sacrilege suggests that he had conscientious objections to swearing an oath. This would be in keeping with the other evidence of his intention to base his life on the Gospels. He is described, in the Life of Bishop Meinwerk,[1] as living in 'voluntary poverty for Christ, an exile and pilgrim', and this succinctly characterises his life. He left his native Swabia for Hesse at the outset; he went on pilgrimage to the Holy Land, visiting several of the places associated with Christ's life on earth – Bethlehem, the Mount of Olives, Calvary, Jerusalem. He gave away his clothes, having nothing else to give; shared the alms he received with other poor, and urged others to give away all their possessions in response to the Gospel call. Why did he reject monastic vows ? Perhaps because he had been born a serf he especially valued his freedom and found living under obedience irksome. Clearly it was not the austerity of the life he objected to – he chose to live off bread and water and salt, with occasional vegetables, poorly clad and solitary – perhaps it was rather that life within the monastic cloister was not sufficiently closely and obviously related to the Gospels. Certainly the treatment meted out to him by the abbot and monks of Memleben was conspicuously devoid of Christian inspiration.

Heimrad left behind him a local cult, but no other discernible influence. He did not found an Order or even attract a group to live with him. In most places he was regarded with mistrust: in one small town he succeeded in winning favour, until driven out by the now jealous priest, but he was only venerated after he had withdrawn to a mountain hermitage. His piety, at the time, was eccentric.

The New Orders of the Eleventh and Twelfth Centuries: the Cistercians
About a century later many individuals were to be found in caves, on islands and mountainsides, in woods and forests, living austerely in voluntary poverty and imitation of the apostles, and these had more impact. Disciples gathered round outstanding exponents of reform and innovation, and a number of new Orders presently sprang up. In the first half of the twelfth century Orderic Vitalis, a monk of St Évroul in Normandy, wrote a long and detailed Ecclesiastical History in which he 'noted down for the information of posterity this account of present-day teachers, who prefer new traditions. . . .'[2] He wrote:

'Monasteries are founded everywhere in mountain valleys and plains, observing new rites and wearing different habits; the swarm

[1] *Vita Meinwerci*, p. 113.
[2] Orderic Vitalis, *Ecclesiastical History*, ed. and trans. M. Chibnall (whose translation I quote), Vol. IV (Oxford Medieval Texts, 1973), p. 333; what follows is from ibid., pp. 310–35.

of cowled monks spreads all over the world. They specially favour white in their habit and thereby seem remarkable and conspicuous to others. Black represents humility in many places in Holy Scripture: therefore up to now monks in their devotion have chosen to wear that colour. Now however, as if to make a show of righteousness, the men of our time reject black . . . and also by cutting their garments in a novel way seek to differentiate themselves from others. In my opinion voluntary poverty, contempt for the world, and true religion inspire many of them, but many hypocrites and plausible counterfeiters are mixed with them, as tares with wheat.'

He goes on to relate how Robert of Molesme tried to persuade the monks of his community to obey the Rule of St Benedict strictly and literally, without the accretions, modifications and relaxations which had become customary. As they were unwilling, he and some companions seceded and looked for a suitable place elsewhere to obey the Rule in the way they wished. At Cîteaux, in the wilderness, they founded a monastery of great austerity and piety.

'It is now about thirty-seven years since Abbot Robert founded Cîteaux in the way I have described, and in that time such a great multitude of men had flocked there that sixty-five abbeys have been founded from it, all of which with their abbots are subject to the chief abbot of Cîteaux. All dispense with breeches and lambskins, abstain from eating fat and flesh-meat, and by the great good they do shine out in the world like lanterns burning in a dark place. They maintain silence at all times and wear no dyed garments. They toil with their own hands and produce their own food and clothing. From 13 September until Easter they fast every day except Sunday. They bar their gates and keep their private quarters completely enclosed. They will not admit a monk from another religious house to their cells, nor allow one to come with them into the church for mass or any other offices. Many noble warriors and profound philosophers have flocked to them on account of the novelty of their practices, and have willingly embraced the unaccustomed rigour of their life, gladly singing hymns of joy to Christ as they journey along the right road. They have built monasteries with their own hands in lonely, wooded places and have thoughtfully provided them with holy names, such as Maison-Dieu, Clairvaux, Bonmont, and L'Aumône and others of like kind, so that the sweet sound of the name alone invites all who hear to hasten and discover for themselves how great the blessedness must be which is described by so rare a name.'[1]

[1] Ibid., Vol. IV, pp. 311, 313, 325, 327. On the Cistercians, see especially

As Orderic was a 'black' monk, one of those traditionalists condemned by the Cistercians as a violator of the Rule, it was a generous tribute. For contrast, here are some excerpts from the satirical pages of Walter Map (c. 1180). He begins his account of the origins of the Cistercians with Stephen Harding, the Englishman who set Robert of Molesme's foundation at Cîteaux on a secure constitutional basis by composing the *Carta Caritatis*. Like Robert, Stephen started as a black monk. He and three others left the monastery at Sherborne and went to France, which was, according to Map,

'The mother of all mischief. . . . They obtained from a rich man a valueless and despised plot in the heart of a great wood, by much feigning of innocence and long importunity, putting in God at every other word. The wood was cut down, stubbed up and levelled into a plain, bushes gave place to barley, willows to wheat, withies to vines; and it may be that in order to give them full time for these operations, their prayers had to be somewhat shortened. . . . [They] decided upon a rule stricter and harder than that of blessed Basil or of Benedict. Skins they abjure, and linen, and even hemp, contenting themselves with undyed wool; and so wide is the chasm that parts them from the black monks that they wear a habit of white, the direct opposite of the others. No monk ever partook of flesh or blood before the days of Charles the Great, who by urgent prayer obtained from Pope Leo the use of fresh meat for the monks north of the Alps, and also leave to use animal oil because, unlike those beyond the Alps, they had no vegetable oil. This indulgence the Cistercians do not accept, but observe the prohibition of the old path in all its strictness, so that they are wholly strange to the use of flesh. Yet they keep pigs to the number of many thousands, and sell the bacon – though perhaps not quite all of it. The head, legs and feet they neither give away, throw away, nor sell. What becomes of them God knows. In like manner it is a question between them and their Maker what they do with their fowls, of which they have great plenty. They have abjured the ownership of churches, and all manner of unjust acquisitions, living like the apostle by the work of their own hands, to the exclusion of all covetousness. That was for a time. What they may have purposed, or promised in the bud, I know not: but whatever the promise was, such a fruit has followed as makes us fear the tree. At that time they were all that was simple

D. Knowles, *Monastic Order in England* (Cambridge, 1963), 2nd edn, Chaps 12–14; C. Brooke, *Monastic World, 1000–1300* (London, 1974), Chap. 9 and on the beauty of their sites, cf. Walter Daniel's *Life of Ailred of Rievaulx*, ed. F. M. Powicke (Nelson's Medieval Texts, 1950), pp. 12–13.

and submissive: no greed, no self-interest, they were deaf to no cry of distress, did to none as they would not be done by, rendered to none evil for evil, kept their innocence as pure from ill report as nard from mire. Everyone praised their sabbaths and would fain be even as they. Thus they grew to be an exceeding great people, and spread into many establishments; and the names of these always contain some spice of the divine, as Godscot, Godsdale [Vaudey], Port Salvation, Scale-Heaven, Wondervale, Lantern, Brightvale [Clairvaux]. From this last rose Bernard, and began to shine among, or rather above, the rest, like Lucifer among the stars of night. A man of ready eloquence he was, and used to have carts driven round through the towns and castles, in which to carry off his converts to the cloister. . . .'

. . . 'The black monks by rule wear the cheapest cloth of their district, and by special dispensation lambskins only. The white monks wear the woven wool just as the sheep did, innocent of any dye, and though they taunt the black monks for their lambskins, they themselves are provided in equally good measure with numbers of comfortable habits, such as would become costly scarlet for the delight of kings and princes if they were not snatched from the dyers' hands. The black monks sit with Mary at the Lord's feet and hear the word, and are not suffered to go out for worldly cares. The white, though they sit at the same feet, go out to work; they practise all manner of tillage with their own hands inside their precinct; and outside they are artisans, harrowers, herdsmen, merchants and in each calling most active. They have no neatherd nor swineherd but of their own number. For the basest and most menial chores, or for women's work, such as milking and so on, they employ no one but their own novices. They are all things for all work, and so the whole earth is full of their possessions; and though the Gospel does not permit them to take thought for the morrow, they have such a reserve of wealth accruing from their care that they could enter the ark in the same spirit of security as Noah, who had nothing left outside to look to. They are all under one central authority, the abbot of Cîteaux, who has power to make any change he pleases. Such victuals as they do not use themselves they do not set before their guests, no, nor allow within their walls anything that they do not give. It is a sign that they abstain in order to abound; for one of the hands of avarice is tenacity. They will accept the loan of a team and plough, but cannot lend their own. . . . Whatever promotes their interest they appropriate under some pretext of righteousness. . . . In defence of any act of violence or robbery, or whatever covetousness suggests, they say: "We are spoiling the Egyptians and enriching the

Hebrews", as if they were the only ones whom the Lord is bringing out of darkness. They are making the kingdom of God somewhat limited, if no-one is in the right way but themselves.... With the Pharisee they say: "We are not as other men are"; they omit to say: "We give tithes of all that we possess." ... It is prescribed to them that they are to dwell in desert places, and desert places they do assuredly either find or make.... And because their rule does not allow them to govern parishioners, they proceed to raze villages and churches, turn out parishioners, destroy the altars of God, not scrupling to sow crops or cast down and level everything before the ploughshare, so that if you looked on a place that you knew previously you could say, "and grass now grows where Troy town stood".... As to their clothing, their food and their long hours of work, the people to whom they are kind (because they cannot do them any harm) say that their clothing is insufficient to keep off cold, their food to keep off hunger, and the work they do is enormous, and from this they argue to me that they cannot be covetous because their acquisitions are not spent on luxuries. But oh how simple is the answer! Do not usurers and other slaves of avarice clothe and feed themselves most poorly and cheaply? Misers crouch over their treasures on their deathbeds; they do not amass them for delicacies, but for their delight, they mean not to use them but to keep them. If you make a point of toil, cold and food, why the Welsh lead a harder life in all these respects....'[1]

Map was a secular clerk, who started his career in the service of Gilbert Foliot, bishop of London, became a canon of St Paul's and holder of several benefices, while he was also a clerk in the household of King Henry II and canon and chancellor of Lincoln before ending his days as archdeacon of Oxford. His career bears witness to the opportunities open to men with his education and training in the second half of the twelfth century. His prejudice is evident. He acted, in the 1170s, as a royal justice; his friend Gerald of Wales tells of him that he always excepted Jews and Cistercians from his oath to do justice to all men when he went on circuit.[2] Yet in some respects his account tallies closely with that of Orderic. He may indeed have used him. The marked difference in tone is not wholly due to temperament. Orderic wrote his pages on the Cistercians in the 1130s, Map his in the 1180s, by which time popularity had brought a success which inevitably made

---

[1] Walter Map, *De nugis curialium* (see Doc. 13), trans. M. R. James, Dist. i, c. 24, pp. 40–2; and c. 25, pp. 46–7, 49, 53.
[2] Giraldus Cambrensis, *Opera*, ed. J. S. Brewer, J. F. Dimock and G. F. Warner (Rolls Series, 1861–91), Vol. IV, pp. 219ff., especially p. 219.

some, especially among the black monks and canons, jealous of the Cistercian estates, wealth and privileges and cynical of an idealism which had proved so practically advantageous.

Savigny, Tiron and Fontevrault

Robert of Molesme moved to Cîteaux in order to establish a community and to inspire a movement whose specific intention was to return to strict observance of the Benedictine Rule in its primitive state, as then understood, and in this he succeeded. What of some of the others who founded Orders around this time? Did their achievements as faithfully reflect their aspirations? In Brittany at the turn of the eleventh and twelfth centuries there were in the woods 'a multitude of hermits'.[1] Sometimes they lodged in shelters made from branches, ate shoots and berries, and spent their time in prayer and study; at other times they travelled widely about the country, barefoot and preaching. Three friends, Vitalis, Bernard and Robert of Arbrissel, occasionally went on preaching expeditions together.

Vitalis of Savigny.[2] Vitalis abandoned a career as a secular canon and a chaplain to Robert, count of Mortain, to follow Christ in the footsteps of the apostles. The earliest account we have of him comes from Orderic, who emphasised his power as a preacher.

> 'He was a man who had studied deeply, was endowed with great courage and eloquence, sought what he believed right with passion, and spared neither rich nor poor in his public sermons. . . . Many multitudes journeyed to hear his words and, after hearing from his lips the shameful deeds that they had done in secret, withdrew in sorrow and confusion from his presence. Every rank was mortified by his true allegations, every crowd trembled before him at his reproaches; men and women alike blushed with confusion at his taunts. . . .'

After some years as a hermit and wandering preacher he established himself and his followers at Savigny. At first they lived in the huge ruins of the old buildings they discovered in the village and began to build a monastery in the wood nearby. Vitalis chose to regulate his foundations along the lines of the new monastic trends, and in 1147,

---

[1] Gaufridus Grossus, *Vita b. Bernardi Tironiensis*, *PL*, Vol. 172, col. 1380; cf. Grundmann, pp. 43ff.

[2] On Vitalis, see his Life ed. by E. P. Sauvage in *Analecta Bollandiana*, Vol. I (1882), pp. 355–90; Knowles, *Monastic Order*, pp. 200ff. The quotation from Orderic, below, is from Vol. IV, p. 333.

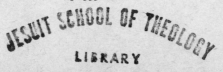

less than fifty years later, Savigny and her daughter houses lost their separate identity and were merged into the Cistercian Order. Vitalis rejected Cluniac customs in favour of the most up-to-date observances, but the quasi-Cistercian régime at Savigny seems in some respects a denial of the life he had been leading. He retained the remoteness and the austerity, but gave up the mobility and the preaching which he had embarked upon with so much vigour and dedication.

Bernard of Tiron.[1] Bernard was a monk of St Cyprian at Poitiers, a Benedictine house of Cluniac affiliations and locally noted for the strictness of its observance. When another monk of that house, Gervase, was made abbot of St-Savin-Sur-Gartempe, he insisted on taking Bernard with him and made him prior. The church of St-Savin was rebuilt and decorated with frescoes during the eleventh century and is today regarded as a splendid achievement of Romanesque architecture and art. But Bernard did not see it in that light. The building programme was very costly. When the abbot wished to acquire a church to increase the endowment of the house, Bernard objected and the two quarrelled. Gervase became so angry that he ordered Bernard to return to St Cyprian. Bernard's biographer is careful to record that such bad temper towards his hero did not go unpunished. Gervase went on the First Crusade, as did many abbots, and in Judea he and the ass he was riding were killed by a lion. His monks planned to elect Bernard as his successor but Bernard was so averse to this that when he realised their intention he left unobtrusively to do what he had long secretly wanted, to live as an anchorite and get his food by the labour of his hands. On the advice of Peter of Stella, a local hermit, he went north to Brittany where he joined Vitalis, Robert of Arbrissel and many other hermits. After three years his retreat was discovered by his community, who wanted him back, and he fled further. The importance he attached to apostolic poverty is clearly brought out by his conduct at this time.[2]

'Out of concern for his poverty another hermit handed one of Bernard's companions eighteen coins, a trifling sum that would at least provide them with something for the first few days of their journey. When the man of God learnt that money was being carried with them he was not a little incensed. "Either you cease to be my companion, he said, or you cease carrying those coins. Do you think to find Christ poor in those parts to which we are going, when we

[1] What follows is based on the *Vita* (Life) by Gaufridus Grossus, op. cit., Vol. 172, cols 1367–1446; see also Grundmann and Knowles; loc. cit.

[2] Grossus, op. cit., cols 1380–4; the quotation which follows is from col. 1384.

know he is everywhere rich? Do not allow yourself to fear poverty, as Christ is rich. For Christ will minister sufficiently to your necessities if first you will seek faithfully the kingdom of God." Having said this, he came upon a poor countryman on his way and ordered the money to be given to him. The poor man was delighted to receive the money, especially as he came by it so easily; Bernard was made even happier at having no money at all. Both rejoicing in their different ways the one went home with his money, the other penniless, having nowhere to rest his head and not knowing where he was going, but confiding in the generosity of God's bounty, hurried to complete as he had intended the journey he had begun and reached the Channel coast.'

He went by boat to an island ten miles out and here he remained for many years, at first quite alone, without bread or fire, sheltering in caves in the rocks, living off the raw roots of plants, and spending day and night in prayer and penitence, tears and contemplation. But the monks of St Cyprian still missed him. They eventually succeeded in persuading his friend Peter of Stella to go to him and use his influence on their behalf and by the urgings of friendship he was persuaded to return. The unconventional ceded to the conventional.

'The monks received Bernard, whom they had not seen for many years, with delight and rejoicing, but they were astonished at this man with long hair and beard, clad in wretched rough clothes such as hermits usually have. Horrified at his clothes they quickly disposed of them, shaved his beard, and provided him with some of their clothes, and after a few days, against his will, made him prior. Thus they changed him superficially, taking from him the habit of poverty, but they did not know how to take from his mind the love of the hermit life.'

His complaisance contented them and when their abbot lay dying he nominated him as his successor. Bernard had no wish for the office but felt obliged to accept. As abbot he bore himself with humility. 'Indeed he abased himself to such an extent that anyone seeing him and eager to see him because of his distinguished reputation would believe he saw not him but the most junior recruit. When he was girding himself among a throng of monks for choir in dress and voice and habit and gait he was the least of all.'[1] While he was abbot he was called upon to defend the liberties of his house, over which Cluny was claiming jurisdiction. His initial response to such a distasteful involve-

[1] Ibid., cols 1393, 1395.

ment was to leave his abbey again and return to the hermit life he had
always wanted. Once more he joined Vitalis and Robert of Arbrissel and
together they wandered barefoot through France, preaching the word of
God in villages, towns and cities. All three were vehement and outspoken preachers, their favourite topic being the denunciation of sin,
sexual sin in particular. Bernard and Robert were present at the Council
of Poitiers at which no less a person than King Philip of France was
excommunicated for adultery. William, duke of Aquitaine, was also
present. As he was guilty of the same offence he suspected that the
clerics were about to excommunicate him as well. He ordered his
retainers to break up the meeting, and cardinals, bishops and abbots
scattered in confusion. But Bernard and Robert stood their ground un-
dismayed and finished delivering the sentence.

They directed their tirades at the clergy as well as the laity. The
clergy were forbidden to marry by canon law, and the enforcement of
clerical celibacy was a principal platform of the papal reform movement.
The practice, however, was widespread and took time to eradicate,
especially in some localities. In Normandy it was quite common for
priests to marry and raise families to whom they left their churches.
Bernard did his utmost to convince the priests that such conduct was
sinful and to persuade them to repudiate their wives. Although he met
with but moderate success, some of the threatened wives plotted his
death and some priests laid traps for him to deter him from preaching.[1]
Once at Coutances, where he was giving a public sermon, an archdeacon who had a wife and family came with a supporting band of
priests and clergy and demanded why, as Bernard was a monk and
therefore dead to the world, he took it upon himself to preach to the
living. Bernard replied with a defence of monastic preaching (Doc. 8),
which is interesting because it represents a viewpoint at the time unfashionable: unfashionable but not inconsistent. There had long been
this element in monasticism: when Gregory the Great sent missionaries
to England he sent monks, and it was English monks in turn who went
as missionaries to Germany. These men were exceptional; and there
were other exceptions. Monks had not normally undertaken parish
duties, but Professor Constable has shown that there were communities
(perhaps many such) which obtained the right to receive and bury the
dead, administer penance and visit the sick.[2] The prevailing tendency
was to frown on activities outside the cloister and to stress the paramount value to the monk of enclosure. That this could produce tensions
is clear from the case of Bernard's younger contemporary and name-

[1] Grossus, op. cit., col. 1397.
[2] G. Constable, *Monastic Tithes from their Origins to the Twelfth Century*
(Cambridge, 1964), especially pp. 165–6.

sake, St Bernard of Clairvaux. St Bernard preached, and preached with outstanding success. It is quite clear that his talents lay this way and that he felt an urge to do so, but he also believed that preaching was not part of the monastic profession and he felt bound from time to time to apologise for doing what he was constantly advocating that members of his Order should not do.

After about four years of this, to him, congenial existence Bernard of Tiron resumed his responsibilities, under pressure from his monks, and went to Rome to press their case against Cluny. He went with a few hermit companions, sitting on an ass and wearing those poor hermit clothes his monks so disliked. The Pope, Paschal II, was so impressed with his sanctity that he heard him with favour, and Bernard was able to govern his monastery for some years in peace. However the dispute flared up again and he went once more to Rome. This time the Pope wanted to make him a cardinal and keep him with him at the Curia. Bernard not only refused this, but he pressed to be relieved of his office and allowed to return to the hermit life.

'The Pope, won over by the constancy and sanctity of a man, who, desiring nothing in the world, sought God alone, as he could not keep him by him, enjoined this office on him: that is, he was to preach to the people, hear confessions, enjoin penance, baptise, travel round the country and conscientiously perform all the duties required of a public preacher. But, having made him his deputy, the Pope did not want a representative of the apostles whom he sent out, without money, to preach, to lack the means of livelihood, and so he admonished him to accept food for the body from those whom he refreshed with the word of salvation. Wanting to begin with himself he invited him to dinner and determined that for as long as he remained in Rome he should eat daily at his table.'[1]

Bernard retired to a remote island with a few disciples, and his monks elected another abbot. The island, however, turned out to be less congenial than expected. It was frequented by pirates who rudely profaned their altar; so they returned to the mainland and the woods. Comparatively more accessible here, Bernard was soon joined by large numbers, attracted by his reputation, and he had to direct and provide for them. He instituted at first a regular routine of Cluniac type. But this involved long periods of psalm-singing; if they were to support themselves by the labour of their own hands, as Bernard wished, they would all have to put in long hours clearing and cultivating the ground.

[1] Grossus, op. cit., col. 1403; and for what follows, cols 1404ff.

Bernard prayed for guidance, and psalm-singing yielded precedence to manual work. But the simple life is not without complications. A local nobleman began to fear that their agriculture would destroy his woods; so he gave them another site. It was actually a better site, with more fertile soil and well supplied with streams, but it was further away from his castle. It also happened to be near Savigny, where Vitalis was already settling with his adherents. As Bernard's biographer put it, two lights were too much for one place. Bernard refrained from intruding and after further search found a site suitable for meditation and prayer in a wooded spot called Tiron, belonging to the bishopric of Chartres, and here finally he established his congregation.

'They were completely unknown to the inhabitants of this region. Burning with the fervour of holiness and ready to bear any and every burden of poverty, they wore clothes monastic in style, but vile, unkempt, filthy, utterly unlike the habits worn by other monks, resembling rather the sheep from which they were taken. For the command of poverty compelled them to have clothes that were the cheapest they could buy, and the least at variance with the Rule of St Benedict which they professed. But the ignorant rustics who lived in these parts abhorred such a habit, which they had not seen before, and believed them to be not monks but Saracens, come by way of subterranean caves to spy upon the citizens. Disturbed by this rumour the local people sent scouts, who directly they came beheld men who were unwarlike and unarmed, devising nothing evil, building modest huts, not erecting castles or towers, who did not make a warlike clamour but sheeplike sang psalms and hymns.

'They returned bringing better hope, beating their sinful breasts and told the rest that they were not Saracens but new prophets sent by God to settle in the desert. When this was known, the people, both rich and poor, hurried along, eager to see. When the man of God saw such a crowd arriving he came forward to a suitable spot and addressed the people. He taught them whom they ought to fear, whom to serve; he urged them to put heavenly things before earthly, to exchange transitory things for eternal. Thus he instructed those who gathered round him. He declared how glorious and wonderful may be the man who is made godlike by participation in the supreme good; he showed how wretched and fleeting are the joys of this life; he proved how dire and permanent remain the torments in hell for sinners after death. Many, afraid and remorseful, renounced the world and putting on the habit of monks submitted themselves to his governance.'[1]

[1] Grossus, op. cit., col. 1410.

Bernard governed Tiron for some ten years until his death in 1117. During this time so many were attracted to his new foundation that a number of daughter houses were set up, while three hundred monks remained at Tiron. By no means all of these were ignorant local peasants, to whom the Saracens were a bogy. A notable proportion were craftsmen. Bernard's biographer singles these out for special mention, and his evidence is corroborated by Orderic, who writes:

'Father Bernard received in charity all who were eager for conversion to monastic life, instructing individuals to practise in the monastery the various crafts in which they were skilled. So among the men who hastened to share his life were joiners and blacksmiths, sculptors and goldsmiths, painters and masons, vine-dressers and husbandmen, and skilled artificers of many kinds. They industriously carried out the tasks imposed on them by their superior and handed over for the common good whatever they earned. So in the place where, shortly before, robbers had normally lain hidden in the grim wood, waiting to fall on unwary travellers, and murder them, a noble monastery rose by God's aid. . . .'[1]

It sounds from this as if the monastery may have been well built and richly adorned. The first buildings were of wood but these were damaged by a forest fire and new buildings on a new site were largely paid for by noble patrons, especially Rotrou, count of Perche and his mother, the Countess Beatrice. Rotrou believed he owed his release from sadistic prison treatment at the hands of Robert of Bellême to Bernard's good offices.[2] The monks' living conditions were poor. They sometimes lacked bread and lived on vegetables and herbs, and they had no wine. In winter many were without lambskin cloaks and many without hoods. But they were generous in their hospitality. Bernard would not turn away anyone who wished to join him or anyone who came to his door for help – his biographer expatiates on this more than once – and he taught his monks to do the same. The blind, the lame, the deformed, the orphaned, women with babies at the breast, the ill, the dying, all were taken in. If there was insufficient for all, the monks gave their guests their own food and in winter their own clothing.

[1] Orderic, trans. Chibnall, Vol. IV, p. 331; cf. p. 330n. and the study by L. Genicot there cited, who is doubtful of the validity of this list of crafts; but, as Dr Chibnall says, 'There is nothing improbable in his list of crafts', and it was characteristic of twelfth-century monasticism to recruit craftsmen. M. Genicot's paper is in *L'eremitismo in Occidente nei secoli XI e XII* (Milan, 1962), a volume with many valuable studies of eleventh–twelfth century hermits in various languages.

[2] Grossus, op. cit., cols 1414–15.

No one was turned away empty, and the poorer they were the more gladly they were fed; if they were dying, they were given the last rites.[1]

What are we to make of all this? There is no tidy pattern. Professor Knowles wrote: 'Bernard ... had a troubled and varied career not unlike that of Robert of Molesme, of which his biographer gives us glimpses without supplying the links of causality that might join the disconnected episodes.'[2] Yet in some ways his chequered career is symptomatic of the efforts of a man searching to include in his life a combination of religious endeavours and experience which though they could be found separately were not at that time catered for in combination in existing institutions. I cannot help feeling that if Bernard had lived a century later he would have become a friar. Some of the stories told about him, for example, his refusal to take any money at all on an uncharted journey (see pp. 50-1), his riding on an ass, dressed in old clothes, with a retinue of a few poor hermits, to see the Pope, his success in persuading Paschal II to sanction his chosen way of life, and their treatment of each other (see p. 53), could all have come from a Life of St Francis. They were kindred spirits sharing a zeal for apostolic poverty and apostolic preaching, an inclination for the hermit life of solitude and contemplation, a concern for the poor, the helpless and the sick. It seems to me that Bernard indeed might have founded an Order of friars. He had the beginning of an opportunity. When Pope Paschal II allowed him the office of public preacher with the duty of travelling about, without money, like an apostle, he was in a not dissimilar position to St Francis when he received his first verbal approval from Innocent III in 1210. But whereas St Francis expected all his followers to live as he did despite the difficulties created by large numbers, Bernard seems to have assumed that when his followers became numerous they would have to build a monastery and profess the Rule of St Benedict. When he left Paschal II he looked forward to the life of an anchorite and preacher. He did not anticipate his popularity and was partially defeated by it. His interpretation of the Rule was in harmony with current reforming thinking. Like the Cistercians his monks lived in previously uncultivated and isolated wooded regions, wore undyed sheep's wool clothing, ate frugally, and worked with their hands. The stamp of Bernard's own personality shows in a few particular features: clothes were not only poor but disreputable (see p. 51); seclusion did not result in isolation from the world. His hospitality to all comers meant that the poor, the infirm, the despised, the old and the orphaned flocked to Tiron for relief, and Orderic's account of the work done by

---

[1] Grossus, op. cit., col. 1441.
[2] Knowles, *Monastic Order*, p. 201.

his monks suggests that they plied their crafts outside as well as inside the monastery.[1] But there is no record of any more preaching tours or any more sabbatical leave in a hermitage.

Robert of Arbrissel.[2] Robert of Arbrissel left the household of the bishop of Rennes to become an anchorite in the forest of Craon. Like Bernard and Vitalis he spent part of his time in prayer and study with congenial associates (the woods of Brittany were not lonely just then, they were so favoured by hermits), part in preaching. He too assumed the distinctive style of the wandering preacher, going about barefoot, in poverty and rags, his hair and beard long. His preaching was encouraged by Bishop Ivo of Chartres and formally licensed by Urban II in 1096, when the Pope was in Angers launching the First Crusade. But it was not wholly approved by his former employer, Bishop Marbod of Rennes, who objected to the inclusion in his sermons of diatribes on the vices of the clergy. Criticising the guilty laity was commendable, criticising the clergy was rocking the boat. The bishop wrote to Robert: 'In the sermons in which you are in the habit of teaching the vulgar crowds and unlearned men, not only, as is fitting, do you rebuke the vices of those who are present, but you also list, denounce and attack, as is not fitting, the crimes of absent ecclesiastics . . .' and continued sarcastically: 'But perhaps it suits you that when in the opinion of the common people the Church's order is grown vile, you alone and your like are held in esteem. . . .'[3]

The bishop also took exception to the way he handled his followers. His preaching attracted a number of adherents of both sexes, who forsook their homes and possessions and lived in renunciation under his direction, calling themselves 'Christ's Poor'. Robert, unlike the bishop, thought it quite suitable for men and women to live unsegregated. His encouragement of women is further indicated in a letter written by Roscelin to Abelard: 'I saw that Robert received women flying from their husbands even when their husbands were trying to summon them back, and he obstinately held them to the end of their lives, in disobedience to the bishop of Angers who ordered him to send them back.'[4]

When he had thus provoked the hostility of the bishops of Rennes and Angers, what happened? Robert became the founder of the con-

[1] See above, and p. 55, n. 1.
[2] See Grundmann, pp. 43ff.; the *Vitae* in *Acta Sanctorum Bollandiana*, Feb., Vol. III (edn of Paris, 1865), pp. 598–621; and J. von Walter, *Die ersten Wanderprediger Frankreichs*, Vol. I (Leipzig, 1903).
[3] Quoted Grundmann, p. 42, n. 64.
[4] Quoted Grundmann, p. 43, n. 65.

gregation of Fontevrault, which rapidly rose to be the most celebrated nunnery of north-western France and the haven of royal and aristocratic ladies. Why this sudden transformation? Fontevrault was founded c. 1100, only four years after Robert had been licensed as a wandering preacher. Grundmann, in his classic study of these religious movements, suggests that, although the part played by the Church in this cannot be clearly established, the facts make the inference of such a connection very probable. Robert was summoned to the synod of Poitiers, late in 1100, which was presided over by two cardinals. The immediate outcome was Fontevrault, where he could lock up his female adherents in strict enclosure. It is a reasonable supposition that the issue had been discussed at the synod and that Robert had appeased his critics by promising in future not to go about with adherents of both sexes, but to keep them apart, with the women in convents.[1]

Norbert and the Premonstratensians

Grundmann discerns similar pressures in the career of Norbert of Xanten, founder of the Order of Premonstratensian canons.[2] This is another case of a wandering preacher turned founder. Norbert was an aristocratic canon of Xanten, who was accused at a synod at Fritzlar of preaching without authorisation and of wearing a religious habit while continuing to live off his own patrimony and unattached to a religious Order. He had been reprehending the clergy in his sermons – hence the charge no doubt. In 1118, however, he obtained a licence to preach from Pope Gelasius II. After spending a year in France during which he collected numerous adherents of both sexes he presented himself before the new Pope Calixtus II at the synod of Rheims to request confirmation of this licence. The Pope's answer is not known for certain, but apparently neither Calixtus II nor the bishop of Laon, Norbert's patron, was prepared to allow him to wander around freely with his adherents. Immediately after the synod they sought to end his activities as a wandering preacher and to bring him and his followers within the confines of a strict order. Norbert accepted their plans on condition that he could remain true to his vocation. He had chosen to live the apostolic life, as it could be understood, straightforwardly, from the Gospels. He and his followers were imitators of Christ, living in voluntary poverty in the world but seeking nothing from it, taking neither wallet nor shoes nor two tunics, in accordance with the Gospel

---

[1] Grundmann, pp. 43–5, cf. p. 40, n. 57.
[2] Ibid.; on Norbert and his Order, see H. M. Colvin, *The White Canons in England* (Oxford, 1951); C. Dereine in *Revue d'Histoire ecclésiastique*, Vol. XLII (1947), pp. 352–78; N. Backmund, *Monasticon Praemonstratense* (Straubing, 1949–56).

command. This life of apostolic perfection, he claimed, we could achieve not by our own merits but only through the superabundant grace of God.

After an abortive attempt to put him in charge of a community of Augustinian canons at Laon who resisted his proposals of reform, he was allowed to institute a community of his own, and Prémontré was founded, soon to spread into an Order. Its general organisation owed much to the Cistercians – Norbert was a friend of St Bernard – but something of its origins as a movement led by a wandering preacher can be discerned in the importance originally attached to preaching and pastoral work, and in its provision for women. Norbert's concern for women is categorically stated by Hermann of Laon.[1] 'Norbert studied to convert to God not only men but also troops of women so that today [in the mid-twelfth century] in the several houses in the bishopric [of Laon] we may see more than a thousand women converts serving God in such vigour and silence that it is hardly possible to find the like in the strictest monasteries of men.' He wrote elsewhere, when comparing Norbert and Bernard of Clairvaux: 'In a Cistercian monastery only men are received, but Norbert determined that with the male sex women are also to be received for conversion, so that in his monasteries we may see that the manner of life of the women is harder and stricter than the men's.' He believed there were over ten thousand women, ranging from poor peasant girls to wealthy widows, in the Order as a whole, and concluded: 'If Norbert had done nothing else, but had omitted the conversion of men, yet for attracting so many women to the service of God by his exhortation, surely he would have been worthy of the greatest praise?' Norbert ended his life as archbishop of Magdeburg, the springboard both for missionary work and the settlement of the Premonstratensians in central and eastern Europe.

Gilbert of Sempringham and the Gilbertines[2]
In the 1130s another new Order, this one primarily for women, began in England. Gilbert of Sempringham built a house and cloister adjoining a parish church he served for a group of girls he had educated. On the analogy of the Cistercians he added some lay sisters to do the domestic chores and lay brothers to do the heavier outdoor work. His admiration for the Cistercians was such that he requested their General Chapter to take charge. This was in 1147, the year in which the Cistercians took in the houses inspired by Vitalis of Savigny, and they were not pre-

---

[1] *MGH SS*, Vol. XII, pp. 657, 659; Grundmann, p. 48, nn. 78–9.
[2] On the Gilbertines, see Rose Graham, *S. Gilbert of Sempringham and the Gilbertines* (London, 1901); R. Foreville, *Un procès de canonisation à l'aube du xiiie siècle (1201–1202): le livre de saint Gilbert de Sempringham* (Paris, 1943).

pared to accept further commitments, particularly not an Order of women. But Bernard of Clairvaux helped him to draw up a Rule which was approved by Eugenius III in the following year. To the three existing categories of recruit was added a fourth, of educated men – canons who were to act as priests, instructors and administrators. For communities of religious women could not be self-sufficient; women were debarred from the priesthood. Gilbert's Order enjoyed considerable favour during King Stephen's troubled reign and after, though it never spread outside England. The powerful family of Geoffrey de Mandeville was among its patrons and aroused the jealousy of monks who were being made to appear old-fashioned. 'This man', wrote a monk of Walden of Geoffrey FitzPeter, later Earl of Essex, 'with others who follow after vain new things, was filled with admiration for that Order newly founded by a man called Gilbert of Sempringham, and founded a house of that Order in Norfolk, at the village called Shouldham; and there, as that new way of religion, unheard of through the centuries, demands, he assembled canons with nuns, brothers with sisters.'[1] Not that they can have enjoyed much of each other's company. Though they lived within the same enclosure, the Gilbertine men and women were kept studiously apart. The precautions taken against any intercourse between them and the presumption of impropriety that persisted despite these are shown in Walter Map's account of the Order:

'Master Gilbert of Sempringham, who is still alive, though blind with age, for he is a hundred years old, founded a new fashion of religion, which first obtained confirmation from Pope Eugenius. It consisted of regular canons and nuns, with a wall between them that the males might not see or be seen by the females. They have no access whatever to each other, except in an emergency requiring unction or the viaticum; and this is administered through a window most carefully arranged, and in the presence of a number of people. They already possess many establishments, but have not gone outside England. Nothing sinister is as yet reported of them. But there is fear of it, for too often the tricks of Venus pierce the walls of Minerva. . . .'[2]

The kind of wall and the window mentioned by Map can be shown in the excavations at Watton in Yorkshire. In the nuns' priory church

---

[1] Quoted by Graham, op. cit., p. 41, from the chronicle of Walden (for texts of which see *Heads of Religious Houses, England and Wales* . . ., ed. D. Knowles, C. N. L. Brooke and V. C. M. London (Cambridge, 1972), pp. xxii, 75n.).
[2] Map (see Doc. 13), trans. M. R. James, Dist. i, c. 27, pp. 60–1.

there is a partition wall running the whole length from east to west. It divides the church unequally, the southern side, used by the men, being smaller than the northern, used by the more numerous nuns and lay sisters. The wall was nearly five feet thick. It reached high enough to prevent men and women from seeing each other, but not to the roof, so that the nuns might hear High Mass which was celebrated daily for them by the canons on the south side. There was a turntable window through which the communion was passed to them, and a window for hearing confession, a finger in length and hardly a thumb in breadth and further protected by an iron plate. The women's living quarters were better than the men's, and here again there were turntable windows for the transfer of food, laundry and so forth. The whole complex of buildings was surrounded by a wall and moat.[1]

In houses like these, in the nunneries and double monasteries of Fontevrault, Prémontré and Sempringham, women inspired by the new religious aspirations could lead a communal life of asceticism and fervour. But in spite of stringent concern for propriety, barriers could fail to forestall gossip and could be ineffective – very early in its history one young girl at Watton became pregnant[2] – and the presence of women strictly enclosed in houses of men was soon discouraged. The Premonstratensian Order developed in a way which took it further and further from its origin. Monastic duties took precedence over pastoral care; women came to be excluded from the monasteries, the foundation of double monasteries was forbidden, and finally new convents for women were prohibited. The enthusiasm with which women adopted the religious, and especially the apostolic life, disturbed most of the Church's leaders. It was unseemly for women to wander about and to mix with men. St Bernard in a sermon raised the question of how the Church should proceed against people whose way of life might be disreputable.

'How, they say, are we to condemn those who have not been convicted and have not confessed? A frivolous excuse, no more; not an argument.

'By this alone, even if there is nothing else, they may be easily apprehended, if, as I have said, the men and women, who say they are continent, are separated from each other, and you force women to live with others of their sex who have taken vows, and men likewise with like-minded men. For by this means for both sexes, vow and reputation will be provided for and their continence will be safeguarded at the same time by witnesses and guardians. If they do not

[1] Graham, op. cit., pp. 54–7, with plan facing p. 55.
[2] See F. M. Powicke in Walter Daniel, *Life of Ailred of Rievaulx*, pp. lxxxi–ii.

keep to this they can most justly be eliminated from the Church which they scandalise.'[1]

The difficulties encountered by Robert of Arbrissel and Norbert of Xanten were partly due to their criticisms of the clergy, partly to their womenfolk. It is notable that when St Francis set out to lead an apostolic life he was careful to avoid these two occasions for collision with the authorities. He was humble and respectful to all the clergy, and when St Clare insisted on joining him he immediately shut her up in a cloister. There was to be no emancipation for her.

[1] St Bernard, Sermo 66, *PL*, Vol. 183, col. 1102, quoted Grundmann, p. 39, n. 55.

4

The Preparation: The Heretics

There were others who were not prepared to honour the clergy or to deny women freedom of movement and male society. What happened to them? If, when they fell foul of the authorities, they continued to preach and to inspire and direct their adherents in defiance of prohibition they were condemned as heretics, and risked ending their careers violently or in prison. But details about their lives, their teachings and beliefs all too often escape us, and the evidence we have is often misleading and difficult to interpret. There is little information, and that little comes mostly from their enemies, prejudiced in advance, from converts to orthodoxy, eager to denigrate their former associates, or from later documents. There is enough to tantalise and to intrigue.

Peter of Bruis[1]

All that we know about Peter of Bruis, who gave his name to the sect of Petrobrusians, is contained in a Tract written against the tenets of the heretics by Peter the Venerable, abbot of Cluny from 1122 to 1156. Peter the Venerable regarded Peter of Bruis's teachings as 'stupid' and

[1] This section is based on Peter the Venerable's *Contra Petrobrusianos hereticos*, ed. J. Fearns (Turnhout, 1968), whose preface is Doc. 9 below. To Dr Fearns's edition, to his paper in *Archiv für Kulturgeschichte*, Vol. XLVIII (1966), pp. 311–35, and to his Liverpool University PhD thesis, 'The *Contra Petrobrusianos* of Peter the Venerable', 1963, I am much indebted. On the heretics, see the general survey by C. Brooke in *Medieval Church and Society* (London, 1971), Chap. 7; H. Grundmann, Chaps 1–3; J. Le Goff (ed.), *Hérésies et sociétés dans l'Europe pré-industrielle 11e–18e siècles* (Paris, 1968); W. L. Wakefield, *Heresy, Crusade and Inquisition in Southern France, 1100–1250* (London, 1974), with useful bibliography; W. L. Wakefield and A. P. Evans, *Heresies of the High Middle Ages, Selected Sources* (New York, 1969; useful translated sources, including versions of Nos 9, 10, 12, 13 below, with commentaries). For full blibliography, H. Grundmann, *Bibliographie zur Ketzergeschichte des Mittelalters* (Rome, 1967); for later heresies, G. Leff, *Heresy in the later Middle Ages* (Manchester, 1967), 2 vols. I have found particularly helpful, in the rich literature on the subject, Fearns, Thouzellier, Maisonneuve (works listed in 'Abbreviations' at front of this book), and the studies of Raoul Manselli cited in pp. 66, n. 3 below.

'impious', as infectious and 'lethal', as a 'virulent plague'; and his
avowed intention in writing was to refute his arguments in the possible
hope of persuading his followers of their error and, more positively, of
strengthening the faith of catholics in danger of succumbing (Doc. 9).
He is thus an openly hostile witness, but his integrity and sincerity,
widely acknowledged by contemporaries, are evident. His active concern
to counter threats to the Christian faith led him to study the beliefs of
non-Christians as well as heretics. He wrote a treatise *Against the
Saracens*, and commissioned translations of the Koran and several
Mozarabic works to accompany it, and his treatise *Against the Jews*
displays considerable acquaintance with the Talmud. He evidently
appreciated that the interests of refutation were best served not by the
misrepresentation of obnoxious doctrines but by accurate knowledge
of them. He familiarised himself with the principal features of Petrobrusian doctrine while travelling through the dioceses of Embrun, Die
and Gap in the Hautes-Alpes, where the sect originated. Reports also
reached him at Cluny, but these were conflicting and he specifically
stated, when dealing at the outset with the question of whether or to
what extent the Petrobrusians acknowledged the authority of Scripture,
that, as rumour could not easily be substantiated, he was unwilling to
condemn them on non-proven evidence. A similar caution and desire
to be sure he knew what he was talking about made him refrain from
hastily adding a refutation of the doctrines of Henry of Lausanne,
Peter of Bruis's successor: he would postpone writing until he had
checked his facts (Doc. 9).

The Tract *Against the Petrobrusian Heretics* concentrates on the
beliefs of the sect, classified under five main heads in the introductory
letter, and mention of their leader's life is only very incidental. Bruis, a
village in the Hautes-Alpes, may have been Peter's birthplace or the
parish he once served. It seems he was a priest who was ejected from
his living and then devoted the rest of his life, some twenty years
(*c.* 1119–1139/40), to preaching. He gained adherents at first in the
sparsely populated regions of the Hautes-Alpes. Attempts by the local
bishops to suppress the movement with the help of the catholic nobility
failed to eradicate it on its native ground, and it spread westwards into
the more densely populated areas about Narbonne and Toulouse; no
longer was preaching undertaken only in the countryside but with
increasing confidence in the towns. Glimpses of his activity, although
few, are compensatingly dramatic. He was a rousing orator. Peter
describes how he used to address the crowds from the consular or royal
tribunal on the capitol at Toulouse, and how he was quickly acclaimed
for his compelling oratory. 'All with loud voices rejoiced that you had
recognised the truth, were inflamed with an immense hatred of the

cross, and one and all were armed with swords and with fire to revenge upon the cross the torments of the crucified'.[1] 'And who except you,' continued the indignant and scornful abbot, 'oh stupid donkeys, ever exacted an account for the death of a father or the blood of a brother from gallows or swords, and not rather from the hangmen or murderers?' Stimulated by the preaching the crowd would hack down crosses, pile them together and set them alight. One Good Friday they had the effrontery to cook meat on such a bonfire, and publicly invite people to join their feast. The effects of popular enthusiasm were summarised thus by Peter the Venerable: 'the people are rebaptised, churches profaned, altars toppled, crosses burnt, meat is eaten publicly on the very day of Christ's passion, priests are flogged, monks imprisoned and compelled by intimidation and violence to take wives.'[2] But not everyone received the new doctrine. At last, at the pilgrimage town of Saint-Gilles, while flames consumed the shattered local crosses, a group of scandalised onlookers seized Peter of Bruis and cast him into his own fire (Doc. 9).

The basic assumption underlying the heresiarch's doctrine was the absolute responsibility of the individual for his own salvation. Any promises, prayers or good works of others on his behalf, whether in infancy or after death, would not benefit him, and as they were unavailing were a waste of time. The celebration of mass was no sacrament, but meaningless and void. Peter the Venerable quotes the kind of argument used.

'Oh people, do not believe the bishops, priests and clergy who are leading you astray. As in much else they deceive you when they minister at the altar and lie when they themselves make the body of Christ and offer it to you for the salvation of your souls. Manifestly they lie. For the body of Christ was made once alone by Christ himself at supper before the passion, and once, that is at that time only, was given to the disciples. Since then it has neither been made by anyone nor given to anyone.'[3]

The rejection of the sacraments, of infant baptism and the eucharist was also based upon interpretation of passages in the Gospels. The Petrobrusians accepted the Gospels but were understood to deny the authority of all or part of the rest of the New Testament, the Old Testament and the Fathers.[4] How they lived we do not know. Peter of

[1] *Contra Petrobrusianos*, ed. Fearns, c. 116, p. 69; what follows is from c. 117.
[2] Ibid., c. 4, pp. 9–10; cf. c. 112, p. 67.   [3] Ibid., c. 150, pp. 86–7.
[4] Ibid., cc. 12–14, 26, 31–2, 74–5, 127, 231, pp. 14–15, 23–4, 26–7, 45–6, 74–5, 137–8 respectively.

Bruis travelled around preaching, but there is no explicit mention of poverty. Some priests were beaten up and the monastic ideal was repudiated, but we lack evidence on his moral teaching. There was certainly an element of puritanism. They maintained that God was mocked by ecclesiastical chant as he delighted only in holy affections, nor could he be summoned by raised voices or soothed with musical melodies.[1] They went further than St Bernard, who attacked the sumptuous ornament of Cluny and wanted churches to be plain and unadorned; they said there should be no churches at all. Special buildings for prayer were not necessary or needed. New churches should not be built and existing ones should be demolished, because the word 'church' signifies not the walls of a building but the congregation of the faithful.[2] Peter of Bruis may have attacked the clergy as unworthy, but their state was really immaterial: his attack went deeper. With no churches and no eucharist the clergy were superfluous. The individual must rely on his own faith and his own prayer.

Henry of Lausanne[3]

Peter the Venerable never wrote the tract he planned against the doctrines of the next leader of the movement, Henry of Lausanne. A refutation was written, thought to be by William of St Thierry; there is some mention of him in the *Gesta* of the bishops of Le Mans and in a Life of St Bernard of Clairvaux, and a diatribe by St Bernard (Doc. 10).

Henry was a French monk who left his cloister to become a wandering preacher. His activities are first recorded in Le Mans in 1116. Bishop Hildebert, before setting off on a visit to Rome, gave him permission to preach a series of sermons during Lent. These sermons had an impact not intended by the bishop. Henry preached on moral issues: he called for marriage without dowry and for the abolition of prostitution, but most of all he reproached the clergy, for their worldliness, their avarice, their unchastity. The people were already in a revolutionary mood and, inflamed by his words, they rose against the clergy who had to barricade themselves in their houses and appeal to the count for help. Hildebert had to interrupt his journey and return to the city. When he reached the suburbs he raised his hand to bless his people, but they repudiated and insulted him, shouting:

---

[1] *Contra Petrobrusianos*, ed. Fearns, cc. 93, 273, pp. 56, 162 respectively.

[2] Ibid., cc. 27, 89, 95, 97, 107-8, pp. 24, 55-8, 63-4.

[3] On Henry, see Fearns, Liverpool Thesis, Chap. 3; P. von Moos, *Hildebert von Lavardin* (Stuttgart, 1965), pp. 12-13; the chief studies are by Raoul Manselli, *Studi sulle eresie del secolo XII* (Rome, 1953), pp. 49-66, and in *Bulletino dell'Istituto Storico Italiano per il medio evo . . .*, Vol. LXV, pp. 1-63, including the refutation attributed to William of St Thierry, pp. 44-63.

'We don't want knowledge of your ways! We don't want your blessing! Bless the mud, sanctify the mud! We have a father, we have a bishop, we have an advocate who exceeds you in authority, in honesty, exceeds you in learning! Your wicked clergy are the enemies of this cleric; they contradict his doctrine; they hate and reject him as if he were impious because they fear that with prophetic spirit he may lay bare their crimes, and with his finer learning condemn their misbelief (*haeresim*) and carnal incontinence. But all this will rebound undiluted on their heads. They have had the boundless impertinence to forbid God's saint to utter with the voice of his heavenly preaching.'

The bishop, according to the chronicler, pitying their ignorance and error, bore their abuse mildly.[1] He was helped in his efforts to recover the lost esteem of his people by a timely fire which burnt down the quarter in which Henry frequently preached. Some took this as a bad omen and rallied to their bishop. Dressed in his episcopal robes and accompanied by a suitable retinue Hildebert then sought out the embarrassing preacher and publicly put his liturgical knowledge to the test. He ordered him to recite the psalm appointed for Mattins. Henry was unable to, was discredited and expelled. We know little of his wanderings after this. He met Peter of Bruis probably some time before 1125 and was influenced by him. At the Council of Pisa in 1135 he was ordered to cease his wandering preaching and re-enter the cloister as a monk at Cîteaux.[2] He either never obeyed or soon absconded and returned to his chosen existence. He was condemned as a heretic at the Second Lateran Council of 1139. He is last heard of at Toulouse in 1145. Then St Bernard and Cardinal Alberic of Ostia hunted him down and he disappears: it is thought that he was imprisoned.

Peter the Venerable said that Henry not so much amended Peter of Bruis's doctrine as changed and expanded it (Doc. 9), but Henry's doctrine, as it can be deduced from the surviving evidence, seems very similar to Peter's. He was never, however, a formal adherent, and his own followers were known as Henricians. Henry, like Peter, rejected infant baptism, considered prayers for the dead ineffective, and held that no churches should be built either of wood or stone. It is not clear whether he thought existing churches should be demolished. The extent to which his teaching may have gone beyond or differed from Peter's cannot be assessed in the absence of further knowledge of Peter's

[1] Von Moos, op. cit., p. 12n., quoting the *Gesta* of the bishops of Le Mans, in full in *Recueil des historiens des Gaules et de la France*, Vol. XII (edn of Paris, 1877), pp. 547ff., especially p. 550.
[2] Manselli, *Studi*, p. 64; for the date see C. Hefele-H. Leclercq, *Histoire des Conciles*, Vol. VI, part i (Paris, 1912), pp. 706–7.

teaching. On the evidence we have, Henry had more to say on the sacraments and the priesthood. He held that chrism and oil were of no use in baptism; that marriage was not a sacrament, the consent of the parties being all that was needed to make it: and that to go to a priest for penance was not a Gospel precept. He attacked the wealthy and unworthy clergy: unworthy priests do not make the body of Christ in the eucharist; the priests of this age do not have the power of binding and loosing; bishops and priests ought not to have riches and honours. The bishop's ring and mitre and pastoral staff were, to him, evidence of clerical wealth and privilege that should be abandoned. He accepted the New Testament as binding, but not the Fathers. He conceded that the teaching of St Jerome and St Augustine might be admirable but it was not necessary to salvation. He had a strong sense of personal mission. 'He sent me who said: "Go and teach all nations." '[1] The same claim was later made by St Francis.

Henry did not start out as a heretic. Bishop Hildebert had supposed him a suitable Lenten preacher, and his tirades had been concentrated on moral issues – he had not as yet raised doctrinal questions or preached doctrinal error. Denunciation of abuses could be quite respectable. The papal reformers had as heartily attacked unworthy priests and Gregory VII himself had suggested that the sacraments of unworthy priests might not be genuine. But monks wandering about out of their cloister and making criticisms could cause trouble, as Hildebert discovered. He moved him on. This pattern recurred over a long period, almost twenty years. Then, at the Council of Pisa, the authorities tried to prevent him from making further nuisance of himself by ordering him back to the cloister. At this point Henry's career diverged from that of others such as Bernard of Tiron. He found it intolerable now to live in any monastery, Cîteaux not excepted, and he did not establish a monastic community of his own. He did not attach overriding importance to obedience to the Pope and reverence for priests, as Francis was to do, and when he was thwarted he did not seek to win the authorities over by persuasion. Instead he rebelled, declaring that 'it is necessary to obey God rather than men'. His opinions were condemned, but it was his defiance, his pertinacity in sticking to his opinions and his way of life, that made him a heretic. Attempts to live according to the Gospel were not automatically considered praiseworthy. To St Bernard, Henry had only the appearance of godliness; he was a wolf in sheep's clothing.[2] St Bernard actually

---

[1] William of St Thierry, ed. Manselli, op. cit., pp. 44–6.
[2] Doc. 10; see also St Bernard, *Epistola 242*, *PL*, Vol. 182, cols 436–7. *Epistola* 242 is translated in B. S. James, *Letters of St Bernard of Clairvaux* (London, 1953), No. 318, pp. 389–90; and it is not certain that it refers to Henry of

praised a bishop, Atto of Troyes, who distributed his wealth to the poor when he thought he was dying, and who then recovered, and his words do not read like sarcasm. Yet the bishop obeyed the Gospel precept when in a fever and when he thought he would not have to live with the consequences. The tone in which Bernard described how Henry undertook the apostolic life is very different and leads him into slander (Doc. 10).

Arnold of Brescia[1]

Another 'ravening wolf in sheep's clothing' in Bernard's eyes, and therefore to be hounded to destruction, was Arnold of Brescia. When Bernard heard that Arnold was at Constance he wrote to the bishop urging that he be expelled, or better still imprisoned, so that he would not be able to run about and do more harm. When he heard that he was in Bohemia, staying with the papal legate, he again wrote, describing Arnold as a man whose life is sweet as honey but whose doctrine is bitter poison. That the cardinal harbours him suggests either that he does not know who he really is, or that he hopes to convert him. St Bernard cannot directly criticise so admirable a motive – he much hopes, he says, that he may succeed – but he immediately proceeds to discourage any such attempt. 'Who can fashion a son of Abraham from this stone? . . . You can try!' But the prudent man will avoid a heretic who has been twice warned, and he expresses his confidence that the cardinal will appreciate his letter and cease to countenance Arnold. St Bernard had earlier been responsible for Arnold's expulsion from France. To him he was dangerous, the more dangerous because his manner of life was praiseworthy; he was a schismatic, an instigator of trouble wherever he went, and a heretic, who in Paris had associated with Abelard and stubbornly defended his errors. Abelard was anathema to Bernard, and Arnold's championship of his master, and consequent criticism of himself, doubtless exacerbated Bernard's hostility.

Most of our information about Arnold comes from John of Salisbury's succinct account of him in his *Historia Pontificalis* (Doc. 11). A canon regular and abbot at Brescia, who was also a popular preacher and an outspoken critic of the bishops for their worldliness and avarice, his first recorded clash with the hierarchy came when he roused the

Lausanne. The letter to Atto, bishop of Troyes, is *Epistola 23*, *PL*, Vol. 182, cols 125–8, trans. James, No. 24.

[1] See Doc. 11; the fullest recent study is by A. Frugoni, *Arnaldo da Brescia nelle Fonti del secolo XII* (Rome, 1954), see also G. W. Greenaway, *Arnold of Brescia* (Cambridge, 1931). The letters of St Bernard are Nos 250–1 in B. S. James's translation (here quoted), pp. 329–32; Nos 195–6 in *PL*, Vol. 182.

populace of Brescia against their bishop. For this, Pope Innocent II
banished him from Italy, and it was at this stage in his career that he
studied under Abelard at Paris and made an enemy of St Bernard.
After Innocent's death Arnold returned and was reconciled to Eugenius
III on giving a solemn undertaking of obedience. But the Pope presently
went north to preach the Second Crusade and Arnold became a leader
of the Romans, who had set up a commune in defiance of papal power.
He believed that, in contrast to their actual practice, the clergy should
live in ascetic and apostolic poverty, and he denounced the college of
cardinals as a den of thieves. He accused the Pope himself for not living
an apostolic life and for maintaining his authority by misuse of money
and by armed force.

His indictment was not undeserved. The Popes of this period were
developing their political as well as their spiritual power, enlarging and
consolidating their hold on the papal estates, and contesting the power
of the Normans in south Italy. Innocent II had called in German troops
to fight for him in his war with Roger of Sicily. Papal revenues were
collected with ever greater zeal as increasingly large sums of money
were needed to pay troops and to bribe the feudal nobles and the
Romans. Bribery was taken for granted. St Bernard accepted that
Eugenius III, a Cistercian who had been his pupil, had had to follow
the custom. 'Who can you quote to me in the city [Rome] who acknowledged your position as Pope without a bribe or the hope of a bribe ?'[1]
During negotiations with the Roman commune in 1149, made difficult
by the city's refusal to abandon Arnold, the same Pope agreed to pay
the senators 500 pounds a year, as had been the custom. Hadrian IV,
who succeeded in effecting Arnold's expulsion, and consequent death,
was accused by the well-informed Gerhoh of Reichersberg of paying
the Romans the enormous sum of 11,000 pounds of Lucca.[2]

The behaviour of the Romans cannot be explained in terms of any
single cause or ideal. Motivation was complex. Political issues, social
and economic unrest, were factors, as they had been in the orthodox
popular movement of the Patarini in Milan a century earlier, but the
mainspring of Arnold's programme and appeal was religious. The
Romans welcomed him as a penitential preacher of austere life who
offered some moral justification for their anti-clericalism. Anticlerical
and rebellious they were, but for all that the welfare and prosperity of
their city were inextricably bound up with the papal Curia. In 1155
Hadrian IV, having renewed the Treaty of Constance with the Emperor
Frederick Barbarossa, who was already in northern Italy with an army,

---

[1] St Bernard, *De consideratione*, Bk iv, c. 3, quoted in P. Partner, *The Lands
of St Peter* (London, 1972), pp. 185–6.

[2] Partner, op. cit., pp. 183–5.

placed Rome under interdict. The price of lifting the ban was Arnold's expulsion. He tried to escape but was arrested by the advancing German army, handed over to the prefect, and executed. He was one of a number of monks who, during the eleventh and twelfth centuries, left the cloister to preach and to lead popular movements of revolt against corrupt, worldly and immoral bishops and their clergy. He was distinguished from others of his time in that he was a schoolman, a favourite pupil of Abelard's, an academic of some standing turned revolutionary, a man of the fashion of Wyclif, though unlike Wyclif in temperament.

Waldo[1] and the Cathars

Peter of Bruis and Henry of Lausanne were priests; Waldo was not. He was a layman, a rich merchant of Lyon, and married. One day he heard in the street a troubadour singing in French the tale of St Alexis, who, on his wedding day, forsook his bride, his home and his inheritance and set out as a poor pilgrim for the Holy Land. Profoundly moved, Waldo went to a priest for advice. How could he follow God's will and become perfect? He received in answer the very same text from St Matthew that was first to meet St Francis's eyes when he opened the Gospel book in response to a similar inquiry from his first disciple, Bernard of Quintavalle: 'If you wish to be perfect, go, sell your possessions, and give to the poor, and then you will have riches in heaven; and come, follow me.'[2] So Waldo distributed his goods, assigning his property and furniture for the support of his wife, making restitution of ill-gotten gains, dowering his two daughters, whom he dispatched (how willingly is not recorded) to Robert of Arbrissel's foundation at Fontevrault, and giving the remainder to the poor. On Assumption Day 1173 he took the vow of poverty. Among the disciples who joined him were two priests, who translated the Psalter and parts of the Bible for them into French, as Waldo and other lay members could not read Latin. These French Scriptures they studied, learning long passages by heart and seeking to model their lives accordingly. So they began to preach and at once they ran into difficulties.

Their preaching was unauthorised, and possibly more well-meaning than well-informed. The archbishop of Lyon ordered them to desist. Waldo refused, quoting St Peter: 'We must obey God rather than men' (Acts, 5:29), and was excommunicated. He felt that justice had not been done, and so he and his followers set out for Rome to appeal to the Pope, taking with them their French translations as evidence of their

---

[1] See Thouzellier, especially pp. 27ff.; Maisonneuve, pp. 137ff.; and other works cited above; also K.-V. Selge, *Die ersten Waldenser.*
[2] Matt., 19:21; Maisonneuve, p. 138; see above, p. 22.

good faith. They arrived while Rome was crowded with prelates gathered to attend the Third Lateran Council, 1179. They were eager to prove their knowledge of Scripture, which they believed would demonstrate their fitness to preach, and they were given a hearing. Document 13 is an account by the learned satirist Walter Map of how he himself was appointed to examine them, and of how he won a speedy verbal victory over their simplemindedness.

Map's famous book, *De nugis curialium* (mostly written *c.* 1180–1) is a mixture of history, stories and satire; some of the tales are true, some the invention of a brilliant story-teller; many are poised between, deliberately, not quite one or the other. No doubt he was at the Lateran Council; very likely he was involved in some discussion with the Waldensians; but this particular account sits with others of heretics deliberately garbled, and it is most unlikely that Waldo and his companions were treated quite as shabbily as this. None the less, they were reckoned ignorant folk and consequently Alexander III, though he approved their vow of poverty, did not feel able to allow them the licence to preach that they so badly wanted. They might preach only if invited to do so by the clergy. This amounted to a prohibition as such invitations were unlikely to be forthcoming. Waldo and his companions returned home. The next year, 1180, Henry, abbot of Clairvaux, whom the Pope had appointed cardinal bishop of Albano and papal legate in Languedoc, summoned Waldo to appear before him at a synod in Lyon to establish his orthodoxy. Waldo placed his hands in those of the cardinal and swore that neither he nor his companions were members of a heretical sect. He was also required to make a positive profession of faith (Doc. 12). This profession was based on an ancient formulary of catholic dogma used in episcopal ordinations, adapted to take account of contemporary conditions and dangers.

The Waldensians were centred on Lyon, in an area where heresy was flourishing and endemic. The influence of Peter of Bruis and Henry of Lausanne had never been eradicated, and the rival heresy of the Cathars had a powerful hold. The Cathars had grown so numerous and so confident that in 1167 they had held a Church Council of their own at St Félix-de-Caraman, twenty-five kilometres from Toulouse, at which they set up a completely independent administrative organisation. They elected bishops, whom their pope then ordained, and, on his advice, fixed the boundaries of their sees (Doc. 14). In the diocese of Albi, two years earlier, when the bishop of Lodève excommunicated them they excommunicated him back.[1] The archbishop of Narbonne presently appealed to Louis VII for help, and soon after, Raymond V, count of Toulouse, appealed to the Cistercians, for prayers, and to the

[1] Maisonneuve, pp. 127–8.

kings of France and England – he was vassal of both – for troops.
Louis VII and Henry II nominated a commission of leading ecclesiastical and lay magnates, including Henry, abbot of Clairvaux, charged with
either converting the heretics or driving them from the realm. Their
mission, of 1178, with its combination of ecclesiastical and military
elements, marked a significant stage in a deterioration of communication
which was to culminate in the Albigensian Crusade. Alexander III
was persuaded to substitute a military effort against the heretics for the
proposed crusade to the Holy Land. The Third Lateran Council, at
which Waldo presented himself, enacted several decrees concerning
heresy and encouraged the faithful to take up arms in the cause of orthodoxy with the offer of the same indulgences and spiritual benefits as
could be earned by a visit to the Holy Sepulchre. Waldo's profession of
faith to Henry reflects these concerns. He dissociated himself from the
Petrobrusians by declaring his belief that God was the author of both
Old and New Testaments, that consecration did change the bread and
the wine into the body and blood of Christ, that good works might
benefit the dead, and that singing in church was praiseworthy and infant
baptism efficacious. His readiness to accept the sacraments as valid,
even when performed by a sinful priest, shows that he did not endorse
the strictures of Henry of Lausanne, and others, on this topic. Veneration
of the use of consecrated oil may also be in repudiation of Henry's
teaching, as may toleration – it seems no more – of the sacrament of
penance, but it is not always easy to identify to which heretical group
a particular doctrine belongs. There was considerable variety of heretical
grouping, and variety also of belief within particular heresies.

Cathar beliefs notably lacked uniformity but they were essentially
dualist.[1] The Cathars (though not all of them believed all of what
follows) believed that the world was governed by two opposing principles, good and evil. To the good God belonged everything spiritual,
to the devil, who was created evil, the material world. The body was
irredeemably evil. It was impossible then for Christ to be at once
human and divine. Christ, if he was indeed the son of God, could not
have taken on a diabolical body; he must have assumed the appearance
of a human body but remained wholly spirit. He appeared thus only to
share in human suffering, but could neither eat nor drink, nor feel
pain upon the Cross. He could effortlessly walk upon the waters. There

---

[1] I.e. they believed the material world to be wholly evil, even in its creation;
they differed among themselves whether its creator was a fallen angel or an
evil God – the latter involving a radical dualism, with two independent deities.
On the Cathars, see Thouzellier; Maisonneuve; A. Borst, *Die Katharer* (Stuttgart, 1953); Sir Steven Runciman, *The Medieval Manichee* (Cambridge, 1947),
which is especially helpful for their background in the Balkans and the Byzan-
tine Empire, for which see also D. Obolensky, *The Bogomils* (Cambridge, 1948).

was no resurrection. Reproduction of evil matter was evil; so marriage was condemned and pregnant women were encouraged to resort to abortion or infanticide. The eating of meat was forbidden. The Cathars had their own sacraments: ordination, the breaking and blessing of bread, in the name of Christ, and the laying on of hands, the *consolamentum*, which did duty for the three catholic sacraments of baptism, penance and confirmation (Doc. 15).

Waldo repudiated these tenets and practices, or affirmed their opposites. He ended his profession with a brief statement of the principles on which he and his associates based their lives. Believing that good works are necessary to salvation, and faith alone is not enough, they have renounced the world and intend to obey the Gospel. They have distributed their goods to the poor, will take no thought for the morrow, will accept only food and clothing and not money, but they will not condemn as beyond redemption those who do not choose to take such drastic measures but live good lives in the world. Surely Waldo and Francis were kindred spirits? There is nothing heretical here. But, though the way of life of the Waldensians, based on the Gospels, was approved and vindicated, there was one thing missing: wandering preaching was enjoined by the Gospel, and yet its practice was denied them. The tension and frustration caused by this proved too great a strain on their obedience. They preached. Probably in 1182, only three years after their appeal to the Pope, and two years after the profession of faith, they were excommunicated as contumacious by the archbishop of Lyon.[1] Known too as the Poor Men of Lyon, some groups dispersed into Provence, where they engaged in doctrinal controversy with the Cathars; others crossed the Alps into Italy, where they inevitably formed links with other groups, for example the followers of Arnold of Brescia. Commercial links between Lyon and Milan also brought them into contact with the Humiliati. Expelled from the Church, they remained convinced of their apostolic vocation.

[1] Thouzellier, p. 38.

5

The Preparation: Papal Policy[1]

The Twelfth Century

How was the Church to face the problems posed by heresy and dis-affection? How to prevent its spread, win back its adherents, define exactly what constituted heresy – all these were urgent questions to which there were in practice no easy answers. The boundaries between heresy and orthodoxy were not clear cut. Many of the heretics were comparatively simple folk whose statements of doctrine and sentiment could hardly be compared with scholastic definitions; and some of the statements of eminent theologians, like Abelard, were thought heretical by other theologians of his generation but became accepted orthodoxy in the next. Closely akin to doctrinal deviation, in the common view, was disobedience. When Samuel denounced Saul for his disobedience to the Lord he said defiance was as sinful as witchcraft, as evil as idolatry (1 Kings–1 Sam.–15: 22-3) and this became a commonplace in medieval attitudes to persistent disobedience. In the ancient world, and under Roman law, burning had been the traditional punishment for witchcraft.[2] It was doubtless by a natural analogy that the mob or the secular arm sometimes lit bonfires for heretics in the early eleventh century. By the twelfth century a tradition was being established, though not based as yet on many precedents, that the appropriate fate of the

[1] I have to treat the large problems of this chapter rather cursorily. Many of them are fully treated by Grundmann, Thouzellier (with very helpful and up-to-date bibliography), and Maisonneuve. From all three I have derived much benefit, and I have also found particularly helpful the series of articles by Miss Brenda Bolton in *Studies in Church History:* 'Innocent III's Treatment of the *Humiliati*', Vol. 8 (1972), pp. 73-82; 'Tradition and Temerity: Papal Attitudes to Deviants, 1159-1216', Vol. 9 (1972), pp. 79-91; 'Mulieres sanctae', Vol. 10 (1973), pp. 77-95 (and see p. 81, n. 1 below). On Innocent III see also M. Maccarrone, in *Rivista di Storia della Chiesa in Italia*, Vol. XVI (1962), pp. 29-72.

[2] Cf. C. Brooke, review of Maisonneuve, *English Historical Review*, Vol. LXXVII (1962), pp. 137-8; and on this and on the English incident of 1165-6 (below), see A. Morey and C. N. L. Brooke, *Gilbert Foliot and his Letters* (Cambridge, 1965), pp. 241-3.

obdurate heretic should be burning; and this might seem to minds attuned to persecution particularly suitable, since custom and biblical interpretation conspired to identify heresy with persistent disobedience to authority, persistent disobedience with witchcraft.

Attitudes towards heresy varied. Kings, often with the encouragement of their bishops, and if it was in their interest, treated it as a crime. In England, in the winter of 1165–6, a group of thirty immigrant weavers was apprehended and examined by a panel of bishops at Oxford who pronounced them heretics and handed them over to the king for punishment. Henry II ordered them to be branded on the forehead and then, stripped to the waist, to be whipped out of the town. The people were expressly forbidden to give them any shelter or assistance and they died of exposure. The house in which they had lodged was dismantled, removed and burnt. There seems to have been no native heresy in England, and it was comparatively easy for a king, whose control of the ports enabled him to prevent the import of foreign currency, to discourage the import of heresy. Henry II had extensive continental possessions. Problems, political, social and economic as well as religious, connected with heretical groups and movements in central and southern France, and in Flanders, from which those weavers came, no doubt alerted him to the prudence of denying this European phenomenon a foothold across the Channel.

It was, in the first instance, the duty of the bishops to deal with heretics, and when they co-operated closely with secular rulers the combination could be formidable. In 1183–4 the archbishop of Rheims had a private meeting with the count of Flanders after the discovery of a few heretics at Arras. Shortly afterwards a number of heretics were denounced by a woman informer. Those who failed the ordeal to which they were subjected were burnt and their goods confiscated to the mutual benefit of archbishop and count who presided together over the tribunal. Cruelty was not out of harmony with public opinion. The populace, if asked, often demanded burning. Peter of Bruis was lynched. Seven heretics were burnt at Vézelay because the abbot, during the Easter procession, asked the assembled crowds what should be done with those who persisted in their obstinacy and all cried: 'Let them be burnt, let them be burnt. . . .'[1] But in some areas, most notably in Languedoc and in centres of Ghibelline affiliation in Italy, the population was generally sympathetic to heretics, whose way of life could be admirable and markedly superior to that of the local orthodox clergy.

In formulating policy, the Popes had to take account of the attitudes of rulers and people, and of their own hierarchy, but they were also able to influence and mould these attitudes. Several quite distinct, even con-

[1] Maisonneuve, p. 116.

tradictory, policies were attempted. Heresy was not a single or uniform
phenomenon. It applied to sects like the Cathars, holding rigid or
modified dualist beliefs, and to groups of unsatisfied, simple Christians,
who studied the Bible in order to understand and follow the original
intentions of Christ, and who failed to recognise in the Church as they
saw it authentic exponents of primitive apostolic authority. One way of
dealing with independent groups of poor, wandering preachers who
claimed an apostolic vocation was to segregate the men and the
women and put them into monastic orders. This was the solution
advocated by St Bernard. Intellectual clarification and definition of
doctrinal positions was fostered by intensive study of theology and
canon law in the schools and universities.

Two other possibilities were persuasion and repression, which could
be viewed as opposite sides of the same coin. Persuasion included
preaching and argument, and reform and improvement in the quality
of the clergy. Repression ranged from confiscation of goods and civic
disabilities to exile and death. Until the time of Alexander III (1159–81),
attention had been focused almost exclusively on conditions in the
south of France, where heresy had major political significance, and
Popes had provided the bishops with no clear guidelines on the general
aspects of handling popular religious movements and arresting the
spread of heresy within them. Alexander III, though continuing to
devote much attention and effort to the south of France, viewed the
problems in a wider context and initiated trends in policy which were
capable of much subsequent development and extension. His views
were formulated earlier in his career – he was a lawyer trained at
Bologna – and were based on a continuing tradition of interpretation of
certain passages drawn from St Augustine. He held that coercion of
wrongdoers is permissible if exercised by a properly constituted
authority, but that such coercion must be undertaken not out of any
desire for vengeance but in a spirit of justice and of love for the offender.
Applied to heresy his principles meant not only that he was prepared to
be persuaded to promote military expeditions against heretics as
meritorious action on the part of Christian soldiers, comparable to war
against the infidel which was already encouraged, but that at the same
time he regarded death as the penalty only of last resort, a confession
really of failure, as the purpose of pursuit was to bring heretics back
into the fold. Heretics needed to have their obstinacy overcome and their
minds disabused. Henry, abbot of Clairvaux, whom Alexander appointed cardinal legate in Languedoc, was the embodiment of this
approach, active in mobilising lay and ecclesiastical intervention and
an eloquent preacher. In 1181 he besieged the castle at Lavaur, where
two heretical leaders had taken refuge. When he had captured them he

set about converting them, and he spoke so convincingly and persuasively that both were won over. They confessed their errors, were reconciled, and ended their lives as canons regular.

Evidence is sparse and fragmentary but sufficient to reveal Alexander's initiative. About 1162 the archbishop of Rheims uncovered a group of suspected heretics, but they forestalled his proceedings against them by appealing to the Pope. The archbishop was a brother of the French king, and Louis VII wrote to Alexander urging severity. The Pope's position was delicate. The papal schism which accompanied his election undermined his power. He was not as yet strong enough to take up residence in Rome, was living on French soil, and was beholden to the French king for recognising his title. He received the petitioners with asperity. Their fervent assertion of innocence, however, impressed him, and he ordered the archbishop to hold an inquiry, to refer its report to him for decision, and meanwhile to ensure that no harm was done to the accused or to their property, which was not negligible. He recommended prudence. It was possible to be mistaken, and he held it better to spare the guilty than condemn the innocent. Procedure by inquiry was more rational and just than ordeal, which was superstitious, uncertain and barbaric. But it is not easy to change men's attitudes. The archbishop was used to the old ways. In 1172 he was asked to judge a clerk of Arras accused of disseminating heretical propaganda. Having subjected him to the ordeal of hot iron which inflicted multiple burns on his hands, feet and body, he condemned him to be burnt. Inquiry, when instituted, though an advance, was not automatically all that satisfactory. Archbishops and bishops were encouraged, for example by letters in 1170, to co-opt prudent and religious men to assist them. But who were chosen as investigators? All too often they were men less charitable, less conciliatory, less understanding than the Pope. Inquiry could also have other applications besides fact-finding. The Flemish petitioners had come to the Pope at Tours. At a council held there in the same year, 1163, Alexander denounced secret conventicles which helped the spread of heresy. The bishops were to seek out any that existed in their dioceses and suppress them. Princes and people were to be reminded not to harbour, help or do business or trade with heretics.

After Alexander's death there was a hardening of attitude. Lucius III and the Emperor Frederick Barbarossa agreed to a joint policy of ecclesiastical and secular repression. *Ad abolendam* (1184) condemned an assortment of heretics by name, including Cathars, Patarini,[1] Humiliati, Poor Men of Lyon (Waldensians), Arnaldists and in general

[1] The word had originally been used of the orthodox, reforming insurgents in Milan of the mid-late eleventh century; by the late twelfth century it had

all who dared to preach without papal or episcopal permission, all whose beliefs were at variance with approved doctrine, and all who abetted heretics. The bishops were to investigate parishes rumoured to contain heretics and to require reputable local people under oath to denounce conventicles, heretics and any who were behaving suspiciously. Refusal to take an oath was regarded as an automatic indication of heresy. The convicted were excommunicated and handed over to the secular authority. This legislation lumped together doctrinal heretics and devotees of voluntary poverty; it threatened the strict dualist and the befriender of a poor, wandering preacher with the same fate. A statute of the synod of Toul, 1192, instructed the faithful to bring any Waldensians they could find in chains to the bishop for punishment. In 1194 the king of Aragon decreed that anyone who helped Waldensians or other heretics, or listened to their sermons, was guilty of *lèse-majesté*. Heretics were warned to leave the country promptly or face persecution. These sanctions were reinforced by his son, Peter II, in 1198. Heretics were to be expelled and their goods confiscated. Any found remaining in the country were to be burnt on conviction. Informers were to receive one-third of the confiscated goods.[1]

Innocent III

When Innocent III became Pope in 1198, prospects for recovery and reconciliation were bleak. By the time of his death in 1216, diametrically opposite policies, employed concurrently, were both yielding results. Crusaders enlisted in northern France had overrun Languedoc where heresy was now savagely persecuted, and the culture of a whole region was in the throes of destruction; but men were permitted to form communities dedicated to voluntary apostolic poverty and preaching.

At the beginning of his pontificate, Innocent III issued the decretal *Vergentis in senium* (1199). Lands belonging to heretics were to be confiscated, by the Church if in papal territory, by the secular rulers elsewhere. The justification given for this was that heretics offended the majesty of Christ – were guilty of *lèse-majesté* against Him – but the intention was ostensibly merciful and remedial, that worldly penalties might correct those whom spiritual sanctions had failed to touch. If penury prompted conversion, lands might be restored. Meanwhile persuasion was reinforced. The Pope's confessor, Rainier, was entrusted with a special mission to preach against heresy in the south of France.

become a synonym for the Cathar heretics: the explanation of this is not known. On *Ad abolendam* see Maisonneuve, pp. 151ff.

[1] Thouzellier, pp. 133ff.

Rainier was much respected, upright, pious, learned, active and
eloquent, a Cistercian and a friend of Joachim of Fiore, the mystic
and prophet, whose ideas were to exercise so powerful an influence in
the later Middle Ages.[1] Another Cistercian was seconded to help him.
Mercy and circumspection were recommended. Bishops could be over-
zealous, and Innocent reminded them that though God's judgements
cannot err the judgement of the Church is fallible. He ordered that the
dean of Nevers, who had been deprived of his benefice after being
accused of heresy, should be allowed to purge himself and that his
revenues should be restored to him, as it would bring shame on the
clergy to reduce him to beggary. Some burghers of La Charité, accused,
acquitted and reaccused, were to be carefully examined. If their guilt
was proved beyond doubt they were to be handed over to the secular
power – and a Cathar knight, Évrard of Châteauneuf, uncle of the dean
of Nevers, was so handed over to his lord, the count of Nevers, and
burnt – but they were not to be punished on suspicion alone. They
were to be warned, and given a penance that was moderate, which would
test the sincerity of their conversion without dismaying them, and they
were to be protected from the hostility of the populace.

A community at Metz uncovered by the bishop, of lay men and women
who met privately to read and discuss parts of the Bible, the New
Testament, the Psalms and other books which they had translated into
French, and who listened to Waldensian preachers who had come
north after being expelled from Montpellier, benefited temporarily from
the Pope's intervention. Innocent stated that their desire to study and
understand scripture was laudable, though they should be brought to
realise that the Church had the preachers properly qualified to interpret
them and that secret conventicles were reprehensible. The bishop was
to act in such a way that the faith of simple people was not weakened;
he must not be too severe, as that would tend to drive them into the
arms of the heretics, nor too indulgent as that would make the heretics
more bold. The bishop found such a delicate balance hard to maintain.
His letters failed to make clear whether their errors were trifling or
fundamental. Innocent demanded that he find out the truth regarding
the opinions and way of life of their translators and teachers and their
attitude towards the Church: without this necessary information he
could not decide on the case. The bishop assured him that they were
thoroughly disobedient, but the Pope was still not convinced and dispatched three Cistercian abbots who, together with the bishop, were

[1] Thouzellier, pp. 139ff.; on the relations of Joachim and contemporary heresy,
see pp. 110ff. The fundamental study of Joachim and his influence is Marjorie
Reeves, *The Influence of Prophecy in the Later Middle Ages: A Study of
Joachimism* (Oxford, 1969).

to interview the translators and their followers, in the hope of correcting any errors in their work, and to send him a detailed report of their investigation. The Cistercians seem to have agreed with the bishop. The translations were burnt and the sect suppressed. Possibly as a result of this, the papal legate in the Netherlands sought to curb the dissemination of vernacular Bibles, both French and German, in the diocese of Liège. All such books were to be handed in to the bishop.

The Humiliati fared better.[1] Included in the general condemnation of heretics by Lucius III in 1184, one group at least was subsequently reinstated, though forbidden to preach. Innocent III favoured conciliation to win them back, and in 1198 or 1199 two of their leaders came to him seeking recognition. He asked them to present a statement of their way of life, and as this differed substantially from the traditional forms he said he would have to reflect upon it but would give it careful consideration. One bishop and two Cistercian abbots were detailed to examine it. Their report was favourable, and in 1201, two to three years after their approach, Innocent III formally approved three categories of Humiliati. The first Order came nearest to the traditional. Its members all received the tonsure and enjoyed the status of canons. They were allowed to build their own churches, so long as other churches were not prejudiced and the bishop gave permission, and they might possess tithes. They were cloistered but might leave freely if they wished. The second Order provided for lay men and women living in separate communities. The third, the Tertiaries, the original and most numerous section of the movement, was experimental, an innovation. It was designed for ordinary lay folk who continued to live at home with their families and to engage in trade and industry – many were weavers and cloth-workers – but who regulated their lives in accordance with strict evangelical principles. Innocent allowed them to meet together on Sundays to hear sermons on devotional and pious subjects delivered by members of their own congregations. He also excused them from taking unnecessary oaths. The Humiliati responded to these concessions by actively supporting the Church against heresy in the northern Italian towns where they mainly flourished. When Jacques de Vitry visited Milan in 1216 he estimated that they had as many as 150 conventual houses in the city as well as innumerable family groups. Popular ballad was quick to highlight their distinctive features:

[1] See B. Bolton in *Studies in Church History*, Vol. 8 (1972), pp. 73–82; and her forthcoming study, 'The Poverty of the Humiliati' – see summary in *Collectanea Franciscana*, Vol. XLIII (1973), pp. 412–13.

Sunt In Italia Fratres Humiliati,
Qui jurare renuunt et sunt uxorati.[1]

But although the Humiliati were won back and enlisted against their former associates, the results of conciliation were on the whole felt to be discouraging. Despite his efforts Innocent admitted that La Charité remained a 'Babylon of heretical depravity'. The Cathars continued to flourish in Italy, and not only in cities of Ghibelline allegiance but even in the papal states, a deliberate protest against the landed wealth and political and economic power of the Church. The strong community of Cathars at Orvieto was in control of the city for several months in 1198, and in 1200 Innocent menaced Viterbo with the loss of her episcopal see if she persisted in favouring heretics. But five years later they were still prospering there, with two consuls Cathars and the chamberlain an excommunicate.[2] In an attempt to counter heresy and recover control of territory, mercenaries and the armies of rival cities were utilised, supported by a wide variety of spiritual, political and economic sanctions. Recalcitrant cities such as Parma, Piacenza and Milan were crippled by the sequestration of their merchants' goods. Bologna was threatened with the removal of her schools. There were some successes. For example in 1204 the *podestà* and fifty leading citizens of Assisi swore to obey the papal mandates; in 1206 Prato expelled heretics and incapacitated suspects from the consulate.[3]

Meanwhile in Languedoc Innocent increased his reliance on the Cistercian Order, which was required to put some of its top-ranking personnel at his disposal. The abbot of Cîteaux itself, Arnaud-Amaury, was appointed legate and two monks of Fontfroide near Narbonne, Peter of Castelnau and Ralph, were chosen to conduct an intensive preaching mission. In the bull *Etsi nostri navicula* of 1204 Innocent explains why he is choosing Cistercians: preaching to be effective must be undertaken by men full of zeal for God, learned in theology, powerful in word and in works, by men exemplary and above reproach. Lack of proper instruction and worthy example had made the population fall easy prey to heretical propaganda. In 1200 Innocent had rebuked Berengar, archbishop of Narbonne, for his failure to visit his province even once during the ten years he had held the see. The archbishop by a timely repentance evaded deposition, but the legates were empowered to discipline the bishops and the local clergy, and the quality of the

---

[1] Quoted Bolton, *Studies in Church History*, Vol. 8, p. 74.

[2] D. Waley, 'Viterbo nello stato della Chiesa nel secolo XIII', offprint from *Convegno di Studio: Viterbo 18–19–20 Ottobre 1970*, p. 5.

[3] Thouzellier, pp. 162–4, 167; and for what follows, see especially pp. 156ff., 187ff.

higher clergy notably improved. The task allotted to the Cistercians was a tough and discouraging one, uncongenial to monks who had opted for seclusion, but Innocent answered their appeals to be released and allowed to return to the cloister with brisk exhortations to obey the call of duty and to abandon the delights of contemplation for the fruitful labour of evangelism. One reason for the failure of this preaching to make much impact may have been the general strategy of threats and reprisals into which it was fitted. Innocent commissioned the Cistercians to preach, and at the same time gave them full authority to wipe out the pollution of heresy with the usual battery of exile, confiscation of property and the help of the secular arm. He also wrote to the French king encouraging him to confiscate the lands of his vassals, be they counts or barons, who showed themselves hostile to the repression of heresy.

At this juncture the Cistercians encountered two Spaniards, Diego, Bishop of Osma, and Dominic, an encounter which was to have far-reaching consequences. Diego suggested that perhaps the image was wrong. He suggested that they should rather silence the heretics by the example of poverty. Diego sent home his own episcopal retinue and his horses, keeping only Dominic for his companion. Ralph and Peter of Castelnau emulated him. This new-style preaching quickly received papal approval.[1] In a bull of November 1206, Innocent III instructed Ralph to gather suitably qualified men to help in his mission, men who, imitating the poverty of Christ, might convince the heretics of their error by example and word. In the spring of the next year the abbot of Cîteaux selected as reinforcements twelve learned and eloquent Cistercian abbots prepared to assist in this, to them, novel approach. They travelled cheaply with one companion each to emphasise their apostolic mission. On arrival each was assigned a region, and they proceeded to tour on foot, preaching and holding discussions and debates. The bishop of Osma held one such debate in September 1207 at the court of Raymond-Roger, count of Foix, who left heretics in his territories unmolested because he had friends and relations among them and because their way of life was edifying. His wife was a convinced Cathar, as was one of her sisters, but another sister was a Waldensian, and by the end of the debate the bishop had succeeded in winning over a group of Waldensians led by Durand of Huesca, an early disciple of Waldo and a dedicated opponent of the Cathars. Unfortunately the bishop died as the year ended, and the Cistercian mission faltered. The abbots were not convinced that the new techniques were preferable; they found the results incommensurate with the effort and returned home. The Pope also was growing impatient. Conversions were far

[1] Ibid., pp. 196ff.; Doc. 17, cc. 19ff.

fewer than he had hoped and were coming principally from among the
ranks of disaffected Christians. The Waldensians were in origin and
intention orthodox, convinced of their apostolic vocation. The Cathars
were proving obdurate. In November 1207 Innocent called on the King
of France to inflict the miseries of war on them – let iron conquer
those whom persuasion had not convinced. In January 1208 Peter of
Castelnau was assassinated and the Pope redoubled his pressure on the
king, the bishops and the barons of France. The Albigensian Crusade
was launched.

The Albigensian Crusade[1] and Durand of Huesca

Command was given to the abbot of Cîteaux, Arnaud-Amaury.
Although as a priest and a monk he was debarred from shedding blood
himself, he is described as fervently desiring the death of Christ's
enemies. Ecclesiastical leadership did not mitigate the horrors of war.
The abbot led the army which took Béziers in 1209. The town was
pillaged and burnt; the inhabitants massacred. Over one hundred
castles capitulated in fear. Carcassonne was taken. The viscount, who
had fought bravely, was taken prisoner and shortly afterwards died in
chains. Simon de Montfort was invested with his fief and went on to
conquer and occupy the county of Toulouse. The war was fought
savagely, with fanaticism. The chronicler Peter of Vaux-de-Cernai
recorded more than once that the soldiers, 'our pilgrims', burnt the
heretics in the lands they overran, at once place 140, at another 60,
burnt them 'with exceeding great joy'.[2]

Durand of Huesca and his followers escaped the beginning of the
crusade. They had been sent to Rome for absolution, and there their
beliefs and proposed way of life were carefully examined and approved.[3]
In 1208 Durand placed his hands in those of Innocent III and swore to
his faith and vocation, his detestation of heresy, his obedience to the
Pope and to ecclesiastical authority. His profession of faith and proposed way of life were based on that already sworn to by Waldo,
although the Poor Catholics, as his reconciled group was called, wore
open shoes to distinguish them from the still unreconciled Waldensians.
It stated:

'We have renounced the world, and what we had we have given to
the poor as God counselled: we are determined to be poor. As we do
not wish to take thought for the morrow we will not accept gold or

---

[1] See Thouzellier, pp. 204ff.; Maisonneuve, pp. 199ff.
[2] Ibid., p. 222 and nn.
[3] On Durand, see Thouzellier, pp. 212–32; cf. Bolton in *Studies in Church
History*, Vol. 9, pp. 88–9.

silver or anything other than daily food and clothing. We intend to observe as precepts the counsels of the Gospel. . . . As the majority of us are clerks and almost all are literate, we have decided to devote ourselves to study, to exhortation, to teaching and to disputation against all heretical sects. Disputations will be conducted by the more learned brothers, of proved catholic faith and instructed in the law of God, that the adversaries of the catholic and apostolic faith may be confounded. We propose that the worthier and better instructed in the law of God and the writings of the Fathers should expound the word of God to the brothers and their friends in our schools. Suitable brothers, instructed in Scripture and strengthened in sound doctrine, with ecclesiastical permission and due deference, shall argue with the erring, to draw them by all means to faith and recall them to the bosom of the Holy Roman Church.'[1]

So Durand had succeeded, where Waldo had failed, in securing for himself and his followers permission to preach. Even the laymen among them, if judged competent, might deliver exhortations and dispute with heretics. The Poor Catholics received papal letters declaring their orthodoxy. Their lay members were exempted from military service against Christians and they were not obliged to take oaths in civil cases. They could now return home and assist the depleted band of missionaries in Languedoc. The local clergy, however, and even the archbishop of Narbonne, unwontedly zealous, viewed them with suspicion, because they consorted with their old associates and because their preaching attracted audiences away from the parish churches. The atrocities committed by the crusaders, indeed the whole concept of the crusade, were offensive to a sect which objected to the death penalty and created a further barrier between them and the leaders of the Church in the area. In 1210 Durand and his followers went again to Rome to apprise Innocent III of their grievances. Innocent listened sympathetically, for he felt that these enthusiastic converts might well induce others to imitate them. He told the bishops to receive and protect them and to allow them to preach, though at convenient hours which did not clash with other services. Encouraged by the Pope's confidence in their sincerity and usefulness, the Poor Catholics had a modest success, establishing communities of educated preachers in Catalonia, Narbonne and Lombardy. Durand himself continued energetically to proclaim his own faith and to attack heresy. He wrote a treatise against the heretics, the *Liber contra Manicheos*,

---

[1] Thouzellier, p. 220 nn., especially nn. 22, 24; G.-G. Meersseman, *Dossier de l'Ordre de la Pénitence au XIIIe siècle* (Fribourg, 1961), especially pp. 282-4.

which he submitted and dedicated to Cardinal Leo of Santa Croce whom he called his protector.[1] Cardinal Leo also befriended St Francis, another of Innocent III's visitors in 1210.

The same year we hear of yet another would-be preacher coming to the Pope on the same errand, seeking recognition for his group. Bernard Prim, also a disciple of Waldo, swore allegiance in the Pope's hands and submitted a confession of faith.[2] This contained a repudiation of errors of which he and his companions were accused and of which they repented, and a statement of life. They fasted, prayed, educated themselves, exhorted others, and worked, if necessary, for a moderate wage. They would accept none to their fellowship who would not restore all ill-gotten gains, and they paid their dues to the clergy. They were opposed to bloodshed, but accepted the propriety of oaths required by truth or justice. They were less educated than the Poor Catholics, though they studied and respected the Fathers as well as the Gospels, and they sought leave to preach penitence, aimed at preventing the simple from migrating into heresy. They wished to defend the faith manfully against heretics to the utmost of their ability. Innocent accepted them and allowed them to exhort to penitence at suitable times with ecclesiastical permission. He warned them, however, to avoid questionable contact with women. Thus made respectable, the group was quite quickly transformed from a lay to a mainly clerical movement.

Papal Policy and the Fourth Lateran Council of 1215[3]

What then can we say of papal policy towards popular religious movements? Innocent III was both arch-persecutor of heretics and most sympathetic towards protest groups. There has been a tendency recently to emphasise his more attractive side and achievements – and I would not wish to belittle them – but the harsher side, the calling of the Fourth Crusade, in which the Christians of Byzantium were attacked and slain by their supposed assistants, and the Albigensian Crusade, cannot be overlooked. Innocent III was both a theologian and a lawyer; and he provided a legal answer, one moreover which was successful: the Franciscan and Dominican Orders grew out of his method. His human sympathy inclined him to give people who appealed to him a chance and not then to listen too readily to criticisms against

[1] Thouzellier, pp. 296ff., and pp. 303–466; and her edition, Une somme anti-cathare. Le 'Liber contra Manicheos' de Durand de Huesca (Louvain, 1964).

[2] Thouzellier, pp. 232–7, 262ff.; cf. Bolton, Studies in Church History, Vol. 9, p. 89.

[3] See Doc. 16; Raymonde Foreville, Latran, I, II, III et Latran IV (Paris, 1965), sec. on Latran IV, especially pp. 237ff., 327ff., 345–7; Grundmann, pp. 135ff.

them. If they were prepared to swear obedience to him and to agree to follow a way of life outlined in a written statement and subject to approval, he was prepared to allow them a certain liberty to establish and prove themselves. The phenomenal success of the Franciscans was not apparent until after his death. He probably thought St Francis not noticeably different from others who came to him, like Durand of Huesca and Bernard Prim. In 1210 he gave Bernard Prim a provisional authorisation, pending further consideration, made formal two years later. He gave Francis a verbal approval of his Rule and said he would do more for him later if his movement prospered. He perhaps envisaged more clearly the need for the Church to provide the service the Dominicans were to render. He tried hard to extract from the Cistercians a band of trained apostolic preachers, and the message was implemented by St Dominic who had worked with them.

The foundations for Innocent's achievement had been prepared by Alexander III. It is possible to discern his contribution here, as in the extension of holy war to cover heretics. Alexander too was a theologian and a lawyer, subtle and cautious, though he had need of caution, being in a less strong position. He too, was accessible. It is striking how easy it seems to have been for humble, unknown men to come directly to these Popes with their problems. Alexander too had listened sympathetically and, if they seemed deserving, had had their beliefs and way of life examined carefully and at length, finally requiring a public profession of faith. He too had been careful not to accept without question criticisms against the humble and had sought to make the bishops more open-minded in their dealings with them. He baulked at allowing laymen to preach and therefore failed to contain within the Church men determined to obey God alone and to preach in poverty. That Innocent was able to make this concession was partly because he came later and had the lessons of experience in his favour. The difficulty was overcome by drawing a distinction between penitential and doctrinal preaching and permitting the former fairly widely, and by giving the tonsure to laymen who wished to preach, thus making them clerks. Francis and his companions were tonsured before they left Rome.

In 1215, at the close of his pontificate, Innocent III held the Fourth Lateran Council. Here an attempt was made to undermine part of his work by a majority of bishops more conservative than himself, who read the signs differently. Heresy was condemned outright. Hard-bitten Cistercian abbots, who had admittedly been given a tough assignment in the south of France where catholics were seemingly becoming a threatened minority, and where some of their number had been murdered, demanded tough measures for their protection. Count

Raymond VI was deprived of his lands. Only Provence was reserved for his young son, and the rest, Toulouse, Narbonne and Béziers-Carcassonne, were assigned to Simon de Montfort, though Arnaud-Amaury, now archbishop of Narbonne, disputed his title to Narbonne.[1] The war was bound to recommence as Raymond sought to recover his lands. The Lateran Council also expressed its disquiet at the proliferation of small new Orders, such as the Poor Catholics, and enacted that in future anyone wishing to enter religion was to join an Order already approved (Doc. 16). This attempt to put the clock back and to consign the numerous aspirants, who for so long had been showing their desire to serve God in new and different ways, either to monastic establishments of the traditional type or else to the heretical groups that would gladly accept them, in fact failed. It did not prevent the emergence of the Franciscans and Dominicans, the new Orders of friars.

[1] Maisonneuve, pp. 232–3, 232 n. 187.

6

St Dominic[1]

The Problem

Dominic was born at Caleruega, in Old Castile, between 1171 and 1173, and died at Bologna in 1221, when he was about fifty years old. In those fifty years the saint and the Church he served had gone a long pilgrimage. When he was born, the Cathar missionaries were actively at work in the south of France and north of Italy, and were soon to spread into the regions close to Dominic's birthplace. Peter of Bruis was dead; Waldo in his prime, not yet a heretic; St. Bernard of Clairvaux was dead, but his influence was still powerful; the prestige of the Cistercian monks and the Premonstratensian canons was very high among those who admired both Mary and Martha. When Dominic died, the machinery of the Inquisition was beginning to be planned, and his devout friends included Cardinal Hugolino, who as Pope Gregory IX was to canonise him in 1234 and in the early 1230s to confirm the formal structure of the Inquisition and to harness his Order to its service. But Hugolino also counted Francis of Assisi among his friends; the Inquisition was perhaps only an unlooked for by-product of Dominic's work, and the formation of the two Orders of friars, Dominic's and Francis's, like and yet unlike, was well under way by 1221.

Like and yet unlike: that is the key to and the theme of our study of St Dominic. Was his Order like Francis's because he knew and studied Francis's work and his Order? Or did they start apart and draw together by some process of mutual attraction? Or again, as many historians and almost all of the Order of Preachers have supposed,

[1] On St Dominic, see Vicaire, 1964 and 1965–7; the pictorial biography by L. von Matt and Vicaire, *St Dominic* (Eng. trans., London, 1957); on the Order, D. Knowles, *Religious Orders in England*, Vol. I (Cambridge, 1948); R. F. Bennett, *The Early Dominicans* (Cambridge, 1937); G. R. Galbraith, *The Constitution of the Dominican Order, 1216–1360* (Manchester, 1925). The main sources are the *De principiis* of Jordan of Saxony, the canonisation process of St Dominic and the early constitutions (Docs 17, 18, 22); the narrative that follows is based chiefly on Docs 17–18.

were they independent of each other's influence, each a faithful reflection of the ethos of their age and of its challenge and opportunities?

And the differences? Do these represent the deep convictions of minds of a different cast, or are they due to chance, or the effect of environment? In the twelfth century there had already appeared in Castile the first harbingers of the parliamentary movement of the thirteenth century.[1] Is it chance that it should be in the constitutions of an Order founded by Dominic, a Castilian, that the most sophisticated representative structure of the thirteenth century appeared? Can one, in contrast, see in Francis the mingling of courtly romance and heroic anarchy which made the twelfth and early thirteenth centuries witness the rise of the anarchic city republics of north and central Italy?

Dominic's Early Life

The course of Dominic's life unfolds, with a clarity at times deceptive, in the official life by his successor Jordan of Saxony (Doc. 17). He seems to have experienced no reactions or crises similar to Francis's, but was prepared slowly and carefully for a life which at first, and for many years, seemed set in a tolerably conventional mould. He was dedicated to the clerical life at an early age by his devout parents, Felix and Jane, small landowners in Caleruega; after long study in the schools, in his early or mid-twenties he became an Augustinian canon regular in the cathedral community of his own diocese, at Osma. Even before this he had shown his insistent need for long periods of silence and prayer, of opportunities to meditate and to study, slowly and quietly, his own vocation, which was so marked a characteristic of his middle and later years. His love of solitude and solitary prayer – often at night, alone (sometimes in fact observed, as several witnesses at the canonisation process reveal) in a church – might lead one to expect a call to the anchorite life; no doubt, like Francis, he felt its attraction. But Dominic's search was for an apostolic life of practical usefulness, and the canons regular were still the obvious choice.

Dominic and Francis between them changed the Church and the world; their personalities are stamped on the history of the religious life in the thirteenth century. Yet Dominic was deeply and sincerely self-effacing. These two facts are the key to much of what follows; not the sole key, for he was a complex man and his achievement had many sides. But he preached and practised a humility akin to St Benedict's, and with like success.

---

[1] In the local *Cortes* (i.e. courts) of Castile. However, there was undoubtedly a great difference between the gatherings of notables in the kingdoms of northern and central Spain in the twelfth century and the fully worked-out representative system of the Order of Preachers.

In 1196 he became an Augustinian canon. It is interesting to observe that he was named after one of the greatest of the Spanish Benedictines, Santo Domingo de Silos, whose monastery lay only twenty-five miles away to the north of Caleruega; but Dominic was never a monk. He declared for Martha early in his career and never wavered, outwardly at least, in his allegiance.

The early chapters of Jordan of Saxony's *De principiis*, our chief source for the facts of Dominic's life, are actually more concerned with the career of Diego, bishop of Osma; and confusing as this has been to many readers, it has the effect of effacing Dominic himself for a while and revealing one of the powerful influences of his life. Diego was an impulsive idealist and devoted to Dominic, who saw a great deal of the world as well as of Osma in his company. Diego twice went to Denmark on embassy for the King of Castile, first to arrange a marriage, then to collect the princess, both times with Dominic in his train. When he reached Denmark on the second occasion, the princess was dead, so that the immediate purpose of the visit was frustrated. For both, however, it provided a deeper purpose, for they had learned that there were still communities of non-Christians on the north-eastern frontiers of Europe, and they conceived the plan of leading a mission to convert them. Diego took Dominic with him to the papal Curia where the bishop requested permission from Pope Innocent III to abandon his diocese and pursue his new idea. The Pope refused, reckoning that such zeal was as much needed in Castile as in the Baltic. But the appeal of the conventional routine of cathedral life had loosened its hold. On their way back, as they journeyed through Provence and Languedoc, they were struck more forcibly than on their earlier passage by how wide and deep was the problem of heresy there, especially of the Cathar heresy at the height of its power in the years preceding the Albigensian Crusade.

1206–17

In Montpellier they encountered the Cistercian missionaries who were trying to handle the problem of heresy in Provence and Languedoc, led by the papal legate Arnaud-Amaury from Poblet in Catalonia, now abbot of Cîteaux. Tough and zealous though they were, they were oppressed, so it seems, with something of the discouragement Dominic himself was to feel ten years later. They wanted to abandon their mission; the bishop of Osma characteristically urged them to try even harder and to outdo the heretics in poverty, humility and religious zeal; and he prepared to join them. Diego and Dominic made Narbonne their headquarters and set to work to help the Cistercian missionaries. Undoubtedly they had some success; stories are told of Dominic's skill

in public debate, of individual Cathars converted, of the book which
leapt from the flames when his doctrine was tried by the ordeal of fire.
Yet progress was evidently extremely slow; Catholic missionaries nearly
always found Cathar territory as stony ground for conversion as Christian missionaries have found Moslem lands in more recent centuries.
Yet Dominic was not easily discouraged, and there is no reason to
suppose that in these years he felt any inclination to criticise the approach
of his superiors to the problems of heresy. They tried persuasion, and,
when that failed, force; throughout the later years of the Cistercian
legation, of the Albigensian Crusade and the power of Simon de
Montfort the elder – until the very brink of Simon's death in 1217 –
Dominic worked alone and with preachers and crusaders. His attitude
to the crusade and to persecution has been much debated, and the
debate will continue, for there is almost no evidence. But his activities
between 1206 and 1217, and the sudden change of that year, strongly
suggest full acceptance of his colleagues' and superiors' activities at
first, with growing doubt and a sudden change of heart at the
end.

Through the period of the Albigensian Crusade and its aftermath,
Dominic carried on, never directly involved in the politics of the
Crusade, yet never unaffected by them. The archbishop of Narbonne
belied his reputation by helping him to found his first community and
base, a convent of nuns at Prouille, in 1207. In the early 1210s he
enjoyed the patronage of the ex-Cistercian Fulk, bishop of Toulouse,
and then of Simon de Montfort himself, and Toulouse became his
centre. Early in 1215 a wealthy citizen of Toulouse, Peter Seila, joined
Dominic and gave him and his companions some fine houses near the
castle. Bishop Fulk for his part, with the consent of his chapter, assigned
to them a sixth of all the tithes of the diocese, to cover the purchase of
books and necessaries. Thus provided with accommodation and
revenues, Dominic went with Fulk, who was attending the Fourth
Lateran Council, to seek confirmation from the Pope for an Order of
Preachers (Doc. 17, cc. 38–40).

This first attempt was frustrated by the decree of the Fourth Lateran
Council itself forbidding new Orders, or, as it was interpreted, new
rules (Doc. 16, canon XIII). This decree was a challenge both to
Francis and to Dominic, and each reacted in a characteristically
different fashion. Francis took his stand on divine revelation and the
Pope's verbal approval before 1215; he bided his time and won formal
recognition for his own Rule eight years later. Dominic very rapidly
conceived the idea of making the Rule he already served, St Augustine's,
the basis for his new community, adding his own regulations to it (Doc.
22).

The Making of the Order

At first the Order confirmed by Honorius III in January 1217 was an Order of canons regular vowed to preaching; a small community with its base in Toulouse and its vocation in the lands of the Cathars. But quite unexpectedly, later in 1217, Dominic dispersed his followers. We have a first-hand account of what happened from one of the brothers, John of Spain, a witness at the canonisation process, and his evidence is very revealing.

'While the witness was at the convent of the church of St Romain at Toulouse with brother Dominic, he, against the will of the count de Montfort, the archbishop of Narbonne,[1] the bishop of Toulouse and several other prelates, and against the brothers' own inclination, sent him to Paris with five brothers who were clerks and one lay brother, to study, preach and found a convent there. He told them to be without fear as everything would go well with them. To the prelates, the count and the brothers he said: "Do not oppose me; I know quite well what I am doing." At the same time he sent other brothers to Spain with like words and like instructions. While the witness was studying at Paris with his companions, Master John, dean of the chapter of Saint-Quentin, then regent in theology at Paris, together with the masters and scholars of the University of Paris, granted them the church of Saint-Jacques, near the Porte d'Orléans. They established themselves there, built a convent, and received there many worthy clerks who entered the Order of Friars Preachers. They were given a number of benefactions and revenues, and everything succeeded with them as Dominic had predicted. It was at this time that the Order of Preachers was also given towns and numerous endowments in the regions of Toulouse and Albi. The Order of Preachers then possessed in these regions these towns and numerous possessions; the brothers carried money with them on their travels, rode on horseback and wore surplices. Brother Dominic prevailed to such effect that he induced the brothers of his Order to abandon and despise all temporal goods, to remain in poverty, to travel no longer on horseback, to live off alms and to carry nothing with them on their journeys. Thus it was that their endowments in France were given to Cistercian nuns, and those in other lands to other communities. So that the brothers might apply themselves with more energy to study and preaching, Dominic wished the uneducated lay brothers of his Order to have authority over the educated brothers in temporal matters. But the clerical brothers were not prepared to allow themselves to be ruled by lay brothers, for

[1] By now, Arnaud-Amaury, former abbot of Poblet and Cîteaux.

fear that it might happen to them as had happened to the religious of the Order of Grandmont through their lay brothers. . . .'[1]

This sudden change is the central event of Dominic's career, and on its interpretation depends much of our view of the man and his work. Jordan of Saxony states that the imminent fall of Simon de Montfort was the signal for his action, but some modern historians have doubted if this can explain more than 'the timing of the move'.[2] What were his underlying reasons? First, it is clear, Dominic did not consult his colleagues. The dispersal took them by surprise and they acquiesced out of loyalty and deference to him. It seemed imprudent, an impulsive act of faith, or folly, when the Order was only just instituted and its members were few and for the most part meagrely instructed to divide them up and send them on widespread missions. But Dominic insisted, against the arguments of common sense, which condemned such a venture as calculated rather to engulf the young community than promote its fortunes, whether proffered by his followers or by his patrons.

The new way involved fundamental changes of outlook and behaviour. Paris and Bologna became the headquarters, not any longer Toulouse. More time and thought were given to recruiting, and universities were the most fruitful centres for recruits as well as for study. Interest in the Cathars ceased to be paramount. The conversion of the Cathars had seemed an eminently sensible, limited objective. Dominic's initial easy success in converting a heretic innkeeper had probably inclined him to be sanguine, but years of unremitting effort had made little impression on the numbers of the Cathars. When a Cathar was converted the penance imposed on him was harsh (Doc. 20, no. i). The terms were not introduced by Dominic – they had been imposed by the Cistercian missionary abbots he had served under – and it could be said of them that they basically required a repentant Cathar to live as he had done before only with a new significance. All the same, it perhaps helps to explain why few Cathars were converted. Dominic never abandoned his role as a missionary; rather he extended his field to embrace people of all creeds, Christian and pagan, Saracen, Jew and Cathar: the

[1] Canonisation Process, Bologna depositions, c. 26; *MOPH*, Vol. XVI, pp. 143–5; Vicaire (1965), pp. 52–3. In the Order of Grandmont considerable administrative authority was given to the lay brothers; increasing power among the clerical brothers seems to have been the cause of rebellion by the lay brothers in the 1180s, which was serious enough for the Pope to intervene and insist on a compromise.

[2] C. Brooke, *Medieval Church and Society* (London, 1971), p. 227. For what follows see especially Jordan of Saxony, c. 62, *MOPH*, Vol. XVI, p. 54; Vicaire (1967), pp. 101–2.

emphasis shifted. Having prised his followers out of what he had come to regard as a rut, Dominic presently caused them to go a stage further. Already in 1215 they had all agreed not to have the ownership of lands and houses; now they renounced rents as well and adopted a visibly apostolic life-style (Doc. 17, cc. 42–53). They became friars.

Dominic did not consult his followers: did he consult anyone else? Another witness at the canonisation process, William of Montferrat (Doc. 18), became Dominic's friend when he was a student staying in the house of Cardinal Hugolino in Rome during Lent 1217. The two discussed ways of drawing themselves and others to salvation, and, before they parted, agreed to meet two years later in Paris, 'when Dominic had organised his Order'. This suggests that Dominic talked over his problems and plans with William. Did he also consult William's host, Cardinal Hugolino? As he met William through his frequent visits to the cardinal he probably did, though Hugolino is not mentioned among the distinguished patrons who advised him on this important matter. If he did, Hugolino would almost certainly have advised against the move. We know that, probably in the same year, he strongly disapproved of St Francis sending out his friars to establish distant provinces and insisted on Francis himself remaining in Italy instead of going to France as he intended.[1] Did Dominic's inspiration come from a meeting with Francis? This is a controversial question. Much of the inspiration of both Francis and Dominic, and especially their emphasis on poverty, evidently grew out of the environment in which both worked. The difficulty in pinpointing where influence lay, or finding precise evidence for it, has enabled a number of scholars to doubt if Francis influenced Dominic, to doubt even if they ever actually met. Yet both a Franciscan and a Dominican source tell of their meeting. Thomas of Celano, in his *Second Life* (cc. 148–50), says that both were on one occasion in Rome talking together with Cardinal Hugolino, who suggested it would be a good idea if some of their followers were promoted to bishoprics. Both humbly declined, and as they left the Cardinal Dominic asked Francis to give him his girdle, and expressed the wish that the two Orders might be merged. Gerard of Fracheto, in his *Lives of the Brothers*, recorded a story told by 'a certain Friar Minor, observant and reliable, a man who had been for long a companion of St Francis . . . to several friars, one of whom put it in writing for the Master of the Order'. Dominic was in Rome, appealing to the Pope 'for the Order's confirmation'. He had a dream in which the Virgin presented him and a man he did not know to Christ, as two who would bring the world back to him. The next day he saw Francis in a church and recognised him as the man he had seen in his dream. He embraced

[1] I Cel., cc. 74–5; *SL*, Nos 79–82; *EFG*, pp. 62–4.

him and said: 'You are my colleague, you and I will run the race together; we will stand as one man and no adversary will prevail against us.' He told Francis of his dream, and from that moment they were 'one heart and one soul in God'.[1]

Clearly these stories refer to the same occasion. But confusion as to its possible date – Celano's story has sometimes been dated 1221, Fracheto's 1215, both dates being open to serious objections – has led to doubt being cast on the meeting itself. Can a satisfactory date be found?[2] Dominic obtained the confirmation of his Order from Honorius III in Rome in January 1217. We know from William of Montferrat that he remained in Rome, visiting Hugolino frequently during Lent. Francis's movements are less certain. He called on Hugolino in Florence probably later that year, and Celano says that he did not previously know him well, but that does not preclude their having met before. Francis did visit the Curia – he was present at Innocent III's deathbed in Perugia in 1216 – and Rome on a number of occasions. If Dominic and Francis met in the early months of 1217, we may well think it had some bearing on Dominic's change of heart. In any event, both founders enlarged their fields of activity by sending out small groups to other countries to inaugurate provinces in 1217. Dominic persuaded his followers to renounce endowments and live in poverty, obtaining their sustenance if necessary by begging, not to carry money or ride on horseback – all characteristic of Francis's requirements for a Friar Minor. Dominic ceased to concentrate all his energies on the Cathars. Francis, brought up in another region where Cathars were probably numerous, or at least conspicuous, shows in his life and writings no overt interest in them, much interest in every kind of living soul, whether Christian, heretic or infidel. There are major similarities between the first two Orders of friars, and minor similarities too. Dominic, like Francis, at this time set another of his brothers as official head of the Order, while retaining overriding authority for himself.[3] Dominic, too, attempted to delegate the administrative responsibilities of the Order to his lay brothers, but failed to gain the consent of his educated clerical followers to this. Their objection looked back to unfortunate experiences of other Orders in the recent past, but Francis was currently stressing the positive contribution lay members could make. To begin with, the Preachers contained more educated men, the

[1] Gerard de Fracheto, *Vitae Fratrum*, i, i, 4, ed. B. M. Reichert, *MOPH*, Vol. I (Louvain, 1896), pp. 9–11; cf. C. Brooke, *Medieval Church and Society*, p. 224. 'One heart and one soul' echoes Acts, 4:32.

[2] Cf. C. Brooke, op. cit., pp. 225–6; Vicaire (1964), c. 12; on the date of Francis's meeting with Hugolino in Florence, *EFG*, pp. 62–4.

[3] Doc. 17, c. 48; I have discussed in *EFG*, pp. 76–83, my reasons for believing that Francis put Peter Cathanii in charge of the Order in 1217.

Minors more laymen. During Francis's lifetime and for a few years after his death lay brothers played an important part in his Order. But the educated clerics who joined the Minors in increasing numbers shared the attitude of their opposite numbers among the Preachers; in 1242 they repudiated Francis's policy and passed constitutions disqualifying laymen from holding office and drastically curtailing their recruitment.[1]

It would be a mistake to oversimplify motives or influences. Dominic's adoption of an apostolic way of life for himself and his followers harked back to the earlier example of Bishop Diego. But he had moved some way from there in the meantime. If his return to it owed something to the example of Francis, it shows how sensitive and receptive, in spite of his conventional upbringing, Dominic was; even more, it shows his humility.

Major Differences between the Orders: the Constitutions and Learning
The primary documents for the origin of the Order of Preachers are the *De principiis*, alias Life of St Dominic, by Jordan of Saxony, who became Master General in 1222 (Doc. 17), and the early constitutions, which represent the development of the Order under Dominic and Jordan (Doc. 22). In theory the Preachers, like the Minors, were governed by a Rule – in their case the Rule of St Augustine – and a body of constitutions. But the difference in their attitude to these instruments was deep. In the Rule lay the essence of the Franciscan way of life, and it was some while before the Minors in general accepted constitutions as more than a practical excrescence: even the elaborate code of 1260, the Constitutions of Narbonne, is in form a commentary on the Rule.[2] Augustine's Rule had been chosen by the Dominicans to satisfy the legal requirements of the Fourth Lateran Council decree (Doc. 16) and all that was distinctive to their Order was contained in their constitutions, more especially in the second of its two sections or Distinctions, which described their system of provinces, officials and committees or chapters. They considered observance would be best fulfilled and safeguarded if everything they were supposed to know and to do was clearly written down and fixed.[3] The *generalissimum* chapter of 1228, an exceptional chapter – three normal General Chapters rolled into one with authority to effect legislation that would otherwise have taken three years (Doc. 22, Preamble and Dist. II, c. V) –

---

[1] *EFG*, especially pp. 243–5.
[2] Ibid., Chap. 9, especially pp. 275ff.
[3] Doc. 22, Prologue, c. 1. For the contrast with St Francis's attitude to Rules, see pp. 25–6, 207.

divided the constitutions into three categories: the few basic requirements which could never be changed; those which could only be
changed in exceptional circumstances; and the rest, which could be
changed but only if agreed by three consecutive General Chapters. This
eminently reasonable provision enabled change to take place but
prevented it from being hastily or factiously achieved. The General
Chapter was composed two years running of elected diffinitors, one
from each province, and every third year of the provincial priors, so
that three consecutive General Chapters ensured the discussion of
measures and assent being obtained both from official and non-official
representatives.

Before 1228 the idea of government by an ordered structure of committees was evidently already well established; after 1228 the main
lines of the system became fixed but never inflexible. The Dominican
Order came to have the most mature constitutional system known in
the thirteenth century and one evidently calculated to give all the friars
a sense that they were involved in the running of the Order. The system
of elections and the hierarchy of committees known as provincial and
General Chapters are described in precise and maturely worded detail
in the early statutes printed below, though there are occasional ambiguities (Doc. 22). The Order was governed by committees formed of
officials, themselves elected, and of elected diffinitors. Every brother
had a voice in the election of those who represented him and was bound
by the decisions reached by his representatives. The idea of involvement, and of representative government, went back to Dominic;
stability and order were consolidated in the régime of Jordan of Saxony.
Although there are clear indications that Dominic could be impulsive
and believed in some measure in his own divine guidance,[1] he achieved
his purposes by consent. The original constitutions of 1216, which
mostly related to the inner life of the convents and were incorporated
in the First Distinction, were agreed after discussion with all his
followers (Doc. 17, cc. 41–2). To the first General Chapter, held at
Bologna in 1220, Dominic ordered the convent at Paris to send four
friars, one of whom was Jordan of Saxony. According to the prior of the
convent at Bologna, who was present, Dominic caused the chapter to
institute diffinitors, with authority to consider policy, to legislate and to
punish. The chapter, or rather these diffinitors, then passed a number
of constitutions.[2] There were still not many friars in the Order at that
time: in 1219 the community at Paris consisted of about thirty.[3] There

[1] See pp. 93–6, 180; C. Brooke, op. cit., 221ff.
[2] Doc. 17, cc. 86–7; Canonisation Process, Bologna depositions, c. 2, *MOPH*,
Vol. XVI, pp. 123–4; Vicaire (1965), pp. 35–6.
[3] Jordan of Saxony, c. 59, *MOPH*, Vol. XVI, p. 53; Vicaire (1967), p. 97.

were a few other houses, at Orléans and Segovia for example, but only friars from Paris and Bologna seem to have composed the chapter. The constitutions were not passed even by the whole convent at Bologna plus the four from Paris, but by the diffinitors. It seems clear that Dominic at this early stage decided to put authority in the hands of a small committee. In that way decisions could be reached quickly and efficiently. Very different was the atmosphere of the early Franciscan General Chapters, to which all the friars could come and where the proceedings were crowded, informal and somewhat confused (see Doc. 25, cc. 16–18, under 1221).

The aim of the Friars Minor was to follow the Gospel, and this involved living in poverty, wandering and preaching; the aim of the Friars Preachers was to care for souls, and in order to be effective pastors they preached and lived in poverty. This initial difference of approach affected the training and preparation of the preacher for his task. St Francis constantly reiterated that example was a more powerful argument than precept; and simple, fervent prayer more moving than cleverness. St Dominic wished his friars to be trained theologians. The necessary accommodation was provided as part of the normal conventual equipment. When there were about sixteen of them, and they were given their first church in Toulouse, in 1216, they quickly built a cloister with cells above it large enough for study as well as for sleep (Doc. 17, c. 44). The priority given to the requirements of study was explicitly stated at the outset of the constitutions. The constitutions were designed to benefit, preserve and strengthen the Order, but if in practice any of the provisions had the effect of hindering a friar in his studies his superior had authority to dispense from their observance (Doc. 22, Dist. II, c. XXIX). Cells were assigned to promising students to facilitate their work. If they failed to fulfil expectations they lost their allocation, but if they made satisfactory progress their cells were havens to which they might legitimately withdraw, to read, write, pray, sleep, sit up working all night long if they wished. They, and those who had qualified as preachers, were as far as possible spared from taking their share of administrative cares and chores that were distracting and time-consuming (Doc. 22, Dist. II, c. XXXI). When St Dominic first dispersed his followers in 1217, however, expansion was too rapid to wait upon preparedness, and some of those sent out to found houses were inexperienced. St Dominic also on occasion ordered friars to preach before they were qualified. Brother Buonviso told how, while he was a novice at Bologna and before he had begun to study Scripture, St Dominic ordered him to go to Piacenza and preach there. He protested his insufficiency but St Dominic said to him: 'Go with confidence, because the Lord will be with you and will put on your lips the words you ought to preach.'[1] He obeyed, and after his sermon, three of his hearers entered the Order.

The Personality of St Dominic

This and other glimpses of unexpected or seemingly inconsistent actions on Dominic's part, recorded in the Canonisation Process, suggest that the tendency to characterise him as conventional and efficient, worthy but unexciting, does him less than justice. Dominic suffers from the inevitable comparison with Francis; he did not inspire stories or biographies like those of Francis. Jordan of Saxony's portrayal of him is properly respectful, but scrappy and detached. Some of those who came forward to testify for his canonisation knew him considerably better. Dominic died in 1221 and was buried in his friars' church at Bologna. Brother Rudolf, the procurator of the convent, responsible for the burial, took the precaution of covering the coffin with heavy stones bonded together with strong cement to discourage possible theft,[2] but no immediate fame attached to his resting place. Some pilgrims came to be healed, but the friars themselves kept no record of cures and were initially reluctant to appear to exploit the relics of their founder for gain. The success of the house however led to the expansion and rebuilding of convent and church. The translation of Dominic's body to a new, and this time marble, tomb in 1233 provided the occasion for an outburst of popular enthusiasm, encouraged by the preaching of brother John of Vicenza, and for a request to Gregory IX for his canonisation. The Pope who, as papal legate and bishop of Ostia, had known and admired Dominic, and had attended his funeral, warmly approved and ordered the necessary inquiry into his public and private life.

Two investigations were held, one in Bologna, the other in Toulouse, Dominic's earlier headquarters. The process completed, Dominic was duly canonised in July 1234. As a source, the process has evident limitations. The commissioners drew up a list of characteristic saintly qualities as a basis, which ensured a large measure of unanimity, but some of the testifiers could and did add spontaneous personal reminiscences and illuminating detail, particularly William of Montferrat and Stephen, two student friends of Dominic's (Doc. 18). The prior, the procurator and other members of the convent at Bologna had also, as they all emphasised, been in a position to observe the conduct of his

---

[1] Canonisation Process, Bologna depositions, c. 24, cf. c. 26; *MOPH*, Vol. XVI, pp. 142–3; Vicaire (1965), pp. 51–2.

[2] Ibid., c. 34, *MOPH*, Vol. XVI, pp. 152–3; Vicaire (1967), pp. 60–1. For what follows, see Jordan of Saxony, c. 98, *MOPH*, Vol. XVI, p. 72, etc.; Vicaire (1965), p. 127.

life day and night, at church, at table and on the road, in health and in sickness. It seems clear that Dominic pernoctated all his life. As a young man he had occupied his nights with study;[1] later he devoted them to prayer. The prior recalled that towards the end of July 1221 Dominic returned from Venice where he had been visiting Cardinal Hugolino, who was then papal legate. The weather was exceedingly hot and he arrived quite exhausted. But in spite of his fatigue he spent the greater part of the night with the prior, who was newly elected, and the procurator discussing the affairs of the Order. The procurator, who was tired, then suggested that Dominic had better retire and not get up that night for mattins, but he, on the contrary, proceeded to the church to pray until mattins, which he attended as usual. After mattins a severe headache heralded his final illness.[2] He never allowed himself sufficient sleep and never slept on a comfortable bed. He would pray until he fell asleep at the foot of the altar, and he frequently dropped off to sleep during meals, the more easily as he ate little. He denied his body all comfort, and a streak of morbid imagination led him to express a desire for an excruciating martyrdom. The story told by Jordan of how he confounded some heretics near Albi who had intended to ambush him by assuring them he would have chosen the most barbaric torture in preference to an ordinary assassination (Doc. 17, c. 34) cannot simply be dismissed as lurid embellishment. Brother John of Spain testified that he had many times heard Dominic protest his desire to be flogged and cut in pieces and done to death for the faith of Christ.[3] It was rumoured among the brothers that he flogged himself with iron chains, but there is little early evidence of excessive flagellation. Only one of the witnesses at the Canonisation Process mentions it, brother John of Spain, and he is careful to state that he had heard it said, whereas the bulk of his evidence is given from his own personal knowledge. Several witnesses remarked that he punished offenders severely, but that he did so with such gentle and humble words that they were comforted. He saw life as a battle. This is brought out by his words to Stephen when he arbitrarily enlisted him – words in Dominic's mouth more than the conventional metaphor of warfare in Christ's service – 'I will give you arms, with which you are to fight the devil all the days of your life' (Doc. 18, c. 36) and by his letter to the nuns at Madrid. Now that they have suitable buildings, he exhorts them to fight the old adversary constantly with their fasts, and not to be sparing with stripes and vigils (Doc. 20, no. iii).

[1] Jordan of Saxony, c. 7, *MOPH*, Vol. XVI, p. 28; Vicaire (1967), pp. 51–2.
[2] Canonisation Process, Bologna depositions, c. 7; *MOPH*, Vol. XVI, pp. 127–8; Vicaire (1965), p. 39.
[3] Ibid., c. 29; *MOPH*, Vol. XVI, p. 146; Vicaire (1965), p. 55; for what follows, cf. ibid., cc. 25–6, 32, 48.

The witnesses at Toulouse knew Dominic in the period when he was
exclusively engaged in combating heresy by preaching and debate,
before the dispersal and effective launching of the Order in 1217. They
were unaffected by the pressures on the friars at Bologna, far removed
from the manifestations of sanctity that attended the translation, the
cures at the tomb. They were not, as were the witnesses at Bologna,
Friars Preachers, but an assortment of men and women who had known
and remembered Dominic. They included a Cistercian abbot and his
sacrist, two other abbots, a canon, a converted heretic, a married
woman, a nun. They were agreed in endorsing the list of his saintly
qualities, stressing in particular his fervent prayer and his chastity,
and they held that he was generally esteemed as exceptionally religious.
Their testimony is notably sober and restrained. Indeed, what they
offer in the way of proofs of sanctity is remarkably underplayed: he had
refused a bishopric; he had lagged behind his companions in a wood
for private prayer although there were wolves about. The women's
evidence is more homely, and it is warmer and more personal. Wil-
liamette, the wife of Elie Martin, testified that she wove material for
his hairshirts. He had sat at her table more than two hundred times,
and she had never seen him eat at one meal even a quarter of a fish or
more than two egg yolks, or drink more than one glass of wine, which he
diluted with three parts water. She had never seen him eat more than
one slice of bread. He was very often in great pain and those about
him would then lay him on a bed, but she had seen him get up quickly
and stretch himself on the floor because he was not in the habit of resting
on a bed. Another woman said that she also made shirts for him of
goat's hair. Beceda, a nun of Sainte-Croix, said that she used to collect
ox-tails from which to make hairshirts for him, and also for Fulk, bishop
of Toulouse. She had never heard him utter the slightest idle word,
and this although she had lived much in his company. Many was the
time she had made his bed for him only to find he had not slept in it;
in the morning she would find the bed untouched, exactly as she had
made it. It was the same when he was ill. What is more, she would often
find him stretched out on the floor without any covering. If, after she
had covered him up, she returned, she would find him this time at
prayer, either standing or prostrate. She had, indeed, a deep concern
for him. She added that when he took his meals in the house in which
she lived – and he would have done so more than two hundred times –
he would eat at the most two eggs, although several dishes were offered
him.[1] Women, it seems, liked to mother him, and their kindly concern,
even if it had to be shown in the making of hairshirts, provides us with

[1] Canonisation Process, Toulouse depositions, cc. 15-17; *MOPH*, Vol.
XVI, pp. 181-2; Vicaire (1965), pp. 81-2.

an insight into an otherwise quite unrecorded aspect of his life in the south of France, a life more informal, more domestic, than we would otherwise have imagined, sandwiched between his regular life as a canon of Osma and the final phase in the convents of the Friars Preachers.

Dominic and Jordan of Saxony

Our sources for St Francis are outstandingly good; those for St Dominic much less impressive, both in quality and quantity. Why is this? In selecting and presenting information the official biographer played initially a crucial part. I cannot help feeling that Dominic could have been better served. Why did Jordan of Saxony, who, as Master General, was much occupied with the administration and affairs of the Order, choose to write about him himself, instead of entrusting the task to one of the friars who had known him better? There were several well qualified by education and position to choose from. I would have liked William of Montferrat to be chosen. He and Dominic had become friends in 1217, when William was staying in Rome (Doc. 18, c. 12). They talked together with enthusiasm of their ideals and hopes and planned to go together as missionaries to north-eastern Europe to convert the pagans – a yearning Dominic retained from his earlier association with Bishop Diego of Osma. They agreed to meet again in Paris after Dominic had organised his Order and William had pursued his theological studies. They kept their promise and duly met in Paris. William joined the Order and became Dominic's principal companion, travelling with him to the Curia, to Bologna, to Viterbo and to Lombard cities, but they did not achieve their ambition to go off together as missionaries. Or Stephen, provincial prior of Lombardy, would have written a lively biography. He recounted delightful snatches of conversation and had a sense of humour (Doc. 18, cc. 35ff., esp. c. 36).

Thomas of Celano concentrated on Francis's life and attributes, saying very little about the development of the Order; Jordan of Saxony chooses the double theme of the beginnings of the Order and the life of the founder, but where he might be telling us more of Dominic he seems to take any and every opportunity to talk of someone else. He begins not with Dominic but with Diego; the mention of another Dominic leads to a digression on him; later, there are digressions on Jordan's friend Henry, even on Jordan himself. Perhaps we should rather say that they would have been digressions in a life of Dominic, but Jordan intended from the outset to write of other friars as well (Doc. 17, Prologue). Jordan shows no personal warmth for Dominic. Not that he was incapable of feeling or of expressing it: he speaks warmly of Reginald, who was responsible for his own entry; and his long account of the self-questionings and idealism of Henry, the student friend with whom he shared lodgings and whom he persuaded to join the Order with him so that they should not be parted, his eulogy on his character (Doc. 17, cc. 67ff.),[1] and his letters to Diana Dandalo of the Dominican convent for nuns in Bologna (Doc. 21), sufficiently show his sensibility.

Francis died in 1226 and was canonised expeditiously in 1228 when Gregory IX also laid the foundation stone of the splendid new double church built in his honour. His translation took place in 1230. Interest in procuring Dominic's canonisation was effectively aroused in 1233. Jordan wrote in the months between the translation and canonisation, 1233–4. Did he write himself, and write as he did, because he wanted to restrain an incipient personality cult?[2]

Founder and Saint

Although the two Orders were popularly called Franciscan and Dominican, Francis was intimately associated with the fundamental ideals and inspiration, and with the vicissitudes, of his Order in a way that Dominic was not. He was the source of authority to which his followers turned in difficulty or dispute, and that is one reason why so many stories about him, in addition to the official lives, were treasured and preserved. Francis's followers were, in a measure, his disciples; Dominic's were his colleagues. The relation of the founder to his Order could present problems. Francis had attempted, through his Testament, to continue his influence beyond the grave. When Dominic died his friars did not immediately appreciate his potential usefulness. They thought of him as a man, some of them at least as the most religious man they had ever met, but as a man like themselves. His friend William of Montferrat, when people told him that they had been cured of various infirmities through Dominic's merits, paid no attention. He did not know these people, had never seen them before, and besides, he was one of the diffinitors, and busy (Doc. 18, c. 16). The prior of the convent at Bologna displayed a similar attitude. He believed, on reflection, that Dominic had performed many miracles of healing: many men and women had brought candles, images and thank offerings to the tomb. Some had wanted to cover the tomb with silk draperies and erect a screen round it, but the friars had vetoed the suggestion. They thought they might be accused of cupidity or vainglory if they allowed anything of the kind, and they also feared that if the tomb became too

[1] See the whole section in Jordan of Saxony, cc. 67–78, MOPH, Vol. XVI, pp. 56–62; Vicaire (1967), pp. 104–9.
[2] For a full discussion of this problem, see C. Brooke, op. cit., Chap. 11.

popular they would find the crowds inconvenient and disturbing.[1] They had important work to do. They could not, however, after Francis's death, fail to notice the advantages that accrued to the Minors, who exploited their asset to the full.

Both Jordan of Saxony, the Master General, and the prior of the convent at Bologna, which possessed the tomb, recollected Dominic to have said that he would be more useful to his friars after death than he had been in life.[2] Brother Stephen gave it as his opinion that the publicity given to Dominic's virtues through the preaching of brother John of Vicenza and the subsequent translation had greatly enhanced the Order's influence, inspiring the brothers to more fervent preaching and inducing the crowds to listen to them. In Lombardy many heretics had been burnt at the stake – a harsh concomitant – and thousands of people who might have been tempted to join the heretics had, through their preaching, been converted to the catholic faith and been turned actively against those with whom they had formerly sympathised. Many cities in Lombardy and the Marches were entrusting the preachers with the regulation of their affairs, the reform of their statutes, and the curtailment of their feuds (Doc. 18, c. 39). So, for the benefit of his Order, rather than simply for his own sake, the cult of St Dominic was promoted in moderation.

[1] Canonisation Process, Bologna depositions, c. 9 and cf. Jordan of Saxony, cc. 97–8, 122; *MOPH*, Vol. XVI, pp. 130–1, 72, 83. Vicaire (1965), p. 41; Vicaire (1967), pp. 126–7, 137–8.
[2] Doc. 17, c. 93; Canonisation Process, Bologna depositions, c. 8, *MOPH*, Vol. XVI, p. 129; Vicaire (1965), p. 40.

7

The Coming of the Friars

When the Minors and the Preachers first received papal approval they were small groups; only a handful of individuals controlled by a dedicated and enthusiastic leader was involved in each case. When Francis and his companions approached Innocent III in 1210 they numbered twelve in all; in 1216, a year after Dominic made his request, there were some sixteen Preachers.[1] At this stage they must have seemed little different from numerous other groups that were proliferating about the turn of the twelfth and thirteenth centuries, some determinedly orthodox, others as determinedly heretical, others still of doubtful allegiance. They were part and parcel of a widespread upsurge of religious sentiment which, in varying degrees and contexts, emphasised the spiritual value of voluntary poverty and manifested an imperative need to preach. They arose in the same milieu as the Waldensians and the Humiliati, and that they were associated with such in the minds of some who came across them in the early days is shown, for example, by the account of them given in the chronicle of Burchard of Ursberg (Doc. 23). When the Minors undertook their first missions to France and Germany they were asked if they were heretics, a natural confusion, since the reputation of the Albigensians, or Cathars, and the Waldensians had preceded them (Doc. 25, cc. 4, 5).

Why did the friars emerge so decisively and succeed and prosper so rapidly? Francis's and Dominic's initial success was in part due to their absolute loyalty and orthodoxy, to their sense of vocation and their persistence; and they were fortunate in the Popes they had to deal with. Yet it was not simply papal recognition that differentiated their movements from the rest. Innocent III also sanctioned the groups led by Durand of Huesca and Bernard Prim; but Durand and Bernard did not achieve more than local and limited appeal and influence. Nor did Dominic, until he dispersed his followers and turned them into mendicant friars. There are bound to be unanswered, and inadequately answered, questions, and it is not possible here to do more than suggest

[1] I Cel., cc. 24–32; Doc. 17, c. 44.

some lines of inquiry. Some Orders foundered or maintained a precarious existence. The Friars Minor and Friars Preachers overcame the
obstacles to growth. From 1217 both Orders grew rapidly. Francis's
qualities of character and his outstanding gifts as a teacher made him
personally responsible for a good number of recruits, but the great
majority joined the fraternity without meeting him. Jordan of Giano,
laughing at himself, tells how he thought Francis somehow human,
since he had known him when he was alive, and so was taken by surprise when the friars greeted him, carrying Francis's relics, with a
solemn procession (Doc. 25, c. 59). The Preachers enjoyed a popularity
comparable with the Minors. Dominic favoured Paris and Bologna,
Francis Assisi, but both Orders were soon paying particular attention
to university towns. Jordan of Saxony in a letter to Diana Dandolo
speaks of his hopes of a good catch in Oxford (Doc. 21, no. 16). The
friars clearly answered a need, and not only among the young. University masters were attracted as well as their students, and so were some
members of the clergy, and knights, burghers, merchants, minstrels, a
wide variety of established folk. The Franciscans, up to 1242, also
attracted and accepted illiterate laymen, peasant labourers and men of
little or no substance.[1]

The families and friends of those who joined were not always pleased,
especially towards the beginning, before the Orders had acquired
reputation and prestige. The first young man to join the Minors in
England, brother Solomon, so upset his sister by coming to her door to
beg for alms that she turned away her face and cursed him.[2] The entry
of Jordan of Saxony's friend, Henry, troubled the canon who had reared
him and his colleagues; they had not heard of the Order – this was in
1220 – and thought his profession unwise (Doc. 17, c. 76). A wealthy
man who welcomed the Minors to Northampton and housed them on
his own land took a different attitude when his own son proposed to
join them.[3] Some members of the hierarchy had their misgivings.
Jacques de Vitry, bishop of Acre, voiced the opinion of responsible
conservatives when he commented on the rashness of sending couples of
young, inexperienced converts all over the place, without training them
and proving them through conventual discipline. The administration of
his diocese was disrupted by the defection of some of his clergy to this

---

[1] *EFG*, pp. 51–3, 154–6, 243–5.
[2] Thomas of Eccleston, *Tractatus de adventu Fratrum Minorum in Angliam*,
ed. A. G. Little (rev. edn, Manchester, 1951), col. 3, p. 12. There are translations of both Eccleston and Jordan of Giano (Doc. 25) in *The Coming of the
Friars Minor to England and Germany*, trans. E. Gurney Salter (London-
Toronto, 1926, for this passage, see p. 17).
[3] Eccleston, op. cit. (ed. Little), col. 4, p. 23; Eccleston, op. cit. (trans.
Salter), p. 32.

idealistic but unregulated new Order. But his critical comment was subsequently deleted from the letter in which it occurred and replaced with a flattering reference to Francis (Doc. 24). The bishops at the Fourth Lateran Council had voted against the creation of any further new religious Orders (Doc. 16, c. XIII), lacking confidence in Innocent III's more flexible policy; but his successor Honorius III (1216–27) enabled the friars to circumvent this provision.

It was Honorius III who gave official approval to Francis's final version of his Rule in 1223, and who also in fact regularised the position of the Dominicans. The Rule he approved for them in 1217, based on the Rule of St Augustine with additional constitutions taken in the main from those of Prémontré, was specifically drawn up to conform to the Lateran decree. But Dominic set in motion the series of changes which transformed the life style of the Preachers only months after he had secured this confirmation, and the further constitutions passed in 1220 to ratify this in effect created a new Order (Doc. 17, cc. 86–7; Doc. 22). The Curia played a vital role in launching and safeguarding the friars. Both Dominic and Francis realised the help it could give and actively sought its support. In the last six years of his life Dominic made regular, and prolonged, visits to Rome in every winter save one, and this gave him the opportunity to make regular contact with the Curia.[1] Francis was emphatic that he did not wish for papal privileges but he did ask for, and receive, direct access to the Curia through Hugolino, and this direct access was in itself a kind of privilege. Sections of his followers had got out of hand while Francis was in the East and as Cardinal Protector Hugolino saved the Minors from disintegration (Doc. 25, cc. 11–15).[2] Francis's choice of Hugolino may have been arrived at independently, but Dominic was the first to engage the Cardinal's interest and friendship and it is possible that Francis profited from his observation of the relationship between Hugolino and Dominic.

Hugolino's part in the fortunes and development of the Orders of friars, particularly of the Minors, first as cardinal then as Pope Gregory IX, has been the subject of controversy, and has been distorted and maligned. It is difficult for students of any persuasion studying him today to forget and forgive his role in founding the Inquisition. No doubt he was an old and experienced Curial official; perhaps several

[1] See Vicaire (1964), pp. 191, 202, 216, 240, 277, 330, 336 and notes; cf. C. Brooke, *Medieval Church and Society* (London, 1971), pp. 223–4 and notes. In most winters between 1215–16 and 1220–1 he spent a considerable time in Rome over Christmas. In 1217–18 he did not reach Rome till around February 1218 (he stayed till the summer); in 1218–19 he was in Spain; in the winter of 1219–20 the Curia was at Viterbo – he called there on his way to and from Rome. On all his other visits the Pope was in Rome.

[2] *EFG*, Chap. 2, especially pp. 59–76.

different characters were combined in his powerful personality. Yet it
is possible to see a link between his impulsive, and violent, measures
against the Emperor Frederick II and against the heretics, and his
equally impulsive surrender to the inspiration of St Francis. He
remains a puzzling figure, summarising a major problem for the modern
scholar: how to reconcile two of the most striking features of the
thirteenth-century Church, often seen in the same person – intense
pastoral concern and a brutal readiness to persecute.

We have only incidental information, in Jordan of Saxony's *De
principiis* for example (Doc. 17), and in the *Vitae fratrum*, about the
spread of the Dominican Order. For the Franciscans we have a detailed
record for two provinces, Germany and England: Jordan of Giano's
Chronicle (Doc. 25) and Thomas of Eccleston's *Account of the Coming
of the Friars Minor to England and their Spread and Increase There*.[1]
These valuable sources enable us to form a picture of how missions were
organised and how they were received; how the friars coped with their
difficulties and learned from their mistakes; who their benefactors
were and what they gave; the conditions of daily life at the outset and
how they changed; the administrative arrangements; the complications
of success. Jordan of Giano's personality shows through vividly in
anecdotes which reveal the attitudes and reactions of a man who wished
to be thought an ordinary friar, and the progress of his career illustrates
how the friars could utilise and develop their raw material, this immature
and reluctant member of the missionary expedition being presently
entrusted with positions of responsibility, guardian, custodian, vicar-
provincial, which he creditably fulfilled (Doc. 25, cc. 17–18).[2] Thomas
of Eccleston's chronicle, completed probably in 1258, records a wealth
of facts and stories he had taken pleasure in collecting during the course
of the twenty-six years he had spent as a member of the Order.

The first abortive missions to Germany and Hungary (Doc. 25, c. 5
and p. 210, n. 1) had highlighted the need to master basic tactics, like
learning the languages of the countries they visited or at least taking some
native of the country with them. The successful mission to Germany in
1221 was led by Cesarius of Speyer. The mission to England in 1224
was planned in France, and three members of the group of nine were
English. They were transported across the Channel by the generosity
of the monks of Fécamp and were helped on arrival by the monks of
Canterbury cathedral and by the Dominicans, who had established

---

[1] For edition of Eccleston and translations of both Eccleston and Jordan of
Giano, see p. 107, n. 2 above; Jordan of Giano was edited by H. Boehmer
(Paris, 1908).
[2] Cf. Boehmer's introduction to Jordan of Giano, op. cit., pp. lviff.; *EFG*,
pp. 20–1.

their province in England in 1221.[1] At their house in Holborn the Friars Preachers treated the Minors as they would members of their own Order, accommodating them for a fortnight, until a house was hired for them in Cornhill by John Travers, who was a sheriff of London from 1223 to 1225. Similarly in Oxford two Minors lodged with the Preachers, eating in their refectory and sleeping in their dormitory for a week, after which they were able to hire a house in the parish of St Ebbe's. Eccleston speaks with pride of the high standard of observance maintained by the English province and delights in giving examples of scrupulous obedience to the Rule, concern at contracting debts, zeal for poverty. One particular attribute of the province was an idiosyncratic ability to combine enthusiasm for the Rule with enthusiasm for learning. Eccleston recalls that the friars were so concerned to preserve the utmost simplicity and a clean conscience and were at the same time so keen to study theology, that they would willingly walk long distances in bitter cold or deep mud, barefoot, in order to attend lectures.[2] One example may serve to show how the simplicity and directness of the early friars could affect their audience. A knight of Northampton, Richard Gobion, provided a house for the Minors, but when his young son joined the Order he told them to leave. St Francis insisted that his Order should own no property and wished their lack of rights to be no fiction but a reality. The ownership of all houses was to remain vested in the donor, either individual, family, guild or municipality, or failing such, in the Papacy. If a donor rescinded his gift the friars were to acquiesce and relinquish their lodging without protest. The Northampton friars filed out, while the knight waited angrily outside the door to watch them go. Last went an infirm old man carrying a Psalter. The knight was suddenly moved by their humble obedience to their principles, repented and begged them to remain.[3] Practising what they preached won them respect and support, just as the good life of the Cathars commanded the respect and support of their relatives and neighbours.

The Orders of friars persuaded some Cathars to abandon their former tenets and join their ranks (see Doc. 15) and they provided a sufficiently satisfying alternative to many who, if the way of life they offered had not been available, might have become heretics (see Doc. 18, c. 39). In the south of France heretics were decimated by military action and the

[1] Eccleston, coll. 1–2, ed. Little, op. cit., pp. 3–11; trans. Salter, op. cit., pp. 6–16.

[2] Ibid., col. 6, ed. Little, op. cit., p. 27; trans. Salter, op. cit., p. 38. The contrast with St Francis's attitude to learning is striking.

[3] Ibid., col. 4, ed. Little, op. cit., pp. 23–4; trans. Salter, op. cit., pp. 31–3.

remnants were then systematically mopped up by the Inquisition. In north Italy, where Cathars and unreconciled Waldensians were also numerous, there was no crusade; yet the numbers of heretics notably declined. The activities of the Inquisition alone can hardly account for this. The new orthodox alternative played a part in contributing to this lessening of the threat to the Church. The papacy very quickly appreciated this, actively promoted their apostolate with letters and privileges, and was soon turning to the friars for ambassadors and inquisitors, as well as confessors, bishops and preachers of crusade. The crusade was no longer confined to expeditions to the Holy Land but embraced a variety of warfare in the Church's cause, and the concept, never a happy one, became increasingly devalued. Among the documents collected by the Inquisition was a record of a conversation in 1247 between Peter Garcias, a citizen of Toulouse, and William Garcias, a relative, who was a Friar Minor. Other Friars Minor listened concealed, with William's knowledge. Peter, on their evidence condemned as a heretic, spoke frankly about his Cathar beliefs. He included a sharp criticism of the friars for urging men to take the cross; it was not meritorious to take arms against the Emperor Frederick II, or against the Saracens, or against a castle, such as Montségur, as the infliction of death was wrong. He damned every Order – except the Order of Friars Minor, perhaps out of consideration for his relative – but added that even the Friars Minor were worthless, since they preached the crusade.[1] Indeed, the use made by the Papacy of the friars for its own ends and purposes, though it produced tangible and often beneficial results, undermined the efficacy of their original appeal, since it tended to identify them with the Curial establishment. Thus they provoked hostility and jealousy in the universities, among the parish clergy and in the traditional monastic Orders (Doc. 26).

In the eleventh and twelfth centuries the idea of the apostolic life of wandering preaching and voluntary poverty exercised a powerful appeal to the imagination and conscience. An increasing number desired a more active participation in the world than the older monastic orders allowed. Their concern for their fellow men was more outward looking; they wanted to go among them and work among them, instead of concentrating their charity and their instruction on those who came to them, as did monks within the cloister. By the late twelfth century, furthermore, the fashion for endowing large monasteries was on the wane, that for founding hospitals, institutions of social welfare, on the increase. There was concern that the individual should achieve his own salvation through his own efforts, instead of relying on the prayers and

[1] W. L. Wakefield, *Heresy, Crusade and Inquisition in Southern France, 1100–1250* (London, 1974), Appendix 5, pp. 242–9, especially p. 246.

intercessions of monks on his behalf. This led to lay people reading the Bible in the vernacular and attempting to live according to the Gospel precepts. The motive behind orthodox and heretical movements was primarily religious. Both were the sign of intense spiritual concern. Some opted for orthodoxy, others for heresy, and at times only a knife edge seemed to separate the two interpretations. Choice was conditioned by a host of factors – local and international, social, demographic, economic, intellectual and political (besides religious sentiment). Heresy was a response of unsatisfied believers, resentful of a corrupt and neglectful clergy, disillusioned with the pace and the insufficiently radical nature of reform; and religious rejection could be and often was combined with political and economic objectives.[1] The religious ideal of voluntary poverty, in its orthodox and heretical forms, found favour just at the time when socio-economic dislocations caused by a rapidly changing and expanding society were creating more acute problems of actual involuntary poverty than had existed in the earlier Middle Ages. In a predominantly rural society, underdeveloped and underequipped, in which technical progress was extremely slow, existence was, for most, hard and precarious, but destitution was comparatively rare, except when adverse weather or the ravages of war brought famine and deprivation to whole areas. Poverty was a condition of weakness, to which no stigma attached, the misfortune of the widow, the orphan, the old, the sick, the retarded, and its sufferers were individually known and were normally supported by the solidarity of the family, the village, the parish, the abbey. Poverty was regarded as a necessary evil, a test for its victims, an opportunity for charity for the more fortunate. But with the increase of population, urbanisation, mobility, trade, the disintegration of the traditional order and relationships, deficiencies of production and distribution, rising prices, wealth and opportunities grew, and also the numbers of the poor. More and more flocked to the towns, where, dependent on market and labour fluctuations and on the occasional distributions of large-scale charity on major festivals, or the weddings and funerals of the great, many lived in collective, anonymous misery and want. By the thirteenth century these urban poor, socially and economically deprived, were the object of anxiety; they could so easily be bribed or incited to disorder and violence. It was becoming easier to look on the involuntary poor

[1] In what follows I am greatly indebted to the searching papers by M. Mollat, 'La notion de la pauvreté au moyen âge: position de problèmes', *Revue d'Histoire de l'Église de France*, Vol. 149 (1966), offprint, pp. 1–17; and Janet L. Nelson, 'Society, Theodicy and the Origins of Heresy: Towards a Reassessment of the Medieval Evidence', *Studies in Church History*, Vol. 9 (1972), pp. 65–77.

not as Christ but as a nuisance. Mobility as well as poverty received contrasting religious and social connotations. By the twelfth century many people were on the move; younger sons of overprolific families in search of adventure and fortune, merchants, pilgrims, crusaders, shared the roads with wandering preachers, who found welcome and reverence, and also with fugitives, outlaws, unemployed bands of mercenaries. These displaced soldiers, who lived by brigandage, were so hated and feared that they were excommunicated along with heretics by the Third Lateran Council of 1179. By a paradox, mendicancy became a fashionable religious virtue, and thousands of friars were supported by door-to-door begging when those who were vagrant beggars from necessity, not choice, were increasingly unwelcome and despised.[1]

[1] See Mollat, op. cit., and Nelson, op. cit.

DOCUMENTS

1. St Francis's Testament

(*Opuscula*, pp. 77–82.) This is Francis's final statement, which every reader will interpret for himself. See pp. 24–8.

The Lord granted me, brother Francis, to begin to do penance in this way, that when I was in sin, it seemed to me very horrible to see lepers, and the Lord himself led me among them and I helped them. And when I left them that which had before seemed to me horrible was transformed into sweetness of body and soul. After that I remained only a little time before I left the world. And the Lord gave me such faith in churches that I used to pray simply, like this, and say: 'We adore you, Lord Jesus Christ, here and in all your churches in all the world, and we bless you because with your holy cross you redeemed the world'.

Afterwards the Lord gave and gives me such faith in priests, who live according to the model of the holy Roman Church, on account of their orders, that even if they should persecute me I wish to run back to them. And if I had as much wisdom as Solomon, and found poor and humble secular priests in the parishes in which they lived, I would not wish to preach against their will. I wish to fear, love and honour them and all others as my masters; and I do not wish to consider sin in them, because I discern in them the son of God and to me they are masters. I do this because in this world I see nothing of the son of God most high in a tangible sense, except his most holy body and blood, which priests receive and priests alone administer to others. This most holy mystery I wish to honour and venerate above all others and to house in precious pyxes.

God's most holy name and words of Scripture, whenever I find them in unseemly places, I like to collect, and I ask that they be collected and put in a suitable place. And we ought to honour and revere all theologians and ministers of the divine word, as those who minister to us spirit and life.

And, after the Lord gave me brothers no one showed me what I ought to do, but the Most High himself revealed to me that I ought to live according to the pattern of the holy Gospel. And I had it written down simply, in few words; and the lord Pope confirmed it for me. And those who came to take up this life, all who had the means, gave to the poor and were content with one tunic, patched inside and out if they wished, with a girdle and breeches. And we did not wish to have more.

We clerics said the office as other clerics; laymen used to say 'Our Father'. And we were happy to live in churches. And we were ignorant and subject to all people. And I used to work with my hands and I wish to work. And it is my firm wish that all the brothers work at some good and worthy occupation. Those who are not trained to one shall learn, not through desire to receive pay for their work, but for the example and to repel idleness. And when pay for our labour is not given we shall run to the table of the Lord, begging alms from door to door.

We used to say a greeting which the Lord revealed to me: 'The Lord give you peace.' Let the brothers take care that churches, humble lodgings and all other things that will be built for them are never accepted unless they are in harmony with holy poverty, which we have promised in the Rule, always living there as strangers and pilgrims.

I firmly order all the brothers on obedience that, wherever they are, they are not to dare to ask for any letter from the Roman Curia, either themselves or through an intermediary, not for a church or for any convent, not on the pretext of preaching or on account of physical persecution; but if they are not received anywhere they are to flee to another territory to do penance with God's blessing. And I firmly wish to obey the Minister General of this brotherhood and any guardian whom it may please him to give me. And I wish to be as a captive in his hands, that I may neither go nor act without his will and command, because he is my master. And although I am simple and infirm, I want to have a cleric with me always to say the office for me as it is in the Rule.

All the friars are likewise bound to obey their guardians and to say the office according to the Rule. If any are found who are not saying the office according to the Rule, and want to vary it in any way or are not catholic, all the friars, wherever they are, are bound by obedience, wherever they may find any such, to bring him before the custodian of the convent nearest to where they find him. And the custodian shall be firmly bound by obedience to keep him strongly guarded as a man in chains day and night so that it is not possible for him to escape from his hands, until he can personally transfer him into the hands of his minister. And the minister shall be firmly bound by obedience to send him in the charge of friars capable of guarding him day and night as a man in chains until they bring him face to face with the bishop of Ostia, who is the lord, protector and corrector of the whole brotherhood.

And the brothers are not to say: 'This is another Rule': because this is a record, admonition and exhortation, and my testament, that I, brother Francis, small as I am, make for you, my blessed brothers, so that we may observe more catholicly the Rule we have promised to the Lord. And the Minister General and all the other ministers and custodians shall be bound by obedience not to add or subtract from these words. And they shall always have this document with them, next to the Rule. And in all the chapter meetings they hold, when they read the rule they shall read this too. And I absolutely order all my brothers, clerics and laymen, on obedience, that they shall not put glosses on the Rule or on these words, saying: 'They want to be understood in this way': but, just as the Lord granted me to speak and write simply and purely both the Rule and these words, so simply and purely they shall be understood and put into practice until the last.

And whoever shall observe this shall be filled with blessing, in heaven with the blessing of the Holy Father, in earth with the blessing of his beloved Son, with the Holy Spirit the Paraclete, and all the heavenly virtues and all the saints. And I, your poor little brother Francis, and your servant, as far as I am able, confirm to you inwardly and outwardly[1] this holiest blessing.

---

[1] I.e. apparently for the inner and outer man, a favourite idea in the writings of Francis's companions (*SL*, p. 25).

2. The Rule of the Friars Minor

The original Rule presented to Innocent III does not survive; it was altered and extended over the years, and the earliest surviving Franciscan Rule appears to be in the shape it had assumed by *c.* 1221. This is commonly known as the First Rule or *Regula Prima* (*Opuscula*, pp. 24–62, trans. Sherley Price, pp. 204–26). After the *démarches* of 1220–3 (see *EFG*, pp. 64ff., 88–95 and Doc. 25, cc. 11ff.) the final version was enshrined in the papal bull *Solet annuere* still preserved in the Treasury of the Basilica of St Francis at Assisi (*Opuscula*, pp. 63–74), hence called *Regula bullata* or *Regula II*.

Two common difficulties in translating Francis's writings are most acute here. The first is to render his use of the present subjunctive with the right balance of authority and tact – I have translated it 'shall', perhaps giving too peremptory an impression, but Francis meant to be obeyed. The second is to determine how vernacular the style is meant to seem. The text of the Rule is based on a version approved, and perhaps tidied, by the papal chancery. In some of his other writings, such as the Testament, there are doubtful readings, not so much affecting the meaning as suggesting that what Francis originally wrote was deliberately ungrammatical or vernacular in flavour.

I. In the Lord's name: here begins the life of the Friars Minor
The Rule and life of the Friars Minor is this, to observe the holy Gospel of our Lord Jesus Christ by living in obedience, without property and in chastity. Brother Francis promises obedience and reverence to the lord Pope Honorius and his successors lawfully succeeding and to the Roman Church. And the other brothers are held to obey brother Francis and his successors.

II. Of those who wish to take on this life, and how they should be received
If any wish to take on this life and come to our brothers, the brothers shall send them to their own provincial ministers; for to them alone and to no others is granted the licence to receive new brothers. The ministers shall diligently examine them in the Catholic faith and the sacra-

ments of the Church. If they believe all of this, wish faithfully to confess it and firmly to observe it to the end, and if they have no wives – or, if they have, if the wives have already entered a monastery, or given them leave with the authority of their diocesan bishop, and if both have taken already the vow of continence and the wives are of such age as to be beyond suspicion – then the ministers shall declare to them the Gospel saying, that they shall go and sell all their goods and take care to give them to the poor.[1] If they cannot do so much, the good will and intention shall suffice. The brothers and their ministers are to be careful not to be concerned with their temporal goods, so that they can freely do with them whatever God inspires them to do. But if advice is needed, the ministers shall have permission to send them to God-fearing men by whose advice they may distribute their goods to the poor. After this they shall give them the clothes of probation, that is, two tunics without cowl, girdle, breeches and hood as far as the girdle, save if on occasion something else seems right, under God, to the ministers. When the year of probation is finished, they shall be received to obedience, promising to follow this life always and to keep the Rule. By no means shall they be allowed to leave this religious Order, according to the Pope's mandate;[2] for according to the holy Gospel, 'No one who sets his hand to the plough and looks backward is worthy of the kingdom of God'.[3] Those who have already promised obedience shall have one tunic with a hood, and those who want may have another without a hood. Those who really need can wear shoes. All the brothers shall wear wretched clothes and can patch them with bits of sackcloth and other fragments with God's blessing. But I warn and urge them not to despise or judge men whom they see clothed in soft raiment of many colours, or eating choice food and drink; rather let each judge and despise himself.

III. On the divine office and fasting, and how the brothers should travel in the world

Clerks shall perform the divine office according to the order of the Holy Roman Church, except for the Psalter, because they can have breviaries.[4] Lay brothers shall recite twenty-four Pater nosters for mattins, five for lauds, seven each for prime, terce, sext, none, twelve for vespers, seven for compline; and they shall pray for the dead.

[1] Matt., 19:21.
[2] The bull, *Cum secundum*, of 22 September 1220; Sbaralea, p. 6 (Honorius III, No. 5).
[3] Luke, 9:62.
[4] For the various possible interpretations of this clause, see S. J. P. Van Dijk and J. H. Walker, *The Origins of the Modern Roman Liturgy* (London, 1960), pp. 206ff.

They shall fast from All Saints [1 November] to Christmas. Those who are willing shall fast for the holy Lent beginning from Epiphany and running through the forty days which the Lord consecrated by his holy fast; those who willingly follow this fast have the Lord's blessing; those who are not willing are not bound to all this but shall observe the usual fast of Lent till Easter. At other times they are only bound to fast on Fridays. At times when their need is manifest the brothers shall not be bound to bodily fasting.

I advise, warn and urge my brothers in the Lord Jesus Christ, that when they travel through the world, they shall not go to law or dispute or pass judgement on others; they shall be gentle, peaceful, modest, kindly and humble, speaking good words to all,[1] as is right. They ought not to ride on horseback unless manifest need or illness compel them. Into whatever house they enter, first let them say: peace be to this house. And according to the holy Gospel, they are allowed to eat of all the foods which are set before them.[2]

IV. That the brothers shall not accept money
I firmly order all the brothers not to accept coins or money in any form, either themselves or by an intermediary. For the needs of the sick, however, and for clothing other brothers, the ministers and custodians alone shall exercise responsibility with the help of spiritual friends, and take account of special circumstances of place, time and cold regions, as they think need makes expedient; but always preserving the rule given above that they accept neither coins nor money.

V. On the manner of work
Those brothers to whom the Lord has given the grace to work, shall work faithfully and devotedly; in such manner that idleness, the soul's enemy, is kept at bay,[3] that they extinguish not the spirit of holy prayer and devotion, to which other, temporal cares should be subjected. They shall accept as reward of their work, for themselves and their brothers, the body's needs, but never coins or money, and accept them humbly, as befits God's servants and the followers of holiest poverty.

VI. That the brothers take nothing for themselves; on seeking alms; and on sick brothers
The brothers shall take nothing for themselves – neither house nor convent[4] nor any thing. As pilgrims and sojourners in this world, serving

---

[1] Cf. Titus, 3:2 (and II Timothy, 2:14).   [2] Luke, 10:5, 8.
[3] Cf. St Benedict's Rule, c. 48.
[4] 'Locum', an ambiguous word, meaning anything from a place, via the site of a house or convent, to the convent itself.

the Lord in poverty and humility, they shall go confidently for alms;
they ought not to be ashamed, since the Lord made himself poor for our
sakes in this world. This is that eminence of loftiest poverty which has
set you up, my dearest brothers, as heirs and kings of the kingdom of
Heaven, has made you poor in goods but eminent in the virtues. This
shall be your portion, which leads to the land of the living.[1] Live wholly
in it, beloved brothers, and you will wish for nothing else under heaven
for the name of Our Lord Jesus Christ, for ever.

Wherever the brothers are or happen to be, they shall act as intimate
friends one to another. Each shall show his brother confidently what
he needs; for if a mother nourishes and loves her son after the flesh,
how much more lovingly should not we love and nourish our brother
in the spirit? If any of them falls into sickness the other brothers should
serve him as they would like themselves to be served.

VII. The laying of penance on brothers who sin

If some of the brothers, urged on by the Enemy, commit mortal sin –
that is, any of the sins for which it is laid down among the brothers
that it should be presented to the provincial minister alone – they are
bound to hasten to the ministers as swiftly as they can, without delay.
The ministers, if they are priests, shall enjoin penance on them with
mercy; if they are not priests, they shall have other priests of the Order
enjoin penance on them, such as with God's help they think expedient.
They should take care not to be angry or upset by anyone's sin, since
anger and distress are a hindrance to charity in themselves and in other
men.

VIII. On the election of the Minister General of this brotherhood and of the Whitsun chapter

All the brothers are bound always to have one of the brothers of this
religious Order as Minister General and servant of the whole brotherhood, and are bound firmly to obey him. When he dies, the election of
his successor shall be made by the provincial ministers and custodians
in the Whitsun chapter – in which the provincial ministers are bound
always to meet together, wherever[2] the Minister General shall arrange,
and this once in three years or at some other term, greater or less, as the
Minister General orders. If at any time it seems to the whole body of
provincial ministers and custodians that the Minister General is insufficient for the service and common good of the brothers, these
brothers, to whom the duty of election is given, are bound in the Lord's
name to choose another brother to guard over them. After the Whitsun
chapter each minister and custodian can, if he wishes and thinks it

[1] Cf. Psalm 141 (142):6 (5).   [2] Or 'whenever'.

expedient, gather his own brothers together to a chapter in his own custody.[1]

IX. On preachers

The brothers shall not preach in the diocese of any bishop, when he has told them not to. None of the brothers shall presume to preach at all, unless he has been examined and approved by the Minister General of this brotherhood, and granted the office of preaching by him. I warn and urge these brothers also, that when they preach, their utterance be purified and chaste,[2] calculated to help and edify the people, by showing them the vices and the virtues, punishment and glory, in a brief sermon, for a short word made the Lord upon the earth.[3]

X. On the admonishment and correction of the brothers

The brothers who are ministers and servants of the other brothers, shall visit and warn their brothers, and humbly and charitably correct them, but not order them to do anything contrary to their soul's health and our Rule. The brothers who are subject shall remember that for God's sake they have renounced their own wills. And so I firmly command them to obey their ministers in every way in which they have promised the Lord their observance, and which is not contrary to their soul's health and our Rule. Wherever brothers are, who know and recognise that they cannot spiritually observe the Rule, they can and should hasten to their own ministers. The ministers shall receive them charitably and kindly, and show such friendly care of them that they feel able to speak and act towards the ministers as lords speak to their servants; for this is how it should be, since the ministers shall be servants of all the brothers.

I warn and urge the brothers in the Lord Jesus Christ to beware of all pride, vain glory, envy, avarice,[4] anxiety and thought for this world, detraction and grumbling. The illiterate shall not seek to learn letters, but shall take note that they should always desire above everything to have the Spirit of the Lord and his holy work within them, to pray always to Him with a pure heart, to be humble, patient in persecution and sickness, to love those who persecute us and rebuke us and criticise us, since the Lord says: 'Love your enemies, pray for those who persecute you and speak ill of you. Blessed are those who suffer persecution for righteousness' sake, for theirs is the kingdom of Heaven. He who perseveres to the end shall be saved.'[5]

---

[1] The wording is ambiguous, but presumably allows both for a provincial chapter and for a chapter in each custody.

[2] Cf. Psalm 11 (12):7 (6); and Psalm 17 (18):31 (30).

[3] Romans, 9:28.   [4] Cf. Luke, 12:15.   [5] Matt., 5:44, 10; 10:22.

XI. That the brothers shall not enter convents of nuns

I firmly command all the brothers to have no discussions with women which would arouse suspicion, nor give them counsel; they shall not enter convents of nuns, save only those brothers to whom the Holy See has granted special licence. Nor shall they form close friendships with men or women, so that no scandal arise between brothers or on their account for any such reason.

XII. On the brothers who go among the Saracens or other infidels

Whichever brothers wish by God's inspiration to go among the Saracens and other infidels shall seek licence to this end from their provincial ministers. The ministers shall give such licence to none save those they reckon suitable for the task.

In addition I order the ministers on obedience to seek from the lord Pope one of the cardinals of the Holy Roman Church, who may be governor, protector and corrector of this brotherhood, to the end that we be always submissive and subject to the Holy Roman Church, firm in the Catholic faith, and always observe poverty, humility and the holy Gospel of Our Lord Jesus Christ, as we have firmly promised.

3. St Francis's Seventh Admonition

(*Opuscula*, p. 10.) This admonition illustrates St Francis's use of St Paul.

VII. That good deeds may follow knowledge

The Apostle Paul says: 'The letter kills, the spirit gives life.'[1] They have been killed by the letter, who want only to know words in order to be reckoned wiser than other men, and to acquire great riches to give to their friends and relations. Those religious have been killed by the letter who are not willing to follow the spirit of the divine letter, but only desire to know words and interpret them for other men. Those have been given life by the spirit of the divine letter, who do not attribute every letter they know and desire to know to the body, but render it by word and example to the Lord most high, to whom belongs every good thing.

[1] II Corinthians, 3:6.

4. St Francis's Fourth Letter

(*Opuscula*, pp. 111–12.) This letter shows us Francis addressing his appeal to a wide circle – it illustrates the universal nature of his message.

Letter 4: to the people's rulers

To all *podestà*, consuls, judges and rectors throughout the world, and to all others to whom this letter comes, brother Francis, your poor, despised little servant in the Lord God, sends greetings, wishing for peace for you all.

Ponder and see that the day of your death approaches.[1] Therefore I ask you with all due respect, do not forget the Lord for the cares and business of this world, in which you are involved, nor depart from his commands, since all who forget him and depart from his commands are accursed[2] and he will give them over to forgetfulness.[3] When the day of death comes, all that they thought they had will be taken from them.[4] The wiser and more powerful they were in this world, the more shall they bear torments in hell.[5]

And so I firmly advise you, my lords, to set aside every care and business, and gladly receive the most holy body and the most holy blood of our Lord Jesus Christ in his holy commemoration; and you will confer such honour on the Lord in the people committed to you that every evening a messenger shall proclaim, or some other signal be given, that all the people give praise and thanks to the almighty Lord God. If you do not do so, you should know that you must render account before your Lord and God Jesus Christ on the day of judgement. Let those who keep this letter by them and observe it, know that they are blessed by the Lord God.

[1] Cf. Genesis, 47:29.   [2] Cf. Psalm 118 (119):21.   [3] Cf. Ezekiel, 33:13.
[4] Cf. Luke, 8:18.   [5] Cf. Wisdom, 6:7.

5. From the *First Life of St Francis* by Thomas of Celano

Cc. 36–7, 80, 84–7 are edited in *Analecta Franciscana*, Vol. X (Quaracchi, 1926–41), pp. 29–30, 59–60, 63–5. Cc. 36–7 illustrate Celano's flowery style; cc. 80, 84–7 his contribution to our knowledge of important aspects of Francis's life.

... 36. Christ's very courageous knight, Francis, went about in cities and towns, proclaiming the kingdom of God, not with the arguments of human wisdom, but the teaching and strength of the spirit, preaching peace, teaching the way of salvation and penitence to the remission of sins.[1] He acted confidently in all things, trusting in the papal authority he had received, avoiding flattery, avoiding blandishments. He was not hesitant but quick to point men's guilt; he did not abet the life of sinners but attacked it with bitter reproof, for he had first induced in his own deeds what he induced in others by words. He feared no gainsayer, but spoke the truth out with confidence, so that even men of great learning, men of glory and position, marvelled at his words, and were afrighted with a healthful fear in his presence. Men came hastening, and women too; clerks hurried to him, religious came in haste, to see and hear God's holy one, who appeared to all a man from another epoch. Men and women of every age rushed to see the wonderful works which God performed anew in the world by his servant. At that time as it were a new light from heaven was seen in the earth, whether St Francis was present, in person or by report, putting to flight all manner of darkness, such as had filled almost the whole region so that scarce anyone knew where he should be going. Thus the mighty depth of forgetfulness of God, the slumber of those neglecting his commands, had covered almost all, so that they scarce allowed themselves to be roused a little from old and inveterate evil ways.

37. He shone as a star in the black of night, like early dawn spreading over the darkness;[2] and thus it came to pass that in a short while the face of the whole province was changed and shone with a more joyful

---

[1] This sentence contains echoes of Matt., 9:35 and I Cor., 2:4–5, Acts, 10:36 and Mark, 1:4. For obvious reasons, I only give very selective notes of biblical echoes in what follows.

[2] Cf. Ecclesiasticus, 50:6–7; Prov., 7:9; Joel, 2:2.

countenance everywhere, shedding the hideous expression it formerly wore. The drought from which it suffered fled, and swiftly grew the corn in the parched land; the untended vine began to sprout the bud of the divine savour, to grow flowers of fragrance, to bring forth likewise fruits of honour and goodness. Everywhere re-echoed the sound of thanksgiving and the voice of praise; and so, many set aside their secular business and found themselves[1] in the life and teaching of the most blessed father Francis and aspired to love and reverence of the Creator. Many of the people, noble and humble, clerks and laymen, were touched by divine inspiration and began to come to St Francis, yearning to fight for ever under his teaching and direction. The saint of God, as a richly flowing stream of heavenly grace, watered them all with showers of heavenly gifts, and adorned the field of their hearts with flowers of virtues. For he was a mighty artificer, and at the proclamation of his way of life, rule and teaching Christ's Church was renewed both in men and in women, and an army in three[2] columns of the saved marched in triumph. To all he gave a pattern of life and truly showed the way of salvation for every order of mankind.

. . . 80. It would take far too long, be impossible indeed, to list and call to mind all that the glorious father Francis did and taught, while he lived in the flesh. Who could ever express the height of affection which he felt for all those things which are of God?[3] Who could adequately describe the sweetness he enjoyed, contemplating the wisdom of the Creator, his power and his goodness, in his creatures? Often he was filled with marvellous, inexpressible joy from this contemplation, when he looked at the sun, when he saw the moon, when he observed the stars and the firmament. O simple piety, and pious simplicity! He even felt the warmth of love for worms, since he had read that saying of the Saviour: 'I am a worm and no man.'[4] And so he collected them from the road, setting them in a safe place where they would not be squashed by the feet of passersby. What shall I say of other lesser creatures, for he had honey or the best wine offered the bees in winter, so that they should not perish in the bitter cold. He praised the efficacy of their work, the excellence of their understanding, to God's glory, with such eloquence that he often passed a whole day in praise of them and other creatures. As once the three young men set in the burning fiery furnace invited all the elements to praise and glorify the creator of all, so this man, full of the spirit of God, never

---

[1] The exact meaning of this clause is not clear.

[2] A reference to the three orders, of Friars Minor, of Poor Clares (the nuns), and the Tertiaries, layfolk living in the world following a simple rule of life but not vowed to chastity or total poverty.

[3] Cf. Matt., 22:21.   [4] Psalm 21 (22):7 (6).

ceased to glorify, praise and bless the Creator and governor of all in all the elements and creatures he had made.[1]

... 84. His highest purpose, his chief desire and supreme aim was to observe the holy Gospel in every way and by every means, and perfectly, with all vigilance, all zeal, entire desire of mind, full fervour of heart, 'to follow the teaching and the footprints of Our Lord Jesus Christ'.[2] He called his words to mind by diligent meditation, and recalled his works by contemplation of him. Above all, the humility of his incarnation and the charity of his passion so occupied his memory that he would scarcely think of anything else. We should recall and ponder in reverent memory the deed he performed in the third year before the day of his glorious death at the town called Greccio, on Christmas Day. There was in that territory a man called John, of good reputation but better life to whom St Francis was particularly devoted, since, though very noble and much honoured in his own land, he rejected earthly nobility and cultivated nobility of mind. About a fortnight before Christmas St Francis sent for him, as he often did, and said to him: 'If you would like us to celebrate this Christmas at Greccio, hurry on ahead and prepare with all care what I tell you. For I wish to make a memorial of that boy who was born in Bethlehem, of the difficult circumstances in which he was born, how he was laid in a crib,[3] and how he was set on a bed of hay with ox and ass standing by, so that we can see all this with our own bodily eyes.' When he heard this, the good, faithful man sped with all haste and prepared everything the saint had said at Greccio.

85. The day of gladness, the time of rejoicing approached; the brothers were called from many places; the men and women of the land, so far as they could, prepared candles and torches with great joy to light up the night, which has lit up all days and years with its glittering star. At length God's saint arrived and found all ready; he saw and rejoiced. The crib was prepared, hay was brought, ox and ass led to the crib. There honour was done to simplicity, poverty exalted, humility honoured; and a new Bethlehem was made in Greccio. The night was lit up like the day,[4] and it gave delight to men and beasts. People came flocking and were glad with a new joy in this new mystery. The wood was filled with voices and the rocks echoed to sounds of rejoicing; the brothers sang, giving praise to the Lord as is his due; the whole night resounded with jubilation. God's saint stood before the crib, full of sighs, touched to the heart in his piety, suffused with wonderful joy.

[1] Cf. Daniel, 3, with an echo also of Genesis, 41:38; and the sentence is a reminder of Francis's Canticle of Brother Sun.

[2] A quotation from the *Regula prima* (see Doc. 1, note), c. 1.

[3] Cf. Luke, 2:7.   [4] Psalm 138 (139):12.

Mass was celebrated over the crib and the priest felt a consolation wholly new.

86. St Francis put on the vestments of deacon, since a deacon he was, and sang the holy Gospel in a resounding voice – his voice was eager, sweet, clear, sonorous, and called all to the highest rewards. Then he preached to the people standing round and uttered honeyed words on the birth of the poor boy born to be king, and the little city of Bethlehem; and often, when he wanted to call Christ 'Jesus', in his burning love he called him 'the boy of Bethlehem', saying 'Bethlehem' like a sheep bleating, filling his mouth with the sound, or rather with a sweet affection. When he named 'the boy of Bethlehem' or 'Jesus', he licked his lips, tasting pleasantly on his palate and swallowing the sweetness of the word. God's gifts there were manifold, and a man of good life saw a wonderful vision. He saw a boy lying dead in the crib, and the saint came to him and woke him as it were from sleep. The vision was not inappropriate, since the boy Jesus had been forgotten in many men's hearts; and by his own grace his servant St Francis revived his memory and printed it sharply on their memories. The solemn vigil was completed and everyone went to their homes rejoicing.

87. The hay in the crib was preserved, so that by it God cured horses and oxen and multiplied his holy mercy.[1] Thus many beasts with different illnesses in the neighbourhood were cured of their diseases by eating some of the hay. Women too, in long and difficult labour, were brought safely to birth when they laid some of the hay on themselves; and a throng of both men and women received the cure they longed for from many misfortunes. The place where the crib was set was consecrated as a temple to the Lord; and in honour of the blessed father Francis an altar was raised over the crib and a church dedicated; where the animals once fed on hay, there from that time men shall eat the flesh of the lamb without blemish or spot, Jesus Christ Our Lord,[2] who gave himself for us with supreme love and beyond recounting, who lives and reigns with the Father and the Holy Ghost, glorious for ever through all the ages. Amen, alleluia, alleluia.

[1] Cf. Psalm 35 (36): 6–8 (5–6).   [2] Cf. I Peter, 1:19.

6. From the Writings of Leo, Rufino, and Angelo, Companions of St Francis

In 1244 the friars assembled in General Chapter issued an appeal for material for a new Life of St Francis, to supplement Thomas of Celano's *Vita Prima*. In 1246 three of Francis's closest companions, Leo, Rufino and Angelo, delivered the material they had collected from their own memories and from other companions of the saint; and this formed the nucleus for the *Vita Secunda* of Celano, completed the next year. Not all scholars are agreed that these stories survive in approximately their original form; but this is the general view and I have defended it at length in the introduction to my edition (*SL*).

The following extracts are taken from my translation in *SL*, pp. 95 (c. 4), 111 (c. 13), 145, 147 (c. 32), 289 (c. 115). The stories are fresh and vivid; yet at the same time chosen partly at least to remind the friars of the 1240s of certain of Francis's principles and attitudes.

No. 115 seems to have been written a little later than the others, for it forms one of a group of stories often called the *Verba S. Francisci*, to which the account of Francis's argument with Cardinal Hugolino quoted on pp. 18–19 also belongs. I personally believe that it was written by brother Leo in the late 1250s, when he collected a few *addenda* to the main stories in the period of anxiety caused by the enforced resignation of the Minister General John of Parma, whom Leo greatly admired. But many scholars think it was written later, and some doubt if it is the authentic work of Leo.[1]

Leo did not die until the early 1270s, but already in or about 1266 his materials seem to have disappeared from view in response to the decree of the General Chapter that all legends of Francis save the Life by Bonaventure should be suppressed. It seems, however, that care was taken to preserve a set – probably the original loose quires and pages of vellum sent in by the Companions – in the friars' library in Assisi; and there they were rediscovered in about 1310 and copied into the earliest surviving manuscript to contain them, now preserved in the Biblioteca Augusta at Perugia.[2]

---

[1] See *SL*, pp. 57–66.
[2] *SL*, pp. 53–6; Brooke in *Latin Biography*, ed. T. A. Dorey (London, 1967), pp. 189ff.

14 [How they obeyed the Gospel to the letter]

In those days, when St Francis was with the friars that he then had, such was his purity that from the hour in which the Lord revealed to him that he and his friars ought to live according to the model of the holy Gospel, he wanted to do this to the letter and tried to observe it throughout his life.[1] He ordered the friar who did the cooking for the brothers, when he wanted to give them vegetables to eat, not to put them in hot water in the evening ready for the following day, as is usually done, so that they might obey that saying of the holy Gospel: 'Take no thought for the morrow.'[2] So that friar put them to soak after the brothers had said mattins. For the same reason for a long time many of the friars in the houses where they were living, and especially in the towns, observed this injunction – being unwilling to acquire or accept alms beyond what was sufficient for them for one day.

13 [St Francis wished cells to be roughly made and poor]

One brother, a pious man with whom St Francis was very friendly, was living in a hermitage.[3] Thinking to himself that St Francis might come there some time, he had a little cell made in a secluded spot near the friary where St Francis could pray when he came there. It so happened that not many days later St Francis arrived. When he had been taken by that friar to see it, St Francis said to him: 'This cell seems to me too attractive. But, if you would like me to stay in it for a few days, have it given some covering of stones and tree branches inside and out.' For that little cell was not walled but made of wood; but as the wood was planed, prepared with axe and adze, it seemed to St Francis too attractive. The friar made it at once more suitable in the way St Francis had indicated. For the poorer and more hallowed the cells and buildings of the friars were, so much the more gladly he viewed them and once in a while stayed in them. After he had stayed and prayed in this one for a few days, he was standing one day outside the cell near the friary, when one of the friars of that house came to where he was. St Francis said to him: 'Where have you come from, brother?' He replied: 'I come from your cell.' St Francis said to him: 'As you have said it is mine, another will stay there from now on, and not I.' We, indeed, who were with him, many times heard him quote that saying of the holy Gospel: 'Foxes have holes and the fowls of the air have nests, but the Son of Man has not where to lay his head.'[4] And he said: 'The Lord when He was in the hermit's cave,[5] when He

---

[1] Cf. Testament, Doc. 1.   [2] Cf. Matt., 6:34.

[3] 2 Cel., c. 59 places this in Sarteano (near Chiusi).

[4] Matt., 8:20; Luke, 9:58.

[5] Cf. Matt., 4:1–2, etc.; *carcer* appears to mean 'hermit's cave' here, not, from the context, 'cell'.

prayed and fasted forty days and forty nights, did not have a cell or any building made there but stayed on the mountain under a stone.' Following His example he wished to have neither building nor cell in this world, nor to have any made for him, but rather, if he should chance to say to the friars at any time: 'Make this cell suitable', he did not wish to remain in it afterwards on account of that saying of the holy Gospel: 'Take no thought for yourselves.'[1]

32 [St Francis corrected the friars who had laid the table specially on Christmas Day]

Once a minister of the friars came to St Francis, who was then staying in the same place, to celebrate Christmas[2] with him. When the friars of the house had laid the table specially on Christmas Day with beautiful white cloths which they had acquired, and glass vessels for drinking, in honour of the minister, it happened that St Francis came down from his cell to eat. When he saw the table put up on a dais and so elaborately laid, he secretly went and took the hood[3] of a poor man who had come there that day, and the staff which he carried in his hands. He quietly called one of his companions and went outside the door of the hermitage, without the other friars of the house knowing. Meanwhile the friars came in to the meal, chiefly because the holy father sometimes used to prefer it so: when he did not come at once at mealtimes, and the friars wished to eat, he wanted them to go in to table and eat. His companion closed the door, staying inside near him. St Francis knocked at the door and he at once opened to him. He came in like a pilgrim with the hood on his back and a staff in his hands. When he came before the door of the building where the friars were eating he cried out like a beggar saying to the friars: 'For the love of the lord God give alms to this poor, sick pilgrim.' The minister and the other friars recognised him at once. The minister said: 'Brother, we also are poor like you. Since there are many of us, the alms we eat are necessary to us; but for the love of God on whom you have called, come in and we will give you of the alms which the Lord has given us.' When he entered and stood before the friars' table, the minister gave him the dish from which he himself was eating and likewise bread. Taking it he sat down on the ground near the fire facing the brothers, who sat at the table on a dais. He said to the brothers, sighing: 'When I saw the table laid with honour and elaborate care I thought this was not the table of poor religious who go daily from door to door. For it is our duty, dearest brothers, to follow the example of humility and poverty in all things more than other religious, because we were called to this and have professed this before God and men. So now it seems to me that I

---

[1] Cf. Luke, 12:22; Matt., 6:31, 34.   [2] Easter in 2 Cel., c. 61.   [3] Or hat.

sit like a friar.' The friars were ashamed, perceiving that St Francis spoke the truth and some of them began to weep bitterly, thinking how he sat on the ground and that he had wanted to correct them in so holy and fair a way.

115 [St Francis refused to seek a privilege to make the friars independent of the bishops]

Some of the friars said to St Francis: 'Father, surely you see that sometimes the bishops do not allow us to preach and leave us to hang about for many days idle in a district before we can preach to the people? It would be better if you would arrange it that the friars might have a privilege from the Pope. It would be the salvation of souls.' He replied to them in great indignation: 'You, Friars Minor! You do not comprehend the will of God and do not permit me to convert the whole world in the way God wills. For I wish to convert the prelates first through humility and reverence, and when they see our holy life and reverence for them, they will ask you to preach and convert the people, and this will serve you better than the privileges you want, which will lead you to pride. If you are free from all avarice and persuade the people to render their dues to the churches, they will ask you to hear the confessions of their people; though you ought not to be concerned with this, as, if they have been converted, they can well find confessors. For myself, I wish to have this privilege from the Lord that I have no privilege from man, unless it be to do reverence to all and through obedience to the holy Rule, by example more than by word, to convert the whole world.'

7. From Thomas of Spalato, *Historia Pontificum Salonitanorum et Spalatinorum*

Ed. L. von Heinemann, *MGH Scr.*, Vol. XXIX, p. 580; also ed. L. Lemmens in *Testimonia Minora S. Francisci saeculi xiii*, p. 10. Thomas of Spalato was an archdeacon, a member of the secular clergy, and gives us a contemporary description not written by a friar of Francis's preaching. For another story showing that Francis's success as a preacher was not due to his appearance, see *SL*, No. 103.

In the same year [1222 or 1223], on the Feast of the Assumption, when I was studying in Bologna, I saw St Francis preaching in the piazza in front of the Palazzo Publico, where almost all the citizens had gathered. The opening words of his sermon were: Angels, men, devils; and he treated of these three rational and spiritual beings so well and so perceptively that many educated men in his audience were filled with no small admiration at the sermon of this uneducated man. He did not deliver his sermon in the usual way, but in a rousing fashion. All he said was aimed at quenching hostility and procuring peaceful agreement. His habit was dirty, his appearance contemptible and his face ill-favoured, but God gave the man's words such effect that many noble clans, whose violence and long-standing feuds had raged with much blood-letting, were induced to agree to peace. So great were the reverence and devotion of the people for him that men and women pressed on him in throngs in their eagerness either to touch the hem of his garment or to carry off a scrap of his clothing.

8. A Sermon of Bernard of Tiron

(From Gaufridus Grossus, *Life of St Bernard of Tiron*, Migne, *PL*, Vol. 172, cols. 1398–9. See p. 52.)

One day while he was preaching publicly to the people in Coutances, a maritime city of the Normans, an archdeacon who had a wife and sons came up with a great company of priests and clerks and demanded to know why he, a monk and dead to the world, preached to the living. Bernard, surrounded as he was by them, replied thus, in the presence of all the people.

'Surely, dearest brother, you have read in the Scriptures how Samson that strongest of men killed his enemies with the jawbone of a dead ass?' [Judges, 15:15]. Taking advantage of the occasion he expounded this chapter of Scripture in his defence, the people listening. 'Samson,' he said, 'who is interpreted as the sun, signifies Christ, the sun of justice; his enemies the demons and the sinful men who join them through malice, fighting against Christ and his law; the dead ass the simple, obedient people, bearing the gentle yoke of Christ and his light burden, following the way of humility, dead to the world, that is, mortifying the sins and vices, as Scripture says [Colossians, 3:3–5].

'The jaw, having the strength of bone, harder than the softness of flesh, the instrument for biting and chewing in the head of the ass, represents the Church's preacher, who ought to have the strength of bone because he ought vigorously to resist sins and vices and bear adversity bravely in the defence of justice and holiness. The preacher ought to be harder than the softness of flesh because he ought to cut away the carnal delight of pleasure from his life and behaviour by the labour of an abstinence more severe, and not spinelessly to submit his mind to softening vices. The preacher is the instrument for eating, if he subtly understands the word of God, which is the food of our souls as our Lord said in the Gospel [Matt., 4:4]; and if he both understands and implements what he says in his works. If he teaches well and lives badly he does not instruct the people but corrupts them. For while he lives badly his preaching is condemned and it is not received, and by his example the people are not edified but destroyed. It is necessary therefore that he lives well and subtly discusses the Scriptures, the food of souls, chewing it over and grinding it; as meanwhile he distinguishes the historical interpretation from the allegorical, divides the allegorical from the tropological and separates the tropological from the anagogical. He swallows the food of the word of God, thus masticated and minutely ground, first himself by right use, tasting the virtue of its savour. Then he passes it over to the body of the dead ass, that is, he draws it down to the capacity of the understanding of the people who are simple and mortifying themselves, as he studies to inform them by all these modes of understanding to strive for eternal life; in order that by instruction through continual preaching, skilfully and wisely planned, he may teach them how to conduct themselves in word and deed, and lead them to a better life. He should not forget that he himself is the instrument by which they bite their food, so that he can tear sinners from the body of the devil by the bite of his reproof and by his rebukes, and restore to Christ's body, which is the Church, those justified by tears of penitence. Just as he is in the higher regions of the ass, in the head that is, through the dignity of prelacy, so he transcends the people, signified by the ass, by the virtue of his works and the holiness of his behaviour.

'You see, therefore, dearest brother, according to the authority of holy Scripture, that if the Christian people, who are symbolised by the dead ass, ought to be dead to the world, how much the more ought that preacher of Christ, who is represented by the jaw, to be nailed to Christ, crucified and dead to the world, just as the great preacher to the world said of himself [St Paul in Galatians, 2:19], he was nailed to Christ crucified that by virtue of his mortification he could chastise those still living in sins and vices, and having chastised them make them conform to him in death, to fulfil what the apostle also said: "Be ye imitators of me, as I of Christ" [1 Cor., 11:1]. Therefore, as the Church's preacher ought to be dead to the world, and his preaching to the people is condemned whose life is not believed to mortify vices and sins, for this reason, because I am a monk and dead to the world, can you prohibit me from preaching when I can profit the people by the example of my life of mortification, and by the word of doctrine move them to better things? As it is accepted that the blessed Gregory and Martin and many other holy monks took on pastoral office in the churches by the merit of their mortification, and with the honour of prelacy the office of preaching, it follows from this that we earn the licence to preach through the virtue of mortification. Therefore, because I am a monk and dead to the world, the right to preach should not be taken from me but rather should be conferred upon me.'

With these and similar words the man of God proceeded, to the applause of the people; and by God's will the archdeacon became somewhat less fierce and arrogant of mind and prevented the priests and their wives from harming him – for such a multitude of priests and ladies had gathered at the feast of Pentecost to make their processions to the cathedral, as is the custom of the country, that there was scarcely space for them. As has been said, Bernard, Christ's warrior, preached to the throng and bore with patience on that account the fight he sustained without and the fear within.

9. Peter the Venerable's Preface to his *Tract against the Petrobrusians*

From *Contra Petrobrusianos hereticos*, cc. 1–10, ed. J. V. Fearns, *Corpus Christianorum, Continuatio Mediaevalis*, Vol. X (Turnhout, 1968), pp. 3–6; also in Fearns, no. 4. See pp. 63–6.)

1. To the lords and fathers, masters of the Church of God, the archbishops of Arles and Embrun and the bishops of Die and Gap, brother Peter, humble abbot of the monks of Cluny, sends greeting and offers his service.

I recently wrote a letter[1] to your reverences arguing against the heresies of Peter of Bruis, but countless important matters hindered my mind from dictating and my pen from writing, and so I had to put off sending it till now. To you in your wisdom I send it now that it may be made known through you to the heretics, against whom it is written, and also to the catholics, to whom it may perhaps be useful. I send it to you since in your dioceses and their surroundings this stupid and impious heresy has, like a virulent plague, killed many and infected more; but stirred by the grace of God and helped by your efforts it has lost ground a little in your area. But it has moved, as I have heard, to places sufficiently close to you, and, expelled from your *Septimania* [i.e. Aquitaine], by your persecutions, it has prepared pits for itself in the province of *Novempopulana* [i.e. Guyenne], which is popularly called Gascony, and the regions adjacent to it. Here, now hiding itself for fear, now assuming the audacity to come out into the open, it deceives those it can, corrupts those it can, and furnishes lethal poison now to these, now to those. It is up to you therefore to whom preeminently the care of the Church of God in these regions pertains and on whom, as on strong columns, she chiefly depends, both on account of your office and your unparalleled learning, it is up to you, I say, to drive it out from those places in which it is glad to find refuge, by preaching, and also if necessary by the secular arm.

2. But because it is more fitting that Christian charity be employed to convert them than to exterminate them let us offer them in argument authority and reason, so that they may be compelled to cede to authority if they wish to remain Christians, to reason if rational men. Perhaps the

[1] I.e. the treatise which follows.

letter which I wrote to you against their errors may be useful to them if
they wish to give heed to this, and if they do not wish to be contentious
and pertinacious, perhaps when they have read it carefully, although
they have certainly been most unwise, they may be able to return to
their senses from the stupidity of such error. If they are given over to
error and choose rather to act foolishly than wisely, to perish than be
saved, to die than to live, perhaps the reading of the letter may satisfy
the hidden thoughts of some catholic men and either heal their minds
from a sickness of the faith unknown to men or fortify them against
those whose tongue was called by the prophet a sharp sword.[1] This
consideration, which I have put last, is the chief cause of my writing,
that even if the reading of it cannot profit the heretics it may yet be of
some usefulness in serving the Church of God. For thus the Church,
as you know in your wisdom, through past centuries has always been
accustomed to act with all the great variety of heresies which have
frequently tried to corrupt its purity: it has never passed over one in
silence, but has purged the blasphemies of all heretics for her own
security and the perpetual instruction of all by the sacred authority of
Scripture and also by reason. Therefore I, although one of the least
among the limbs of the body of Christ, that is of his Church, have
laboured to finish this work, so that what I have written may if possible
be useful to the heretics and may supply catholics, into whose hands it
may come, with precautions against this impious dogma and any like it.

3. Because the first seeds of dogmatic error, sown and multiplied by
Peter of Bruis for almost twenty years, produced five principal poisonous
bushes, I concentrated to the best of my ability on these and applied
my mind and words the more diligently to those in which the greater
damage to faith revealed the greater danger. Since the work is rather
diffuse, and your involvement in a great deal of ecclesiastical business
may not perhaps give you much time for reading, I list the heads briefly
and show the errors which are dealt with at length in the letter in order.

4. The first chapter of the heretics' opinions denies that infants who
have not yet reached the age of understanding can be saved by baptism
into Christ and that the faith of other people can be of benefit to those
who cannot have their own – since, according to them, one's own faith
and not another's saves in baptism, as Christ said: 'He who will believe
and be baptised shall be saved; he who will not believe shall be condemned.'[2]

5. The second chapter says that the building of temples or churches
ought not to be undertaken, and those already built should be demolished: it is not necessary for Christians to have sacred places for prayer,
since God, when invoked, hears as well in the tavern as in the church,

[1] Cf. Psalm 56 (57):5 (4).   [2] Mark, 16:16.

in the market place as in the temple, before the altar or before the stall, and He will listen to those who are deserving.

6. The third chapter directs that holy crosses be broken into pieces and burnt since they are the symbol or instrument with which Christ was so horribly tortured and so cruelly killed. Such a symbol is not worthy to be adored nor venerated nor to have any prayers addressed to it, but in order to avenge his sufferings and death it should be disparaged with all dishonour, chopped up with swords, burnt with fire.

7. The fourth chapter not only denies the truth of the body and blood of Christ consecrated daily and constantly in the Church through the sacrament, but judges it altogether void and that it ought not to be offered to God.

8. The fifth chapter derides sacrifices, prayers, alms and everything else done for the benefit of the faithful departed by the pious living and affirms that these cannot in the slightest degree help the dead.

9. To these five chapters, as God granted me, I have replied in that letter sent by me to you, holy fathers, and, to the best of my ability, I have endeavoured to show how the impiety of the faithless may be either converted or confounded, and also the faith of the pious confirmed.

But after the burning of Peter of Bruis at Saint-Gilles, in which the zeal of the faithful took vengeance for the holy cross which he had lit with flames by burning him – after that manifestly impious man was made to pass from fire to fire, from a transient to an eternal, Henry [of Lausanne], the heir to his iniquity, with some accomplices, not so much amended the diabolical doctrine but changed it. I have seen recently written in a book, which was said to have been dictated by him, not merely five but many chapters set forth. Against these my mind is kindled once again to act and to stop the mouths of demons with God's words. But as I have not yet full confidence that he thinks and preaches thus I put off a reply until I have complete assurance about these reports. But if perhaps you in your wisdom could make a careful inquiry and let me know, I will give what help I can, that the cup of death which the most miserable of men and his miserable associates offer, which is now in some part emptied, may be drained altogether of the remaining dregs through new replies. Meanwhile, if it pleases you, take note of the letter drawn up for the benefit of its readers, pass it to those who need it as time and place may offer, so that, as I have said, it may serve either to correct some of the heretics against whom it is written or to put on their guard catholics for whom it is written in these and similar matters. If it pleases anyone to transcribe it, he should not omit to put this small letter at the beginning by way of a preface, because in this all the origin and substance of the whole large work are briefly indicated.

10. St Bernard of Clairvaux on Henry of Lausanne

St Bernard, Letter 241, Migne, *PL*, Vol. 182, coll. 434–6; also in Fearns, no. 5: another version by B. S. James, *Letters of St Bernard* (London, 1953), no. 317. Bernard writes to the count of Saint-Gilles about the heretic Henry of Lausanne.

How great are the ills we have heard and known which the heretic Henry has caused and is causing daily to the churches of God! A ravening wolf in sheep's clothing is living in your territories; but by God's providence we know him by his fruits. Churches lack their people, the people lack priests, the priests lack the reverence due to them, and the Christians lack Christ. Churches are held to be synagogues; holiness is denied to the sanctuaries of God: the sacraments are rated not sacred: festivals are deprived of their solemnity. Men die in their sins: souls are heedlessly snatched to the dread tribunal, neither reconciled, alas, by penitence nor furnished with holy communion. The little children of Christians are shut out from the life of Christ, while the grace of baptism is denied: nor are they permitted to draw near salvation, although their holy Saviour interceded for them and says: 'Suffer the little children to come to me.'[1] Surely therefore God, who saved men and beasts as he multiplied his mercy, does not withhold his great mercy from innocent children alone? Why, I ask, why in their spite do they grudge the child who is our Saviour to the children, when he was born for them? This spite is diabolical: by this spite death entered the world. Does anyone think that little children have no need of the Saviour because they are little children? If that is so, God almighty made himself a little child for nought, to say nothing of the fact that he was flogged, spat upon, nailed to the cross, that finally he died.

This man is not of God, who thus acts and speaks contrary to God. Alas! Yet he is listened to by many, and he has a following who believe in him. Oh, most unhappy people. At the voice of a single heretic are silenced all the voices of the prophets and apostles which have called every nation to one Church in the faith of Christ and have sung with one true Spirit. Thus the divine oracles have deceived, the eyes and minds of all are deceived, who read what was predicted and contem-

[1] Cf. Matt., 19:14; Mark, 10:14; Luke, 18:16.

143

plate what is done. By a blindness which is astounding, as of the Jews, either he sees not or does not want to see the truth which is manifest to all fulfilled, and he has by some devilish art persuaded the stupid, foolish people not to believe their own eyes in a matter perfectly plain. The ancients spread deceit; the moderns live in error; the whole world has gone to destruction even after the shedding of Christ's blood; only on those whom Henry deceives have come all the riches of God's mercies and the grace of the whole Church! And now for this cause, though very sick in body, I have journeyed to this region, which he ravages fearfully like a singular wild beast, while there is none to resist him, none to cure. From every part of France he had been chased for attempting the like evil; only this region does he find open to him: in it he rages without hindrance under your dominion against Christ's flock, and how this agrees with your good name, illustrious prince, you yourself must judge. Yet it is not to be wondered at if that crafty serpent deceived you, since he has the outward show of piety, whose inner strength he has utterly rejected.

But hear now what manner of man he is. He is an apostate who abandoned the habit of religion (for he used to be a monk), and returned to the filth of the flesh and the world like a dog to his vomit.[1] Not bearing to live, for shame, among his relatives and acquaintance, or rather, not permitted to by reason of the greatness of his crime, he girded up his loins and set out upon a journey into the unknown, making himself a wanderer[2] and a fugitive upon earth. When he had begun to beg he charged his expenses to the Gospel (for he was an educated man) and squandering the word of God for money evangelised that he might eat. If he could elicit something more than food from the simpler people or from some of the women, he basely gave himself up to playing games of chance or, to be sure, to baser deeds. For frequently after a day of plaudits from the people this notable preacher was found the following night with harlots and sometimes with married folk. Inquire, if you please, how the noble man left Lausanne; how he left Le Mans; how Poitiers; how Bordeaux. Nor does it appear he ever had a path open for his return anywhere, since everywhere he left footprints of evil behind him. Did you hope for good fruit from such a tree? Actually the lands in which he is he caused to stink throughout the world, because as the Lord said: 'a corrupt tree cannot bring forth good fruit'.[3]

This, therefore, as I have said, is the reason for my coming. Nor do I

---

[1] Cf. Prov., 26:11; etc.
[2] 'Gyrovagus': the opprobrious word in St Benedict's Rule (c. 1) for a wandering monk.
[3] Cf. Matt., 7:18.

come of myself, but I am drawn as well by the summons of and compassion for the Church; if perhaps that thorn and its viciousness can
be extirpated from the Lord's field while the seeds of it are still small,
not by me, who am nothing, but by the hand of the holy bishops with
whom I am and the co-operation also of your powerful right arm. Chief
among these is the venerable bishop of Ostia,[1] directed to this task by
the Holy See; a man who has done great things in Israel, and God
Almighty has through him in many things given victory to his Church.
It is important for you that you, illustrious prince, receive him honourably, and those who are with him; and so as not to lose the effort undertaken by such great men especially for your own and your people's
safety, give help according to the power given to you from above.

[1] Alberic, a Frenchman and formerly a Cluniac monk, consecrated cardinal–
bishop of Ostia in 1138; he died in 1148.

11. John of Salisbury's Account of Arnold of Brescia

(From *The Historia Pontificalis*, c. 31, ed. and trans. M. Chibnall (Nelson's Medieval Texts, 1956), pp. 62–5, slightly adapted.)

Negotiations for peace were proceeding between the Pope [Eugenius III, 1145–53] and the Romans, and numerous legations sped to and fro between the two parties. But there were many obstacles in the way of peace, the greatest of all being the refusal of the Romans to expel Arnold of Brescia, who was said to have bound himself by oath to uphold the honour of the city and Roman republic. The Romans in their turn promised him aid and counsel against all men, and explicitly against the lord Pope; for the Roman Church had excommunicated him and ordered him to be shunned as a heretic. This man was a priest by office, a canon regular by profession, and one who had mortified his flesh with fasting and coarse raiment: of keen intelligence, persevering in his study of the Scriptures, eloquent in speech, and a vehement preacher against the vanities of the world. Nevertheless he was reputed to be factious and a leader of schism, who wherever he lived prevented the citizens from being at peace with the clergy. He had been abbot at Brescia, and when the bishop was absent on a short visit to Rome had so swayed the minds of the citizens that they would scarcely open their gates to the bishop on his return. For this he was deposed by Pope Innocent and expelled from Italy; crossing the Alps into France he became a disciple of Peter Abelard, and together with Master Hyacinth, who is now a cardinal, zealously fostered his cause against the abbot of Clairvaux.[1] After Master Peter had set out for Cluny, he remained at Paris on the Mont Sainte Geneviève, expounding the Scriptures to scholars at the church of St Hilary where Peter had been lodged. But he had no listeners except poor students who publicly begged their bread from door to door to support themselves and their

---

[1] Hyacinth, Jacinctus or Giacinto, a favourite pupil of Abelard and his supporter against St Bernard of Clairvaux, was made a cardinal by Pope Celestine II (1143–4), and after a long career in the Curia, ended his life as Pope Celestine III (1191–8). Celestine II was one of two short-lived Popes between Innocent II (1130–43) and the Cistercian Eugenius III (1145–53), who are named below.

master. He said things that were entirely consistent with the law accepted by Christian people, but not at all with the life they led. To the bishops he was merciless on account of their avarice and filthy lucre; most of all because of stains on their personal lives, and their striving to build the church of God in blood. He denounced the abbot, whose name was renowned above all others for his many virtues, as a seeker after vainglory, envious of all who won distinction in learning or religion unless they were his own disciples. In consequence the abbot prevailed on the most Christian king to expel him from the Frankish kingdom; from there he returned to Italy after Pope Innocent's death [1143] and, after promising reparation and obedience to the Roman Church, was received at Viterbo by Pope Eugenius. Penance was imposed on him, which he promised he would perform in fasts, vigils and prayers in the holy places of the city; and again he took a solemn oath to show obedience. Whilst dwelling in Rome under pretext of penance he won the city to his side, and preaching all the more freely because the lord Pope was occupied in Gaul he built up a faction known as the heretical sect of the Lombards. He had disciples who imitated his austerities and won favour with the populace through outward decency and austerity of life, but found their chief supporters amongst pious women. He himself was frequently heard on the Capitol and in public gatherings. He had already publicly denounced the cardinals, saying that their college [*conventum*], by its pride, avarice, hypocrisy and manifold shame was not the church of God, but a place of business and den of thieves,[1] which took the place of the scribes and Pharisees amongst Christian peoples. The Pope himself was not what he professed to be – an apostolic man and shepherd of souls – but a man of blood who maintained his authority by fire and sword, a tormentor of churches and oppressor of the innocent, who did nothing in the world save gratify the flesh and empty other men's coffers to fill his own. He was, he said, so far from apostolic that he imitated neither the life nor the doctrine of the apostles, wherefore neither obedience nor reverence was due to him: and in any case no man could be admitted who wished to impose a yoke of servitude on Rome, the seat of Empire, fountain of liberty and mistress of the world.

[1] Cf. John, 2:16; Matt., 21:13; etc.

12. Waldo's Profession of Faith

(From A. Dondaine, 'Aux origines du Valdéisme – une profession de foi de Valdès', *Archivum Fratrum Praedicatorum*, Vol. 16 (1946), 191–235, at pp. 231–2; also in Thouzellier, pp. 27–30; Fearns, no. 12. See pp. 71–4).

In the name of the Father and of the Son and of the Holy Spirit and of the most blessed and ever Virgin Mary. May it be known to all the faithful that I Waldo and all my brothers, setting before us the holy Gospels, believe in our hearts, understand by faith, confess with our lips and affirm with simple words the Father, Son and Holy Spirit to be three persons, one God and the whole Trinity of the Godhead co-essential, consubstantial, co-eternal and co-omnipotent, each person in the Trinity fully God and the whole three persons one God, as is contained in the Apostles' Creed, the Nicene Creed and the Athanasian Creed. That the Father, together with the Son and Holy Spirit, the one God of whom we speak, is the creator and maker and governor and, in suitable place and time, disposer of all things visible and invisible, in heaven and air, water and earth: this we believe and confess with heart and lip. Of the New and Old Testaments, that is the law of Moses and the prophets and the apostles, we believe one and the same God to be the author, who, dwelling in Trinity, as has been said, created all things. We believe John the Baptist to have been sent by him, holy and just, filled by the Holy Spirit in his mother's womb. We believe in our hearts and confess with our lips that the incarnation of God was not made in the Father, nor in the Holy Spirit, but in the Son only, that he who was in Godhead the son of God the Father, true God from his Father, might be true man of his mother, having true flesh from his mother's womb and a rational human soul, both natures in him at the same time, God and man, one person, one son, one Christ, one God with the Father and the Holy Spirit, ruler and author of all, born of the Virgin Mary with a true human birth; and he ate and drank and slept and fatigued with the journey he took rest; and he suffered truly his passion in the flesh and died a true death of his body, and rose by the true resurrection of his flesh and truly came again to life, in which after he

had eaten and drunk he ascended into heaven and sits at the right hand
of the Father; he will come to judge the living and the dead: this we
believe with our hearts and confess with our lips. We believe one
catholic Church, holy, apostolic and immaculate, outside which no one
is saved. Also the sacraments which are celebrated in her, by virtue of
the inestimable and invisible help of the Holy Spirit, although they
may be administered by a sinful priest, while the Church receives him
we in no way reject, nor do we withdraw from ecclesiastical services and
blessings celebrated by such a one, but with a benevolent mind embrace
it as we do from the most righteous. We approve the baptism of infants,
that, if they should die after baptism before they can commit sin, we
confess that they may be saved. Indeed we believe that in baptism all
sins, both that sin originally contracted and those which have been
voluntarily committed, are forgiven. We consider that confirmation
performed by the bishop by the laying on of hands is to be accepted as
holy and venerable. We firmly believe and simply affirm the sacrifice
of bread and wine after consecration to be the body and blood of Jesus
Christ, in which nothing more may be achieved by the good priest or
less by the bad. We concede that sinners by penitence of heart, oral
confession and works of satisfaction according to the Scriptures may be
able to attain God's pardon and we most willingly communicate with
them. We venerate unction with consecrated oil for the sick. We do not
deny that the married may have conjugal intercourse according to the
Apostle;[1] we forbid in all cases the divorce of the formally contracted;
we do not condemn second marriages. We humbly praise and faithfully
venerate all ecclesiastical orders, episcopal, priestly, and others, lower
and higher, and all which is recited or sung with proper authorisation
in church. We believe the devil became evil not by God's creation but
by his own will. We do not at all condemn the eating of meat. We
believe in our hearts and confess with our lips the resurrection of this
body which we carry round with us, not of another. We firmly believe
and affirm that at the last judgement every individual will receive either
rewards or penalties for the things done in this life. We do not doubt
that alms and sacrifices and other good works undertaken by the faithful
may benefit the dead. And because according to the apostle James faith
'without works is dead'[2] we have renounced the world; as the Lord
counselled we have given what we had to the poor and made ourselves
poor so that we may not be careful about the morrow, nor will we accept
from anyone gold or silver or anything other than daily food and
clothing. We intend to observe as precepts the counsels of the Gospels.
But we acknowledge and believe that those remaining in the world with

[1] Cf. especially I Cor., 7:2ff.
[2] James, 2:20.

their possessions and giving alms and other benefits from their goods, observing the precepts of God, may be saved. Therefore we earnestly request you in your wisdom that if it should happen that anyone should come to your regions saying they are from us, if they do not have this faith, know for certain that they are not of our company.

13. Walter Map on the Waldensians

(From Walter Map, *De nugis curialium – Courtiers' Trifles*, Distinctio i, c. 31, 'Of the sect of the Valdesii', i.e. Waldensians; trans. M. R. James (Cymmrodorion Record Series, 1923), pp. 65–6; text in Fearns, no. 11). Map's tales must be read with a wary eye (see p. 72).

At the Roman Council under Pope Alexander III, I saw some Valdesians [Waldensians], simple, illiterate men, called after their leader Valdes [Waldo], who was a citizen of Lyon on the Rhone. They offered the Pope a book written in the French tongue, in which was contained the text, with a gloss, of the Psalter and many of the books of the two Testaments. They pressed very earnestly that the right of preaching should be confirmed to them; for in their own eyes they were learned, though in reality hardly beginners. It is the common case that birds which do not see fine snares or nets think that there is a free passage everywhere. Do we not see that those who practise themselves all their days in subtle discourse, who hardly can either entrap others or be entrapped, the explorers of the deepest depths – are not they, fearing offence, always cautious in their utterance about God, whose state is so high that neither praise nor the strength of prayer can mount to it unless this mercy draws it? In every letter of the divine page there flit on the wings of virtues so many sayings, there is heaped up such wealth of wisdom, that any to whom the Lord has given the means can draw from it fulness. Shall then the pearl be cast before swine, the word be given to the ignorant, whom we know to be unfit to take it in, much less give out what they have received? Away with such a thought, uproot it! From the head let ointment go down to the beard and thence to the clothing; from the spring let the water be led, not puddles out of the streets. I, the least of many thousands who were called, was deriding these, wondering that there should be any discussion or doubt about their petition, when I was summoned by one, a great prelate, to whom that supreme Pope had committed the charge of confessions, and took my seat, a mark for arrows; and in a gathering of many lawyers and skilled men there were brought before me two Waldensians who figured as leaders in their sect, to dispute with me about their faith, not for love of ascertaining the truth, but that I might be put to shame and my mouth shut, as of one that speaketh iniquity. I confess that I took my seat in fear, lest my sins might require that, before so great an assembly, the grace of speech should be denied me. The bishop bade me try my hand against them, and I prepared myself to answer. First, therefore, I put to them very simple questions which ought to be unknown to no one, for I was aware that when an ass eats thistles, his lips count lettuce unworthy of them. 'Do you believe in God the Father?' They answered: 'We do.' 'And in the Son?' They answered: 'We do.' 'And in the Holy Ghost?' They answered: 'We do.' I said again: 'And in the mother of Christ?' And they once more: 'We do.' And by everyone present they were hooted down with universal clamour, and went away ashamed; and rightly, for they were governed by none and yet desired to become governors, like Phaethon, who knew not even the names of his steeds.

These people have no settled abodes; they go about two and two, barefoot, clad in woollens, owning nothing, but having all things in common, like the apostles, nakedly following a naked Christ. They are now beginning in a very humble guise, because they cannot get their foot in; but if we let them in, we shall be turned out. He who believes not, let him hear what has just been said concerning this kind.

14. The Council of the Cathar Church of Saint-Félix-de-Caraman, 1167

(Ed. F. Šanjek, 'Le rassemblement hérétique de Saint-Félix-de-Caraman (1167) et les églises cathares au XIIe siècle', *Revue d'histoire ecclésiastique*, Vol. LXVII (1972), pp. 767–99, especially pp. 772–9; A. Dondaine, 'Les actes du concile albigeois de Saint-Félix-de-Caraman', in *Studi e Testi*, Vol. 125, *Miscellanea G. Mercati*, Vol. V (Rome, 1946), pp. 324–55, with text on pp. 326–7; Fearns, no. 8. Cf. Thouzellier, pp. 13ff., Maisonneuve, pp. 128–9). The authenticity of the document has been strongly attacked; probably most scholars believe it authentic, but it is difficult to expel all doubt, for there is little evidence at this date by which to check its statements with sufficient precision (see especially, Šanjek's and Dondaine's articles, and Thouzellier, pp. 13–14n.).

In 1167, in the month of May, Pope Niquinta gathered (?was gathered by) the Church of Toulouse in the town of St-Félix, and a great crowd of men and women from the church of Toulouse and from other churches nearby collected there to receive the consolamentum, which the lord Pope Niquinta undertook to administer. Then Robert d'Épernon, bishop of the church of the French [i.e. of the north of France] arrived with his council; Marc of Lombardy likewise came with his council, Sicardus the Cellarer bishop of Albi with his council, and B[ernard] the Catalan came with the council of the church of Carcassonne, and the Council of the church of Aran (?Agen) was there. When all this countless number was gathered, the men of the church of Toulouse wished to have a bishop and they elected Bernard Raimund. In like manner Bernard the Catalan and the council of the church of Carcassonne, at the request and instruction of the church of Toulouse and with the advice, will and permission of Bishop Sicardus the Cellarer, elected Guirald the Mercer; and the men of Aran (Agen) elected Raimund of Casals. Afterwards Robert d'Épernon received the consolamentum and the order of bishop from the Lord Pope Niquinta so as to be bishop of the Church in north France; similarly Sicardus the Cellarer received the consolamentum and was ordained bishop of the church of Albi; Marc received the consolamentum and was ordained bishop of Lombardy; Bernard Raimund received the consolamentum and was ordained bishop of the church of Toulouse; Guirald the Mercer received the consolamentum and was ordained bishop of Carcassonne; Raimund of Casals received the consolamentum and was ordained bishop of Aran (?Agen). After this Pope Niquinta addressed the church of Toulouse. 'You have asked me to tell you the primitive customs of the churches both small and great, and I tell you the seven churches of Asia were divided and had their boundaries fixed, and not one of them did anything that was contrary to another. The churches of Romania and Dragovitza and Melenguia and Bulgaria and Dalmatia were divided and defined and not one of them did anything that was contrary to another and so there was peace between them. You should do the same.'

So the church of Toulouse elected Bernard Raimund, William Garsias, Ermengaud de Forest, Raimund de Beruniaco (Baimiac), Gilbert de Bonvilar, Bernard William Contor, Bernard William Bonneville and Bertrand of Avignonet as assessors. The church of Carcassonne elected Guirald the Mercer, Bernard the Catalan, Gregory and Peter 'Calidas Manus', Raimund Pontius, Bertrand de Molino, Martin de Ipsa sala, and Raimund Guibert to be assessors for the church. When these had met and taken counsel they said that the church of Toulouse and the church of Carcassonne were divided as the [Catholic] bishoprics like this: the bishopric of Toulouse is separated from the archbishopric of Narbonne in two places, and from the bishopric of Carcassonne at Saint-Pons, where the mountain [the Montagne Noire] comes between the town of Cabardès and the town of Hautpoul as far as the boundary between the town of Saissac and the town of Verdun and comes between Montréal and Fanjeaux. As the other bishoprics are divided at the boundary of Razès as far as Lérida where it comes by Toulouse, the church of Toulouse is to have this region in its power and administration.

Similarly the church of Carcassonne as it has been defined and bounded has in its power and administration all the bishopric of Carcassonne and the archbishopric of Narbonne and the other territory, divided as said above as far as Lérida where it touches the sea. The churches are divided in this way, as said above, that they may have peace and concord between them and not aim to take each other's rights or to dispute.

These are the witnesses and assessors: Bernard Raimund, William Garsias, Ermengaud de Forest, Raimund de Bauniaco (Baimiac), Gilbert de Bonvilar, B[ernard] William Contor, B[ernard] William Bonneville and Bertrand of Avignonet; and for the church of Carcassonne Guirald the Mercer, B[ernard] the Catalan, Gregory and Peter 'Calidas Manus', Raimund Pontius, Bertrand de Molino, Martin de

Ipsa sala and Raimund Guibert. All these directed Ermengaud de Forest to make a declaration and charter for the church of Toulouse and Peter Barnard in the same manner for the church of Carcassonne and this was done and completed.

This copy was drawn up by the Lord Peter Isarn from the old charter composed on the authority of these assessors, who divided the churches as it is written above; on Monday 14 August [1167]. In 1232, Peter Pollanus copied all this as requested and commanded.

15. Rainer Sacconi on the Rites and Churches of the Cathars, 1250

(From Fearns, no. 10; A. Dondaine (ed.), *Liber de duobus principiis* (Rome, 1939), pp. 65–70). The author was a Dominican who for seventeen years had been a Cathar, and spoke from knowledge, but also from a very hostile viewpoint. This particularly affects his list of 'Cathars' at the end, which is evidently intended to show how few and scattered they have become. Clearly the numbers refer only to 'perfecti', the inner circle of fully committed Cathars, not to adherents or well-wishers; and by 1250 the numbers had been greatly depleted, by crusade and conversion, especially in the south of France. In effect this is a catalogue of the Cathars surviving in north and central Italy, the Balkans and Constantinople. But it is a valuable indication of their distribution and of their earlier centres of influence. Some of the names are obscure: I follow the identifications proposed by A. Dondaine, op. cit. pp. 62–3 and in *Archivum Fratrum Praedicatorum*, Vol. XX (1950), pp. 234–324, especially pp. 282ff., in which he suggests that the obscure *Albanenses* is derived from a personal name, 'the followers of Albanus'.

The sacraments of the Cathars. The Cathars, after the manner of apes, who try to imitate the acts of men, have four sacraments, though these are false and void, illicit and sacrilegious. They are: the laying on of hands, the blessing of bread, penance and ordination, of which I will say something in order.

The laying on of hands. The laying on of hands is called by them consolamentum and spiritual baptism, or the baptism of the Holy Spirit, without which, according to them, neither is mortal sin remitted nor the Holy Spirit given to anyone, but by its efficacy alone are both conferred. However the *Albanenses* hold in this an opinion a little different from the others. These say that the hand itself does nothing, because it has been created by the devil according to them . . . but the Lord's prayer which they then say when they lay on the hands is alone effective. All the other Cathars say that both are there necessary and required, the laying on of hands and the prayer. It is also the common opinion of all the Cathars that through this laying on of hands there is no remission of sins if those who lay on their hands are then in mortal sin themselves. This laying on of hands must be done by two at least, not only by their prelates but also by their juniors and in case of necessity by Cathar ladies.

The breaking of bread. The blessing of bread of the Cathars is a breaking of bread which they do every day at lunch and at dinner. They do this breaking of bread in this way. When Cathars, either men or women, have gone in to table they all say standing: 'Our Father'. Meanwhile he who was professed or ordained first holds a loaf, or more if it is necessary for the number that may be there, and saying: 'The Grace of our Lord Jesus Christ be with us all evermore', he breaks the loaf or loaves and distributes to all of them, seated, not only to the *Cathari* but also to their adherents and to robbers, adulterers and homicides. The *Albanenses* say that this material bread is not blessed and cannot receive any blessing, because bread is a creature of the devil according to them, and in this they differ from all the rest who hold that this bread is truly blessed. Not one of them believes that from this bread is fashioned the body of Christ.

The false penance of the Cathars. Now I must describe what the penance of the Cathars is like. The penance of the Cathars is absolutely false and vain, deceitful and poisonous, as will be hereafter shown. For three things are required in true penance, contrition of heart, confession of mouth and satisfaction of work. I, brother Rainer, once a leader of heretics, now by God's grace a priest in the Order of Preachers, though unworthy, say unhesitatingly and testify before God, who knows that I do not lie, that nothing of these three is to be found among the Cathars or in their penance. The poison of error which they have drunk from the mouth of the old serpent does not permit them to have any sorrow for their sins. Here is a quadruple error: that the eternal felicity is not lessened for a penitent sinner on account of any sin he may have committed; that the pains of hell are not increased by lack of penitence; that the fire of purgatory is reserved for no one; but that by the laying on of hands both guilt and punishment are completely assuaged by God. The traitor Judas is not more gravely punished than an infant a day old, but all will be equal in glory and in punishment, as they believe, except the *Albanenses*, who say that all will be restored to their original condition, though not on account of their own merits, and that in each kingdom, that of God and of the devil, that is, some are greater than others.

To this I say further that many of them, who are infected with the errors I have mentioned, often regret when they call to mind that they did not more often indulge their appetites during the time when they were not yet professed in the heresy of the Cathars. This is also the reason why many believers, both men and women, do not fear to know a sister or brother, a daughter or son, a niece or [nephew], a kinsman or relation, any more than their own wife or husband. Though some perhaps draw back from these through horror and human shame.

It is clearly proved that they do not grieve for their sins, committed before their profession of heresy, since none of the men make restitution for usury, theft or rapine: they keep the fruits of these themselves or rather give them up to sons or nephews remaining in the world. They even say that usury is not a sin.

Moreover I can say without doubt that during the seventeen years I lived with them I never saw a single one of them pray secretly by himself, or show himself sorry for his sins, either by weeping or beating his breast and saying: 'God be merciful to me a sinner', or anything similar that might be taken as a sign of contrition. They never implore the help or patronage of the angels or of the blessed Virgin or the saints, and they never fortify themselves with the sign of the cross. . . .

[He goes on to give details of their manner of confession and penance, almsgiving – or lack of it – prayer and ordination to the four orders, of bishop, elder and younger sons and deacon; and finally he lists their sees in France and Italy.]

These are the churches of the Cathars, sixteen churches in all – and do not lay it to my charge, reader, that I have called them 'churches', but to theirs, since so they call them. The church of the *Albanenses* or of Desenzano; the church of Concorezzo; the church of the *Baiolenses* or of Bagnolo; the church of Vicenza or of the March; the church of Florence; the church of the valley of Spoleto; the church of France; the church of Toulouse; the church of Carcassonne; the church of Albi; the church of Slavonia [the Balkans]; the Latin church of Constantinople; the Greek church of Constantinople; the church of Philadelphia in Romania; the church of Bulgaria; the church of Dragovitsa; and they all stem from the two last.

The places in which they dwell. First, the *Albanenses* live in Verona and in many cities in Lombardy and are in number about 500 both men and women.[1] Those of Concorezzo are scattered through almost the whole of Lombardy and are 1,500 and more both men and women. The

[1] See above. The doctrinal differences which had split the Cathar churches in the late twelfth and thirteenth centuries seem to have combined under persecution with a strong sense of loyalty to the communities from which they came, so that the surviving Cathar *perfecti*, scattered over north and north-central Italy retained allegiance to churches originally French as well as Italian. The fullest studies are by A. Dondaine in *Archivum Fratrum Praedicatorum*, Vol. XX (1950), pp. 234–324, and A. Borst, *Die Katharer* (Stuttgart, 1953), especially pp. 231ff.

Baiolenses live at Mantua, Brescia, Bergamo and in the *contado* of Milan, but only a few, and in Romagnola, and there are 200 of them. The church of the March are not [?] at Verona and are about 100. Those of Tuscany and the valley of Spoleto are about 100. The church of France dwell at Verona and in Lombardy, and are about 150. The church of Toulouse and Albi and Carcassonne with those who were once of the church of Agen which was almost completely destroyed are about 200. The Latin church in Constantinople is about 50; the churches of Slavonia and Philadelphia, the Greek church, and the churches of Bulgaria and Dragovitsa are about 500. Reader, you can safely say that there are not more than 4,000 Cathars, men and women, in the whole world, and this count has often been made among them.

16. The Fourth Lateran Council, 1215

Canons X and XIII in *Monumenta Diplomatica S. Dominici*, ed V. J. Koudelka and R. J. Loenertz, *MOPH*, Vol. XXV (Rome, 1966) pp. 60–3; *Sacrorum conciliorum nova et amplissima collectio . . .* , ed. J. D. Mansi (Florence, Venice, Paris, 1759–1927), 53 vols, Vol. XXII, pp. 998–9, 1002–3; C. J. Hefele, *Histoire des Conciles*, translated from German into French and ed. by H. Leclercq (Paris, 1907–21), Vol. V, pt. ii, pp. 1340, 1344; see especially R. Foreville, *Latran, I, II, III et Latran IV* (Paris, 1965), pp. 295–7, 352, 354; and above, pp. 83, 86–8.

X. On appointing preachers

Among other things pertaining to the salvation of Christian people the nourishment of God's word is known to be especially necessary: as the body is nourished by bodily food, so the soul is by spiritual, for man does not live by bread alone, but by every word that comes from the mouth of God.[1] It often happens that bishops cannot themselves alone minister God's word to the people, since they have a multiplicity of tasks, are sometimes afflicted by sickness or invasion or other hindrances – to say nothing of those who have inadequate knowledge, a state deserving rebuke and by no means to be tolerated henceforth – especially when their sees are large and spread out; and so we sanction by a general constitution that bishops may appoint men suited to fulfil the office of holy preaching in a health-giving manner, powerful in deed and in speech, who shall diligently visit the flock committed to them on the bishops' behalf, when they cannot perform the task themselves, and edify them by word and example. When they are in need, the bishops shall provide suitable support so that they are not forced to abandon the work for lack of anything.

And so we ordain that suitable men be established in cathedrals and other conventual churches, who can be coadjutors and colleagues of the bishops, not only in the office of preaching, but also in hearing confessions, enjoining penances and other tasks pertaining to the salvation of souls. If any neglect to fulfil this, he shall be subject to stern punishment.

[1] Matt., 4:4; etc.

XIII. The prohibition of new religious Orders

So that the variety of religious Orders bring not grave confusion in God's Church, we firmly prohibit anyone to devise henceforth a new religious Order; but whoever wishes to join an Order, shall adhere to one already approved. In like manner any who wishes to found a new religious house, shall take the rule and constitution of one of the approved Orders.

We also prohibit anyone to venture to be a monk in several monasteries, and any abbot to venture to preside over a number of monasteries.

17. From Jordan of Saxony, *On the Origin of the Order of Preachers*

(See pp. 90–105; ed. H. C. Scheeben, *MOPH*, Vol. XVI (Rome, 1935), pp. 1–88.)

Prologue

1. To the sons of grace and co-heirs of glory, to all the brothers: brother Jordan, their servant of little worth, sends greetings and prays for their continuing joy in their holy profession.

2. Many of the brothers have importuned me, wishing to know how this Order of Preachers by which divine Providence guards the world in these last times of peril, first began; what manner of men its early brothers were, how they came to increase and multiply, how they were helped and comforted by God's grace. And so, long inquiry was made of the same brothers who were present at the outset, and who saw and heard Christ's venerable servant Master Dominic, first founder of this Order, master and brother, who conversed and lived in piety with God and the angels while still in the flesh, dwelling among sinners, and was a guardian of the commandments, a follower of good counsel, and in everything that he knew and could do a servant of his eternal Creator, a light in the black darkness of the world because his life was pure and its whole manner and converse chaste and holy.

3. It seemed good to me, who, though I was not at all one of the first, have met the first brothers and lived with them and have seen the blessed Dominic not only when I was outside the Order but after I was within, and knew him fairly well – I confessed to him and at his wish took on the order of deacon; and in the fourth year after the first establishment of the Order I put on this habit – it seemed to me, I say, that the events I saw and heard myself, and knew from the early brothers' narration, of the beginnings of the Order, of the life and miracles of that blessed man, our father Dominic, and also of some other brothers, as opportunity offered and it was planted on my memory, I should commit to writing. Failing this the sons of this Order who shall be born and grow, would know nothing of the beginnings of this Order, and would wish to know in vain, since after a long time has passed no one could be discovered who is adequately informed to relate any certain facts. And so, my brothers and sons, most beloved in Christ,

I have collected what follows, for your comfort and instruction: take it with devotion and be ardent in imitation of the early charity of our brothers.

Here beings the account of Diego, bishop of Osma

4. In the regions of Spain there was a man of venerable life whose name was Diego, bishop of the see of Osma, noted for his theological learning, his native wit in the ways of the world, and still more for the exceptional goodness of his life. He was so possessed by God's love that, casting aside what was his and seeking only the things of Christ Jesus, he turned his mind so totally to this that as a usurer of souls (so to speak) he rendered to his Lord the talent lent to him with mighty interest.[1] He strove to attract men of good fame for honest living and good character, wherever he could find them and by whatever means he could, and procure them benefices in the cathedral over which he presided. Those of his subjects who showed little inclination towards holiness, much towards worldly pleasure, he persuaded by his words and enticed by the example of his deeds to assume the mode of a good life and a holier. So it happened that he strove to persuade the canons of his cathedral by frequent admonition and by constant pressure to submit to the observance of the canons regular under the Rule of St Augustine; and although some held out against him he had such success that he bent the canons' inclination to his purpose.

On St Dominic and his condition as a young man

5. In Diego's time there was a young man called Dominic, sprung from the same diocese, in the village called Caleruega. His mother saw in a vision, before she conceived him, a puppy in her womb with a burning brand in its mouth, which, when it came from her womb, seemed to set the whole world on fire. Thus was forecast the conception within her of a notable preacher, who would wake souls asleep in sin to be alert and watchful by the bark of the sacred learning, and scatter over the whole world the fire, which Jesus came to set upon the earth.[2] He was nurtured from his boyhood years by his family's care, and especially by his uncle, an archpriest; and they had him taught first the rites of the Church, so that one whom God had foreseen to be a vessel of election might while still a boy drink like a new-made jug the odour of sanctity, nor suffer the loss of it thereafter. . . .

[cc. 6–10 describe his years of study.]

[1] Cf. Philippians, 2:21; Matt., 25:14ff. Jordan's Latin is filled with biblical echoes, and I only note the more conspicuous of them.

[2] Cf. the *Vita Secunda* of St Bernard of Clairvaux, by Alan of Auxerre, *PL*, Vol. 185, col. 470–1, where a similar story is told in similar words.

How he was called to the cathedral of Osma

11. The man of God pondered lines of advance, stepped from virtue to virtue, grew day-by-day in moral stature in the eyes of all, shone as a morning star amid the mist by his purity of life, and seemed a marvel. His reputation came to the ears of the bishop of Osma, who made diligent inquiry as to his true worth and made him a member of the community of canons regular in his own cathedral church.

[c. 12 Dominic is promoted supbprior.]

13 It was his frequent practice to pass the whole night in prayer, to close his door and pray to his Father.[1] As he prayed, from time to time he used to groan and cry out from a heavy heart, and could not restrain himself from making his outbursts heard. Frequently and particularly he prayed that God would deign to give him true charity, efficacious to help and assure the salvation of men; for he thought he would only be a true member of Christ when he spent himself wholly, to the limits of his strength, for the welfare of men's souls, as the Saviour of all, the Lord Jesus, offered himself for our salvation. He read a book called the *Conferences of the Fathers*,[2] which treats of the vices and every point of spiritual perfection; he read it, I say, and loved to trace the paths of salvation in it, and strove to follow them with the full force of his mind. This book advanced him with grace's aid to a strong purity of conscience, to an ample light of contemplation, to the pitch of perfection. . . .

How the bishop of Osma set off for the Marches

14. While fair Rachel thus comforted him with her embraces, Leah lost patience and began to demand that he appease the reproach of her weak eyes by visiting her and giving her a numerous progeny.[3] It happened about this time that King Alfonso of Castile decided that he wanted to marry his son Ferdinand to the daughter of a noble of the Marches [of Denmark]. . . .

[cc. 14–16 Diego sets off as ambassador on this account, taking Dominic with him, and on the way finds the neighbourhood of Toulouse full of heretics, one of whom Dominic converts. On a second embassy Diego finds the bride-to-be dead, but takes advantage of his journey to attempt a new project.]

[1] Cf. Matt., 6:6.
[2] John Cassian's classic book on the spiritual life, written soon after 400 to interpret to the West the teaching of the monks of the eastern deserts. See O. Chadwick's *John Cassian* (Cambridge, 1968), 2nd edn, and *Western Asceticism* (London, 1958).
[3] Genesis, 29:16–35, a strangely inappropriate metaphor.

How he went to the Pope and what they discussed

17. And so the bishop . . . with his clerks seized the opportunity and hastened to the papal Curia. He came to Pope Innocent [III] and immediately asked from him permission to resign his bishopric, if it could be granted, claiming that he was insufficient on many counts and that the enormous dignity of the office was beyond his strength. He revealed to the Pope that his real intention was to devote all the strength he had to the conversion of the Cumans,[1] if his resignation should be accepted. The Pope did not accept his resignation, nor, though Diego begged him, was he willing to grant him some of what he asked even for his sin's deliverance, that he should remain bishop and go to the land of the Cumans to preach; for God's hidden providence was to foresee a rich fruit for the toil of this great man on another path to salvation.

How he put on the habit at Cîteaux

18. On his way back he came to Cîteaux, where he saw the observance of many of God's servants, and was allured by their lofty religious life to take on there the monastic habit, and so he hastened back to Spain with a few monks on whose instruction he could learn the fashion of the Cistercian life, knowing nothing yet of the obstacle which God would set in his hastily chosen path.

Of the advice which he gave to those whom the Pope had sent to him

19. At that time Pope Innocent had sent twelve abbots of the Cistercian Order with a legate to preach the faith against the Albigensian [i.e. Cathar] heretics. A council was held of the archbishops, bishops and other prelates of that land, who discussed which was the appropriate technique for fulfilling their mission.

20. While they thus counselled together, it happened that the bishop of Osma journeyed through Montpellier, where the Council was under way. They received him with honour and asked his advice, since they knew he was a holy man, wise, just and zealous for the faith. He, as a man of prudence and knowledgeable in God's paths, began to inquire about the rites and customs of the heretics, and to study the method they used to entice some to join their evil way by persuasion and preaching and evidences of a sanctity assumed. In contrast he saw the great pomp of those who had been sent by the Pope, their costly furnishing in money, horses and vesture. 'No', he said, 'I do not think that this is the way, my brothers. It seems impossible to recall these men to the faith by words alone; we must attack them rather by our

[1] Pagans living in eastern Hungary; one manuscript reads 'Saracens'. See M.-H. Vicaire (1964), p. 461.

example. Look: the heretics put on a show of pious devotion, lying examples of Gospel poverty and austerity, and so persuade the simple to follow in their paths. So, if you have come to demonstrate the opposite, you will do little good, much harm and win no support. Blunt one nail with another;[1] chase feigned holiness away with the true religious life; for the pride of pseudo-apostles would be shown up by manifest humility. Thus Paul was compelled to be a fool, to list his own virtues, to deploy his austerities and the dangers he had faced, to rebut the swelling pride of those who preened themselves on the merit of their life.' They answered him: 'What do you advise, good father?' 'Do as you see me do', he replied; and soon the Spirit of the Lord rose within him and he called his followers, sent them to Osma with the trappings and furnishings of his equipage and all the stores he had brought with him, keeping only a few clerks in attendance on himself. He said it was his intention to stay in that land and spread the faith.

[cc. 21–2 describe how Dominic stayed with him, and the abbots followed Diego's example.]

23. There were frequent disputations under chosen judges at Pamiers, Lavaur, Montréal and Fanjeaux; and on the days appointed noblemen, knights, women and common folk came wanting to be present at the discussion of the faith.

24. It happened that one particular celebrated disputation was arranged at Fanjeaux, for which a large throng of faithful and heretics gathered. Several of the faithful prepared pamphlets first, laying out arguments and authorities to confirm their faith; when they had all been examined the blessed Dominic's leaflet was reckoned the best and received general approval, and was laid before the three judges chosen to determine the disputation by the consent of the parties, beside the heretics' leaflet, which they had written on their own account. The aim was that whichever party's leaflet was reckoned by the judges the more reasonable, their faith should be accepted as superior.

25. After much dispute the judges could not agree to support either party, and they fell on the plan of throwing both leaflets into a fire, so that if either was not burned it would doubtless contain the true faith. And so a large fire was kindled, and they threw in both leaflets. The heretics' book was immediately consumed, but the other, written by Dominic, the man of God, not only remained unharmed, but leapt a great distance out of the flames in the presence of all. It was thrown in a second, and third time, and each time was thrown out of the fire;

[1] A Latin proverb, normally 'to drive out one nail with another'.

and so it demonstrated openly the truth of the faith and the holiness of the man who had written the leaflet. . . .

On the founding of the convent of nuns at Prouille

27. To support some noble ladies, whose parents, through poverty, had handed them over to the heretics to be educated and brought up, Bishop Diego founded a monastery on a site between Fanjeaux and Montréal called Prouille; and there to this day Christ's handmaidens offer their joyful service to their Creator, in great strength of holiness and excelling purity of innocence, leading a life which brings salvation to them, to men an example, joy to the angels, pleasure to God. . . .

[cc. 28–31 treat the bishop's return to Osma, leaving Dominic in spiritual charge, and his death, and of Dominic's life in the period which followed.]

On the preaching of the crusade against the Albigenses

32. After the death of the bishop of Osma a crusade against the Albigenses began to be preached in France. Pope Innocent was vexed that the rebel spirit of the heretics could not be tamed or softened by truth's good works, nor pierced by the sword of the spirit which is God's word,[1] and so he decreed that they must be attacked by the power of the secular sword.

33. While Bishop Diego was still alive, he had in a prophetic spirit predicted by his curse that secular judgement would fall on them. When on one occasion he had manifestly and publicly refuted the false rebellion of the heretics in the presence of many noblemen, and they mocked their attackers in defending themselves by a sacrilegious defence, he was angry and raised his hands to the heavens, saying, 'Lord raise thy hand and touch them';[2] and those who heard this saying had it brought later to mind when the onslaught offered them an interpretation of it.

Of the injuries inflicted on Dominic by the heretics in the region of Albi

34. At the time when the crusaders had taken the Cross, brother Dominic remained a sedulous preacher of God's word till the death of the count de Montfort. How great were the injuries he received from the wicked in those days! Their snares he also spurned. On one occasion they threatened him with death, and he replied unperturbed: 'I am not worthy of the glory of martyrdom; I have not yet earned this death.' Later, passing a place in which he suspected there might be an ambush

[1] Cf. Ephesians, 6:17. On the Albigensian Crusade, see pp. 84ff.   [2] Job, 2:5.

laid for him, he sang and went on his way eagerly. When this was told
to the heretics, they wondered at his unshakable firmness of purpose,
and said to him: 'Do you not fear death? What would you have
done, had we seized you?' But he replied: 'I would have asked
you not to kill me quickly with sudden wounds, but to draw out my
martyrdom by tearing my limbs one by one; then to show me each
piece of my limbs before my eyes; afterwards to tear my eyes out and
leave my trunk thus lying in its own blood, or wholly destroy it. By this
lingering death I would earn a greater crown of martyrdom.' The
enemies of truth were astonished at his words and laid no further
ambush for him nor plotted against the life of the righteous man, since
death would be a boon to him rather than bring him harm. He himself
strove with all his strength and most fervent zeal to win for Christ the
souls he could; and there came to be within his heart a wonderful, almost unbelievable, longing for the salvation of all.

[c. 35 describes how Dominic offers to sell himself to rescue a man
from the heretics; cc. 36-7 are concerned with other events of his life
during the crusade and rule of Simon de Montfort.]

37. The count de Montfort had a special devotion for Dominic, and
with the assent of his counsellors gave a notable town called Casseneuil
to him and to whomsoever joined and followed him in the work he had
begun. Brother Dominic also had the church of Fanjeaux and some
other possessions, from all of which he and his followers could receive
support. What they could spare from these revenues they granted to the
sisters of the monastery of Prouille.[1] For the Order of Preachers had not
yet been instituted; there had been discussion only of the foundation
of an order, although Dominic was engaged in the office of preaching
with all his strength. Nor was the constitution that possessions might
not lawfully be received, or if received kept, adhered to as yet, for it
was only promulgated at a later date [c. 87]. From the death of the
bishop of Osma to the Lateran Council about ten years passed, during
which Dominic remained there on his own.[2]

Of the two brothers who first offered themselves to brother Dominic
38. As the time approached when the bishops began to go to Rome
for the Lateran Council [1215], two men from Toulouse of good
character and suited to the work offered themselves to brother Dominic:
one of them was brother Peter Seila, afterwards prior of Limoges, the
other brother Thomas, a man of grace and eloquence. The first of

[1] See Doc. 19.
[2] Diego died in 1207; the Lateran Council was held in 1215.

these brothers, Peter, gave to brother Dominic and his companions[1] the lofty and noble houses, which he had possessed at Toulouse round the castle of Narbonne. From that time they first began to live at Toulouse in those houses, and from then on all who were with him began more and more to humble themselves and order their way of life in the manner of religious.

Of the revenues from which at first they provided for food and other needs

39. But the bishop of Toulouse, Fulk of happy memory, who was very devoted to brother Dominic the beloved of God and men, seeing the religious life of the brothers, their grace and fervour in preaching, rejoiced that a new light had risen, and with the consent of his whole chapter granted them a sixth part of all the tithes of his diocese, so that with the help of this income they could provide themselves with books and other needs.

How Master Dominic went to the Pope with the bishop of Toulouse

40. Brother Dominic joined the bishop, so that they went together to the Council, and with one voice prayed Pope Innocent [III] to confirm to brother Dominic and his companions his Order, to be in name and fact the Order of Preachers; and also to confirm the revenues granted to the brothers both by the count and by the bishop.

41. When the Pope had heard their pleas, he urged brother Dominic to return to his brothers, to have a full discussion with them, and with their unanimous consent to chose some rule already approved, and that then the bishop might assign them a church. When this had been accomplished he might return to the Pope to receive confirmation of the whole scheme.

42. When the Council was over, therefore, they returned to Toulouse and Dominic expounded the Pope's message to the brothers. The would-be preachers soon chose the rule of that great preacher St Augustine, adding to it some more exacting customs on eating and fasting, on beds and clothes. They proposed and established that they should have no possessions, so that the office of preaching should not be hindered by earthly cares; they were only ready to keep their rents.

43. The bishop of Toulouse with the consent of his chapter assigned three churches to them, one within the city boundaries [St Romain], another at Pamiers [La Trinité, Loubens], the third between Puylaurens

[1] This has been taken to mean that Peter was the first to join Dominic, but it seems clear that Dominic already had companions when Peter made his gift.

and Sorèze, that is the church of St Mary of Lescure,[1] in each of which there was intended to be a convent and priory.

Of the first church granted to the brothers in Toulouse

44. In the summer of the year 1216 the first church in the city of Toulouse, founded in honour of St Romain, was given to the brothers. In the event none of the brothers chanced to live at the other two churches. But at the church of St Romain a cloister was immediately built, with cells adequate for study and sleeping above it. There were then about sixteen brothers.

On the death of Pope Innocent and the ordinance of Pope Honorius and confirmation of the Order

45. Meanwhile Pope Innocent was taken from the world and Honorius was appointed his successor; and brother Dominic soon went to him and obtained in full, according to what had been planned and established, confirmation of the Order and of everything he had wanted to have confirmed.

On the death of the count de Montfort, which Master Dominic had foreseen

46. In the year 1217 the men of Toulouse decided to rise against the count de Montfort, as we reckon that Dominic, the man of God, had a little while before foreknown by the spirit. In a vision a tree was shown him, lofty and fair, on whose branches lived a great number of birds. The tree was felled, and the birds resting on it flew away. Full of the spirit of God, Dominic understood that the moment was near when death would cut down the count de Montfort, that great and lofty prince, and guardian of many wards.

47. He called on the Holy Ghost, gathered the brothers, and said to them that it was the intention of his heart to send them all, few though they were, out into the world, and that they should no longer live there together. They were all astonished when he pronounced the decision to which he had come so suddenly; but the authority of holiness manifest in him inspired them, and they readily agreed, trusting that it would all come to a good end.

48. It seemed to him good that they should choose one of the brothers to be their abbot, by whose authority the rest might be ruled as their elder and head, while he himself retained the power to correct the abbot. Brother Matthew was lawfully elected abbot, and was the first and last in the Order to be called abbot, since the brothers afterwards

[1] See Vicaire (1964), p. 498; the third church seems to be a mistake, probably due to confusion with other gifts.

decided that he who was set over them, as a lesson in humility, should
be called not abbot but Master [i.e. teacher] of the Order.

Of the brothers sent to Spain

49. Four brothers were sent to Spain: brother Peter of Madrid and
brother Gomez, brother Michael of Ucero and brother Dominic; after
these last two had returned from Spain to Master Dominic they were
sent from Rome to Bologna and dwelt there. For they could not make
headway in Spain, as they had hoped, although the other two profited
abundantly and spread the word of God. This other Dominic was a
man of excellent humility, of little learning but great in virtue. . . .

[c. 50 tells more of him.]

Of the brothers sent first to Paris

51. Brother Matthew, who had been chosen abbot, and brother
Bertrand, afterwards provincial prior of Provence, were sent to Paris.
Bertrand was a man of great holiness and remorseless self-discipline, for
he mortified his flesh fiercely, and had absorbed in himself the model
and pattern of Master Dominic in many things – he had been sometimes
his companion on his journeying. These two, I say, were sent to Paris
with a letter from the Pope to make the Order known. With them went
two other brothers to study, brother John of Navarre and brother
Laurence the Englishman. Before they went to Paris brother Laurence
had received a divine revelation – as he foretold and the event proved –
of much that later befell the brothers at Paris, of their dwelling and the
site of their houses, and of the many recruits they received. Separately
from them came also brother Mames, the brother of Master Dominic,
and brother Michael of Spain; and they had with them a Norman lay
brother called Oderius. . . .

52. All these were sent to Paris, but the last three, travelling faster,
arrived there sooner, and entered Paris on 12 September; three weeks
later the others joined them. They rented a house for themselves by the
Hospital of the Blessed Virgin Mary before the gates of the bishop of
Paris.

Of the house of Saint-Jacques and its conferment on the brothers at Paris

53. In 1218 the house of Saint-Jacques was given to the brothers,
though not as an outright gift, by John, dean of Saint-Quentin, and by
the University of Paris, at the request of Pope Honorius; and they
entered the house to dwell there on 6 August.

On the brothers who were sent first to Orléans

54. In the same year some young and simple brothers were sent to Orléans, who lived there as it were as a small seed, the beginning of what later became a richer plant.

Of the brothers first sent to Bologna

55. In 1218, early in the year, brothers were sent from Rome by Master Dominic to Bologna; that is, brother John of Navarre and brother Bertrand, and later brother Christian and a lay brother. They dwelt at Bologna and suffered great deprivation and poverty.

[cc. 56–66 describe the reception and career of brother Reginald, Dominic's visit to Spain, Paris and Bologna, and two visions, the second interpreted to refer to two recruits received at Paris, one of them Jordan of Saxony himself, the other brother Henry.]

Of brother Henry: how and where he was educated

67. Brother Henry was born of good family by the standards of the world and became a canon of Maestricht; there he was taught from his earliest years with care, under the discipline and the fear of the Lord by a holy and deeply religious canon of that church. That good and righteous man crucified his flesh, trod under foot the evil allurements of this world, and abounded in many works of piety; and so he had inspired the tender mind of the young man to every work of virtue, making him wash the feet of the poor, go often to church, abhor vices, despise luxury, love chastity. He was a young man of excellent character, and showed himself in every way conducive to discipline, apt to virtue: and so, as he grew older in years, he grew also in character to the point that if you talked with him you would think him an angel and his goodness inborn.

68. In course of time he came to Paris and immediately devoted himself to the study of theology, having a great natural penetration of mind and orderly power of reasoning. He was lodged with me, and by living together we acquired a pleasant and strong bond of friendship.

69. Meanwhile brother Reginald of happy memory came to Paris and preached vigorously; and I was touched by divine grace and was inspired, and vowed, to join the Order, thinking that I had found the safe path to salvation, such as I had often conceived and pondered in my mind before I knew the brothers. The purpose of my heart became fixed, and I began to toil with every care to draw my companion and friend with me in like desire, seeing that he was cut out by nature and his own disposition to be most effective in the office of preaching. He resisted, and I the more pressed on unceasingly.

70. In the end I succeeded in getting him to make confession to brother Reginald and receive his exhortation; and on his return to me he opened the book of Isaiah to seek guidance, and the first place on which his eyes fell was the text: 'The Lord God hath given me the tongue of the learned, that I should know how to bear up him that has fallen by my word. He raises me early in the morning, he lifts my ear early to hear the Master. The Lord God hath opened my ear; I contradict Him not, neither have I turned away back.'[1] I interpreted the prophet's words as answering his own intention, as it were an echo from Heaven, for he was a man of great eloquence; I urged him to set his young manhood under the yoke of obedience. After a little while we turned to that text which follows: 'Let us stand together'[2] and read it to instruct us on no account to desert one another, but to stand together in this noble kind of society.

[cc. 71–4 describe their doubts and delays, and brother Henry's visions.]

Of the entry of brother Jordan and brother Henry and brother Leo

75. The day arrived when the faithful are reminded by the placing of ashes on their foreheads that they came from ashes, and to ash will return; and this we had chosen as a fitting start to our penance, the start that we had vowed to the Lord, though our other fellow-lodgers as yet knew nothing of it. And so when brother Henry went out of the lodging and one of our companions said, 'My dear Henry, where are you going?', 'To Bethany', he said. The other did not understand, but later realised what he meant when he saw that he had entered Bethany, which is interpreted to mean the house of obedience. The three of us came to Saint-Jacques, where the brothers were singing 'Let us change our garment . . .'; and we came into their midst unexpectedly but fittingly and immediately put off the old man and put on the new, so that the words that they sang were fulfilled in our deed.

76. After brother Henry's entry into the order, the holy man who had brought him up, and two other good and spiritual members of the same church, who also felt a strong affection for him, were greatly upset; for they knew nothing of this novel and (to them) unheard of Order, and reckoned that a youth of great promise was somehow lost. And so they decided that one or two of them should go to Paris to turn him or bring him back from what seemed to them this foolish step. Then one of them said: 'Let us not act too quickly, but let us spend the night in prayer, asking the Lord of his kindness to show us His will in the matter.' Night came, and as they prayed one of them heard a voice

[1] Isaiah, 50:4–5.   [2] Isaiah, 50:8.

from on high answering their prayers: 'This is the Lord's doing and cannot be altered.' Assured by this divine revelation they were troubled no more, but wrote to him at Paris urging him to persevere faithfully, explaining the nature of the revelation they had had; and this letter I myself read, and it was full of piety, and sweet as honey.

[cc. 77–85 conclude the account of brother Henry of Cologne.]

On the first chapter, celebrated at Bologna

86. In 1220 the first General Chapter of this Order was celebrated at Bologna; I myself was present, sent from Paris with three brothers, since Master Dominic had ordered by his letter that four brothers be sent from the house at Paris to the chapter at Bologna. But when I was sent I had not yet completed two months in the Order.

87. In the same chapter, by common consent of the brothers, it was laid down that the General Chapter should be at Bologna and at Paris in alternate years; but that it should be at Bologna the next year. Then it was ordained that our brothers should henceforth hold no possessions or rents, but renounce those which they had in the region of Toulouse. Many other constitutions were made there which are observed to this day.

The appointment of brother Jordan as prior of Lombardy, and the sending of brothers to England

88. In 1221, in General Chapter at Bologna, it seemed good to them to lay on me first the office of prior over the province of Lombardy, although I had spent only a year in the Order, and had not struck such deep roots as I ought, so that I was set to rule over others, before I had learned to rule my own imperfect self. In the same chapter a community of brothers was sent to England with brother Gilbert as prior. At this chapter I was not present.

[cc. 89–91 are on brother Everard, formerly archdeacon of Langres.]

On the death of Master Dominic

92. At Bologna meanwhile Master Dominic, approaching the end of his earthly pilgrimage, began to be seriously ill. He summoned twelve of the wiser brothers, and from his sickbed began to urge them to fervour, to the expansion of the Order, and to perseverance in the holy life; he admonished them to avoid mingling with women such as could cause suspicion, and particularly with young women, since they are especially alluring and able to entangle souls not yet purified in the fire. 'Look!' said he, 'to this hour God's mercy has preserved me without

fleshly corruption; but I confess I have not avoided this sign of im-
perfection, and conversations with young ladies please me more than
speech with the old.'

93. Before his death he said privately to the brothers that he would be
more use to them dead than alive. For he knew to Whom he had
entrusted the safe-keeping of his toil and fruitful life; he had faith that
a crown of righteousness was reserved for him; that when he had
received it, he would have greater power to obtain what he wanted, the
more firmly he was established in the Lord's domain.

94. As the pain of his illness grew sharper, he laboured at the same
time in fever and flux. At length his pious soul was released from the
flesh, took its journey to the Lord, whose it was, changing the melan-
choly life on earth for the eternal comfort of a heavenly abode.

[cc. 95–102 describe a vision at the time of his death, his burial and
early miracles.]

On the qualities of Master Dominic

103. But there is something more brilliant and magnificent than his
miracles, and that is the good qualities in which he excelled, the force of
divine fervour he carried, so that he was revealed beyond doubt as a
vessel of honour and grace, a vessel adorned with every precious stone.
His mind was firm and equable, save when he was stirred to compassion and mercy. A joyous heart lights up the face, and so his countenance showed the calm assurance of the inner man with an outward
expression of evident kindliness and joy. He kept such constancy of
heart in the aims which he had conceived with God's help and careful
thought, that scarcely ever would he agree to change a statement made
with due deliberation. Although great joy shone in his face, as has been
said, from the witness of a good conscience, the light of his countenance fell not to the earth.[1]

104. This quality won him the ready affection of all: he quickly
penetrated the hearts of all who saw him. Whenever he conversed with
his companions on the road, with his host and the rest of the family
in a house, or among great men and princes and prelates, he was always
full of edifying words, abounding in examples to bring the minds of
his hearers to love Christ and despise the world. Everywhere he
showed himself a man of the Gospel in word and deed. By day, with his
brothers and companions, none was more companionable or more
cheerful than he.

105. By night none was more constant than he in vigils and prayers
of every kind. In the evening he spent long hours in weeping, in the

[1] Cf. Job, 29:24.

morning in joy.[1] He assigned the day to his neighbours, the night to
God, knowing that the Lord sent by day his mercy and by night his
song.[2] He wept copiously and often, and his tears fed him day and
night; by day especially because he celebrated mass frequently, daily
indeed, by night since he surpassed all the brothers in tireless vigils.

On his vigils

106. It was his frequent custom to spend the night in churches, so
that he scarcely ever seemed to have a bed to sleep on. He prayed by
night and stayed awake as much as he could force on his body's frailty.
When at last tiredness came over him and his spirit languished, he took
the sleep he must before the altar or elsewhere, sometimes indeed laying
his head on a stone like the patriarch Jacob; and after a short nap he
woke again and stirred his spirit to fervent prayer.

107. He surpassed all in the breadth of his charity, since he loved all
and was loved by all in turn. He asserted his right to rejoice with those
who were glad and weep with those who wept, pouring over in fatherly
care, spending himself utterly in helping his neighbours and showing
compassion on the wretched. The quality which won especial favour
with all who knew him was that he walked on a straight and single
path, never in word or deed showing any vestige of duplicity or deceit.

108. He was a true lover of poverty, and wore vile clothes. In food
and drink he was most temperate, avoiding delicacies, gladly content
with simple food, keeping firm command over his flesh, drinking his
wine watered, so that while it satisfied his body's needs it never blunted
his subtle, delicate spirit.

[c. 109 is a paean of praise for Dominic; cc. 110ff. deal with a brother
Bernard's temptations and Jordan's difficulties with him; cc. 121–30
are an epilogue on the translation of Dominic's body in 1233.]

[1] Cf. Psalm 29 (30):6 (5).   [2] Cf. Psalm 41 (42):9 (8).

18. From the Acts of the Canonisation of St Dominic

The evidence of the witnesses at the canonisation process in 1233 forms a major source for the personality and activities of Dominic; these extracts give an idea of the nature of the material, and its repetitiveness, and I give the depositions of brother William of Montferrat and brother Stephen, the most vivid of the witnesses. The most recent edition is by Walz, *MOPH*, Vol. XVI, pp. 89–194, with the texts on pp. 123ff.; full French translation in Vicaire (1965), pp. 35ff.; on the early history of the process, see E. W. Kemp, *Canonisation and Authority in the Western Church* (Oxford, 1948).

These are the testimonies received on the life, conversation and death of St Dominic, founder of the Order of Preachers

1. Witnesses were received to give evidence on the life, conversation and death of brother Dominic, inspirer and founder of the Order of Friars Preachers, and its first Master, on the authority of Pope Gregory IX, by Master Tancred, archdeacon of Bologna, and by Thomas, prior of S. Maria de Reno, and brother Palmerio of the church of Campagnola, of the dioceses of Bologna, and Reggio. They were introduced by brother Philip of Vercelli, canon[1] of the same Order, made procurator by brother Ventura, prior of the convent and church of St Nicholas of the Order of Friars Preachers of Bologna and by the chapter of the same church, gathered in their chapter house in the manner accustomed at the bell's summons. Witnesses were also received on the miracles which God has worked by brother Dominic's merits before his death and after. And they took their oaths before these examiners in the year of Our Lord 1233, the 6th Indication....[2]

The testimony of brother William of Montferrat

12. On 7 August brother William of Montferrat, priest of the Order

---

[1] Canon, because subject to the Rule of St Augustine and so in a sense a canon regular; the Dominicans were often called canons in early days before the term 'friar', literally simply 'brother', became in any sense a technical term.

[2] I.e. in the sixth year of the current indictional cycle of fifteen years, a method of dating which originated in the taxation cycle of the late Roman Empire, and survived in medieval documents, especially in the papal chancery. Witnesses were also sworn in Toulouse; see Vicaire (1965), pp. 75ff.

of Preachers, spoke thus under oath. About sixteen years ago, he went to Rome to celebrate Lent, and the Lord Pope, then bishop of Ostia, received him in his house. At that time brother Dominic, founder and first master of the Order of Friars Preachers, was at the Roman Curia. He often visited the bishop of Ostia, and it was thus that the witness met him. His manner of life delighted William and he felt drawn to him. They often discussed the paths to salvation for themselves and the rest of mankind. Brother Dominic impressed him as a man of truly religious life, more so than any other he had ever met, even though he had conversed with a great number of holy men; Dominic seemed to have greater zeal for the salvation of mankind than any other of his acquaintance. The same year the witness went to Paris to study theology. Before they parted they had agreed, and promised one another, that when Dominic had organised his Order and the witness had passed two years in theological study, they would go together to labour for the conversion of the heathen in northern lands.[1] Brother Dominic came from Spain to Paris while the witness was studying there. It was then that William received the habit from Dominic's hands and joined the Order. Later he lived with him on several occasions in various places, following him when he went to the Roman Curia and elsewhere, when he came and went, when he lodged, at meals, at rest, at prayer, when he was sick and when he was well. And all the time he was with him, he saw him observe with the utmost rigour the rule and observance of the Friars Preachers, readily granting dispensation to his brothers, to himself never. He saw him observe, whether well or sick, all the fasts prescribed by the Rule;[2] he saw him suffer, on the way to Rome, a severe attack of dysentery, yet he did not break his fast, nor did he eat meat; he only allowed a special dish of fruit and vegetables to be prepared for him from time to time. The witness knows this well since he shared all his meals with him; and besides, he has seen him act in this way in all his illnesses. When asked where else he has seen Dominic ill on other occasions, he replied: at Viterbo, but he does not remember what his illness was.

13. It often happened that Dominic was ill provided with food or drink, endured wretched hospitality, a wretched bed; but all the time

---

[1] One manuscript mysteriously specified 'Pcia' which has been interpreted as Prussia; perhaps 'Dacia', for Denmark, is a more likely reading, for although the Danes had long since been converted to Christianity, Dominic went there as a young man (see Doc. 18, cc. 14–16) and knew there were pagan lands beyond; he and Bishop Diego had planned to go back there.

[2] By 'Rule' is meant the First Distinction of the early constitutions, the Rule of life laid down by Dominic for the Dominican communities; see Doc. 22, and Doc. 17, c. 42.

the witness was with him he never heard him complain, sick or well. He never went to take his rest without a long period of prayer first, often accompanied by such sighs, groans and tears that many times the witness and his companions were woken up by them. William was certain that Dominic thus passed more time in prayer than in sleep. When they were together, he always lay down fully dressed, with cloak, belt and breeches, never on a mattress, but on the ground, on a plank, on straw, or any other kind of bed. He kept silence at the hours laid down in the Rule and customs of the Order. He refrained from idle words, spoke always with God or of God. When the witness was asked how he knew these details, he replied that he had been Dominic's chief companion, and lived with him night and day, on the road, when they stopped: he saw and heard all he reported.

14. It is his conviction that brother Dominic always preserved his virginity. He was witness to his good conduct; he has heard many religious men and other folk of credible witness, who lived long with Dominic, and gave the same opinion. When asked their names, he replied: the bishop of Osma where Dominic was canon; the canons who had been his companions in the world and other men whose names escaped him.

15. He was present when the body of the blessed Dominic was translated from its original burial place to the site where it now is in the church. The provincial prior and the brothers of the church of St Nicholas were afraid that there would be an unpleasant odour in the tomb in which the body lay; for it was low lying and liable to flooding. For this reason they were not willing for strangers or layfolk to be present when the tomb was opened; but they could not prevent the *podestà* and twenty-four noble and honourable citizens of Bologna from being there, some of whom had mounted guard over the tomb for many nights before it was opened. When the stone over the sepulchre was lifted and the wooden coffin appeared in which lay the body of brother Dominic, a sweet and delightful savour came out of the tomb itself. The witness could never determine what aromatic scent could produce such a savour. All those present sensed it as he did. He bent down and kissed the coffin, and he felt the savour grow stronger. The rest of those present, both friars and laymen, did the same and savoured the same perfume. They wept copiously out of joy and devotion. Finally the body was translated to the place it now occupies.

16. The witness saw several persons later on who said they had suffered various serious illnesses and been delivered of them by the merits of the blessed Dominic. But he does not remember who they were, nor their names; for they were strangers to him, as he was one of the diffinitors and had no time to pay attention to them.

The testimony of brother Stephen

35. On 13 August brother Stephen, prior provincial of the Order of Preachers of the province of Lombardy, said on oath that it was a little over fifteen years since he came to know master Dominic, founder and husbandman of the Order of Friars Preachers and first Master; but before he came to know him by sight he heard much good of him from many men of credible witness – to whit that when he was prior or sub-prior of Osma Cathedral, where he was canon, he studied scriptural theology at Palencia, and at that time a fearful famine arose in that region, so that many poor people died of hunger there; and so brother Dominic, moved by compassion and pity, sold the books he had glossed with his own hand, and gave to the poor the money he got from them and his other possessions, saying: 'I do not wish to study on dead skins while men die of hunger.' Following his example some men of great position did the like, and then began to preach with him. And as Stephen understood, after a little while brother Dominic came to the region of Toulouse with the bishop of Osma to preach, especially against the heretics. There he founded and established the Order of Friars Preachers.

36. The witness also said that, when he was a student at Bologna, Master Dominic came to Bologna and preached to the scholars and other good men, and the witness confessed his sins to him, and it seemed to him that he was attracted to him. Late one evening, when the witness was sitting down to dinner in his hostel with his fellows, brother Dominic sent two brothers to him, who said: 'brother Dominic orders you to come to him at once.' 'When I have had my dinner I will come to him', he replied. 'No,' they said, 'come at once.' So he got up, left his companions, and came to Dominic; and he found him with a number of brothers at the church of St Nicholas. Brother Dominic said to the brothers: 'Teach him how to seek pardon.' When pardon had been granted, he took Stephen's hands in his; and before he could draw back Dominic had clothed him in the habit of the Friars Preachers, saying: 'I will give you arms, with which you are to fight the devil all the days of your life.' And the witness was mightily astonished, then and later, by what instinct brother Dominic thus summoned and clothed him in the habit of the Friars Preachers, since they had had no previous talk of his conversion to the religious life. He believes that he did it by divine inspiration or revelation.

37. He also said that brother Dominic was the best and supreme comforter of the brothers and other men in their temptations. He knows this because he himself at the very beginning of his conversion, when he was a novice, had a number of different temptations. In these he was fully comforted by Dominic's instruction and preaching. The

same happened to many other novice friars, as he has heard from them. The witness also said that after his conversion he stayed for about a year in the convent of St Nicholas at Bologna with brother Dominic, and enjoyed his close friendship. All the time he was with brother Dominic he said that he heard no evil, harmful or superfluous word from his lips. Dominic was assiduous and diligent in his sermons; so moving were his words that he often stirred himself and his hearers to tears; never has Stephen heard a man whose words so moved the brothers to penitence and tears. It was Dominic's custom to speak always of God or with God whether he was at home, away from home, or on the road. And he urged the friars to do the same, and even laid it down in the constitutions.[1] This he knows, since he saw, was present, heard and lived with him. Dominic was ardent and devout in prayer above all the men he ever saw. He had this custom, as Stephen himself saw, that after compline and the friars' communal prayer, he made them go to the dormitory, but he stayed in the church to pray. As he prayed by night he broke out and was so moved by groans and lamentation that the brothers nearby were woken up, and some of them moved to tears as well. Often he spent the whole night in prayer till mattins; and yet he was on his feet at mattins, passing round both sides of the choir, urging and stirring them on to sing loudly and devoutly. So long did he pray at night that Stephen could not actually remember to have seen him sleeping in a bed during the night, though a place was set apart for him to lie down, where there was just a coverlet spread over a wooden bench without straw or mattress – and Stephen had lived a long time in a convent with him and made frequent and careful inquiry in case he could discover him in bed.

38. He also said that very often he saw him celebrate mass, and always in the canon of the mass he saw his eyes and beard bathed in tears. He celebrated and uttered the Lord's prayer in mass with such devoutness, that those about him could really feel his devotion. He never recalls to have seen him celebrate mass without being moved to tears, as he said before. All this he said he had seen and heard, as he before bore witness. Dominic, he said, was zealous to preserve the Order and the Rule and to comfort the brothers more than any man he ever saw. He can scarcely believe he will ever have a successor to match him in these qualities. Brother Dominic also loved poverty. He very often heard him preaching and urging the brothers to poverty. If ever he or a community of friars was offered possessions, he was unwilling to accept them nor would he permit the friars to accept them. He wished

---

[1] See Doc. 22, Dist. 2, c. XXXI, 2. The phrase which follows is one of many echoes of the opening of the First Epistle of John – 'That which . . . we have heard, which we have seen with our eyes. . .'.

them to have wretched little homes. He himself wore a miserable habit and wretched clothes. When the witness was asked how he knew this, he replied that he often saw him wearing a miserable, short cloak. Nor would he cover his clothes with a cape even in the presence of the great. Since the brothers at St Nicholas had very wretched and tiny cells, brother Rudolf, who was the friars' procurator, began to raise some of the cells an arm's length when brother Dominic was away. But when brother Dominic returned and saw the cells heightened, he began with tears to rebuke brother Rudolf and the other friars again and again, and say to him and to them: 'Do you want to abandon poverty so soon and build great palaces?' And so he ordered them to stop, and the task remained unfinished while he lived. Dominic had loved poverty in himself, and so loved it also in his brothers. He ordered them to use wretched clothes, never to carry money on the road, but everywhere to live on alms. This he had written in his Rule.[1] Dominic was sparing in food and drink. Asked how he knew, the witness replied that he often saw him in refectory, and when the brothers had two dishes or two courses, he was content with one. Almost always while the brothers ate, Dominic bent over the table asleep because he had been up too long and so was very tired; and he ate little and drank little, and sleep used to take a strong grip on him at table.

39. Stephen said that he firmly believed that brother Dominic was a virgin in mind and body to the end of his life. Asked how he comes to this belief, he replied that he heard brother Dominic's confession, and never heard him confess mortal sin. He was patient and joyful in tribulation: asked how he knows, he replied that he saw him when he and the brothers were in real want and poverty in food and clothing, and that he was happy and joyful at the time when he suffered privation. Stephen said that he firmly believed that the grace conferred on the Friars Preachers in the province of Lombardy and in the other provinces too in recent times was granted or at least increased by the prayers and merits of brother Dominic. Asked why he believes so, he answered that from the time when brother John of Vicenza began to preach the heavenly revelation he had had of brother Dominic and to proclaim his life and converse and sanctity to the people, and Stephen himself and other brothers began to prepare for the translation of brother Dominic's body, from that moment an ampler grace appeared and shone with a new clarity, both in the brothers who preached of his life and holiness and in the people who heard them – as appears by the consequence in the cities of Lombardy in which a mighty throng of heretics has been burnt, and more than a hundred thousand men, who

---

[1] See early constitutions, Dist. 1, c. XIX, Dist. 2, cc. XXVI, XXXIV, all but the last quoted in Doc. 22 below.

had been uncertain whether to adhere to the Roman Church or to the heretics, have been converted in their hearts by the preaching of the Friars Preachers to the Catholic faith of the Roman Church. He knows this because those converts now persecute and loath the heretics whom at first they defended. Almost all the cities of Lombardy and the March submit their deeds and statutes to be set in order and amended at the friar's will, to erase, add, subtract and change as they reckon expedient. And they accomplish this too in stopping warfare, and making peace and treaties between them; also in dealing with usury, with the return of goods wrongfully taken, in hearing confessions and many other good deeds too long to recount.

40. The witness also said that he made arrangements for the day and manner of translating Master Dominic's body, and was present at the translation with many brothers, the *podestà* of Bologna and many respected citizens of the city and many of other cities, in whose presence the witness with the other brothers began to dig with iron picks and shovels. They found hard earth, and very strong, tough mortar, in which the sepulchre was enclosed. Lifting the stone which was laid over the sepulchre, they and those standing by savoured such fragrance as he could by no means describe, since it seemed to have the scent of no earthly thing. On account of this fragrance the brothers and all around prostrated themselves with tears, praising and blessing the Lord, who showed in such a marvellous way that his saint would be glorified. They found the wooden coffin in which was hidden the body of brother Dominic, strongly enclosed and bound with iron nails, and when they opened it, there issued a greater fragrance than the first. Then with reverence and devotion the Master [Jordan of Saxony] with a number of brothers took the bones from the old coffin and placed them in the new; and the witness and Master Jordan, and the other brothers, in the presence of the [arch]bishop of Ravenna, of many other bishops and clerks, of the *podestà* of Bologna and many other citizens of Bologna, translated it to the marble sepulchre in which it now rests. For many days after the translation Stephen sensed the presence of that first fragrance on his own hands and on those of the other brothers who had handled the bones of brother Dominic. All this he knows, because he saw it, was present, handled the bones with his hands and afterwards many times sensed the fragrance on his own hands and on the brothers', who had likewise handled and touched the bones.

19. The Foundation Charter of Prouille, 1211

(In *Monumenta Diplomatica S. Dominici*, ed. V. J. Koudelka and R. J Loenertz, *MOPH*, Vol. XXV (Rome, 1966), p. 181). This charter or *notula* survives in its earliest form only in the text printed by Jean de Réchac, *Le vie du glorieux patriarche S. Dominique* . . . (Paris, 1647), pp. 198–9. Prouille was Dominic's first foundation, to provide shelter for his female followers (see Doc. 17, c. 27).

Let it be evident to all present and future who read or hear this charter that the lord Fulk, by God's grace humble minister [i.e. bishop] of the see of Toulouse gave and granted the church of St Mary of Prouille at the request of Dominic of Osma, made on behalf of the ladies converted to the religious life by the preachers appointed to preach against the heretics and put down heresy: that the ladies who live the religious life there at present and in the future may be free of tithes and first fruits, and possess the church free of tax and service.

Given in 1211, in reign of King Philip [II of France].

20. Letters of St Dominic

i. *c.* 1208: The reconciliation of Pontius Roger, a converted heretic (in *Monumenta Diplomatica S. Dominici*, ed. V. J. Koudelka and R. J. Loenertz, *MOPH*, Vol. XXV (Rome, 1966), No. 8, pp. 16–18; see also p. 94).

To all Christ's faithful to whom this letter comes, brother Dominic, canon of Osma, least of preachers, sends greetings in Christ. By the authority of the abbot of Cîteaux, legate of the Holy See [Arnaud-Amaury], who laid this office on us, we reconcile the bearer of this letter, Pontius Roger, by God's kindness converted from the sect of the heretics, enjoining on him by virtue of the oath we have administered to him that on three Sundays or feast days he shall be led by a priest, clad only in breeches, from the entry to the village to the church, while the priest flogs him. We have also enjoined on him to abstain from meat, eggs and cheese, or anything in the nature of flesh at all times, save on Easter day, Whit Sunday and Christmas Day, when we have ordered him to eat meat as a denial of his old error.[1] He shall have three lents a year in which he abstains from fish; three days a week he shall abstain from fish, oil and wine, thus fasting unless bodily sickness or summer toil make dispensation necessary. He shall wear the clothes of a religious in shape and colour, with small crosses sown on the line of each breast. He shall hear Mass daily, if he has the opportunity, and on feast days he shall go to church for vespers. At the other hours, night and day, wherever he is, he shall make offering to God by saying ten Pater nosters seven times a day, twenty in the middle of the night. He shall preserve his chastity utterly and dwell at Tréville. He shall show this document to his chaplain every month. We order the chaplain to take due care and diligence as to his way of life. He shall observe all this diligently, until the legate shows his will to us otherwise on these points. If he scorns to observe it, we order him to be treated as a perjurer, a heretic and excommunicate, and to be cast out from the company of the faithful.

ii. 1215: Licence for an ex-heretic's lodging (in Koudelka (ed.), op. cit., No. 61, pp. 52-3).

[1] I.e. he had been a Cathar, and so refused to eat any meat.

To all Christ's faithful to whom this letter comes, brother Dominic, canon of Osma, humble servant of the preaching,[1] sends greetings and sincere affection in the Lord.

By this letter's authority you may know in your prudence that we have granted to Raymond William of Hauterive(?), glovemaker, licence to have William Hugo, formerly clothed in the habit of a heretic, as Raymond declared in our presence, as a lodger with him in his house at Toulouse, living like other men with him, until the cardinal gives a more precise mandate to him or me; and this shall not bring ill-repute or loss to Raymond William.

iii. 1220: Exhortation to the prioress and convent of nuns at Madrid, and appointment of brother Mames (see p. 171) to take charge of them (Koudelka (ed.), op. cit. No. 125, pp. 126–7).

Brother Dominic, Master of the Preachers, to his dear sisters the prioress and the whole convent of nuns of Madrid, greetings and the hope for their improvement from day to day.

We greatly rejoice and thank God for the fervour of your holy manner of life and that God has freed you from the evil savour of this world. My daughters, fight the old adversary constantly with your fasts, since none will receive the crown who has not truly striven. Since you have had till now no conventual home in which to keep your religious life, now by God's grace you have not the excuse of not having suitable buildings in which the life of religion may be preserved. Henceforth I will have you keep silence in those places where speech is forbidden, the refectory, dormitory and oratory, and that your order of life be kept in all other places. None may go out of the gate and none may enter, save a bishop or some other superior who comes to preach or to visit. Be not sparing in stripes and vigils. Be obedient to your prioress. Have no wish to gossip with one another or waste your time in idle tales.

Since we cannot help you in temporal matters, we do not wish to burden you by giving any of the brothers the power to receive or introduce any women; this shall be for the prioress alone with the counsel of her community.

Moreover we have enjoined our very dear brother [Mames], who has laboured much and attached you to this holy condition, that he makes disposition for you and orders your life in every way as seems expedient to him, so that you may live in holiness and religion. We grant him power to visit and correct you, to remove the prioress, if need be, with the consent of the greater part of the nuns, and we give him licence to make dispensation for you in any way he sees fit. Farewell in Christ.

[1] Dominic was still a canon and his Order had not yet been formed or approved; down to 1215 he was formally seconded from Osma, where he had professed as canon, to Toulouse and its neighbourhood, for 'the preaching'.

21. From Jordan of Saxony's Letters to Sister Diana Dandolo

(ed. A. Walz, *MOPH*, Vol. XXIII (Rome, 1951), as *Beati Iordani de Saxonia Epistulae*. Diana became a nun under Dominic's influence, very much against the wishes of her noble relations.

No. 16

To his very dear daughters in Christ Jesus, the Sisters of St Agnes at Bologna, brother Jordan, unprofitable servant of the Order of Preachers, sends greetings, and every hope of success in achieving the Bridegroom whom they pursue.

Life and toil are brief; the rest is long to which we hasten our steps, dearest of all my daughters. And so we should rejoice and be happy to run the course which we are on, so that the Lord's righteous deeds be to us a song, while we still are on our journey away from the Lord and in the flesh. I write thus to you so that if any feeling of tribulation rises within the spirit of any one of you, she may know how to support it with patience, or rather with joy.

By tribulations we lay up treasure for ourselves in Heaven, so that when the day comes that sorrow is turned to gladness, according to the number of the present sorrows our souls may receive consolations the more to balance them. It happens that the mind itself is purified in the crucible of tribulations and better prepared against the numerous daily wiles of the enemy and amply filled, furthermore, with divine consolation. The sharp pain of tribulation, therefore, is good and to be desired; it works patience, it gives understanding to those in trouble, it tests the mind, which receives increase of spiritual comfort, which lays up a copious treasure and reward for future joy. Thus says the Lord to the afflicted: 'Rejoice in that day and be glad; lo! your reward is great in Heaven. . . .'[1]

I trust in the grace of Jesus Christ, that you walk in all things according to holiness, instant in prayer, taking time for meditation, prompt in obedience, careful in your work, slow to speak, constant in silence, putting on bowels of mercy, kindness, humility, patience, moderation, charity. Whence also I trust in you, that there is no need to dwell over

[1] Matt., 5:12. Jordan's Latin is here, as always, charged with biblical echoes: the next paragraph has reminiscences of James, 1:19, Colossians, 3:12, etc.

long on arguments to persuade you, but rather to give my God thanks always for you in His grace, which was given you in Christ Jesus, the Son of God, your groom, to whom is honour and glory, virtue and power for ever and ever. Amen.

Fare well in Christ Jesus always. I write to you from England before Candlemas in good health. Pray for me without ceasing to the Lord, that He may open His hand to us generously always, and direct His word in our mouth to His honour, to the Church's profit and the growth of the Order. I was then at the schools at Oxford; and the Lord gave us ample hope of a good catch. Ask the Lord often that His will be perfected, especially in those for whom we are hoping, and in others too.

Brother Gerard greets you and recommends himself earnestly to your prayers.

No. 41

For his dearest sister in Christ Diana, dwelling in the house of St Agnes at Bologna, brother Jordan, unprofitable servant of the Order of Preachers, prays for abundance of the delight of heavenly gifts.

There was no time to write to you just now, my dearest friend, as amply as I could wish, but yet I write to you, and send to you, a word, a little word bounded by a manger, made flesh for us – a Word of salvation and grace, a word of sweetness and glory, a good and pleasant word: Christ Jesus, and Him crucified, lifted on the Cross, raised to the right hand of the Father. Raise your soul to Him and within Him: and may you rest in Him for ever, world without end.

Recite this word in your heart, turn it over in your mind; may it turn sweet in your mouth as honey. Think on it, meditate on it; may it stay with you and live with you for ever. And there is another short, small word, your love and your heart, which will speak for me and do satisfaction for me in your heart to your love. May this word be yours too and may it likewise dwell with you for ever!

Farewell, and pray for me.

22. From the Ancient Constitutions of the Order of Friars Preachers

The earliest Dominican constitutions were composed by Dominic himself in 1216, when he established the interior way of life of his communities, with many borrowings from the Premonstratensian constitutions. In 1220–1 he and the General Chapter passed a number more (exactly how many is not known); in 1221 they laid the foundations of the provincial organisation and the provincial and General Chapters. These were considerably expanded early in Jordan of Saxony's régime, and in 1228 the first 'Generalissimum' Chapter passed a substantial tidying up of the whole framework. Subsequent chapters made further changes, so that in the late 1230s a new edition became necessary, which was undertaken by Jordan's successor, the eminent canonist Raymond de Peñaforte, in the years 1238–41.

So much is tolerably clear, and many details of the changes of the 1230s and later are preserved in the Acta of the General Chapters. But the reconstruction of the precise history, clause by clause, of the early constitutions is a delicate matter. It has been most fully and elaborately worked out by Professor Vicaire, whose findings are the basis for the notes given here. But some details are uncertain, and it is particularly difficult to know what early constitutions and arrangements were erased altogether in the changes of the 1220s and 1230s.

What follows is a substantial extract from the constitutions as they survive in a single manuscript written just before Raymond's reform, c. 1238. From all the internal and external evidence, contemporary references, etc., Professor Vicaire has attempted to distinguish the elements and strata. In general, the first Distinction represents Dominic's legislation of 1216, approved by the Pope early in 1217, the Rule of life of the Order, and was often referred to in early days as the Rule – though the word can also refer to the Rule of St Augustine. The second Distinction is mainly the work of Jordan's early chapters; how much represents ideas already mooted in Dominic's day seems to be an insoluble mystery, though a few passages can be definitely attributed to his lifetime.

The best edition of the early constitutions is by H. C. Scheeben, in *Quellen und Forschungen zur Geschichte des Dominikanerordens in*

Deutschland, Vol. XXXVIII (1939), pp. 48–80; French translation in Vicaire (1965), pp. 161–96; full analysis and study in Mandonnet-Vicaire, Vol. II, pp. 203ff., 273ff.; with references to other editions, etc. I have given fuller references and a detailed comparison of the Dominican and Franciscan constitutions in *EFG*, pp. 293ff.

These are the first constitutions of the Order of Friars Preachers, as they were in the time of Master Jordan, who succeeded St Dominic, out of which Brother Raymond de Peñaforte, third Master of the Order, gave form and order to another version of the constitutions, which is now in force.

[Preamble]

In the year of Our Lord's incarnation 1228 there gathered in the house of Saint-Jacques at Paris the twelve priors provincial together with brother Jordan, Master of our Order, and two diffinitors with each prior, chosen by the provincial chapters to accompany him, on whom all the brothers have unanimously conferred their votes and granted full power, so that whatever they establish or abolish, change, add, or take away, should remain firm and stable; nor could anything be changed by any of their chapters which the same priors and diffinitors have ordained to be immutable for all time. The priors and diffinitors called on the Holy Ghost, and then made diligent inquiry, and promulgated with unanimous agreement certain constitutions for the benefit and good name and life and preservation of the Order, and arranged for them to be inserted in their place among the other constitutions. Among the constitutions, furthermore, they willed that some be observed inviolate and immutable for ever; that is, those which lay down that possessions and rents are not on any account to be accepted; that appeals are not allowed; and that it is not possible for the provincial priors to be prejudiced in any particular by the diffinitors nor the diffinitors by the priors when exercising their offices. Certain constitutions they willed to be so far immutable that only in a like chapter, when new reasons, circumstances or affairs appear, could a change be made for the time; that is those which lay down that constitutions can only be made by the approval of three (consecutive) General Chapters, that the friars are not to ride on horseback, not to carry money for their expenses, not to eat flesh save on grounds of illness – allowing, however, that in such matters a superior may lawfully dispense as time and place dictate.

Here begins the customs of the Friars Preachers

Here begins the Prologue

1. The Rule commands us to be of one heart and one mind in the

Lord;[1] and so it is just that we, who live under one rule and the vow
of a single profession, should also vow to be in unison in the observance
of our religious life according to the canons, so that the outward uniformity of our character and life may foster and reveal that unity which
is preserved within and in our hearts. Surely it can be observed more
efficiently and fully and held in our memories if all that must be done is
committed to writing, if all may know by written testimony how they
should live, and if none may lawfully change or add or subtract any
item by their own will; for if we neglect even trivial items, we may in a
small measure decline.

2. Within his convent a superior may have power to dispense for his
brothers any item of observance which seems to him expedient, and
especially any which seem to hinder study or preaching or the health
of souls, since our Order is recognised to have been founded especially
for preaching and the health of souls, and our zeal should be chiefly and
ardently directed to the end that we can be useful to the souls of our
neighbours.

3. Wherefore we have carefully compiled this book, which we call
the Book of customs, to provide for the unity and peace of the whole
Order, and we have divided it into two Distinctions. The first
Distinction comprises: how the brothers are to conduct themselves in
their own convent by day and by night; the conduct of the novices, the
sick, of the brothers at blood-letting; about silence and about faults;
the second Distinction concerns the provincial and General Chapters,
study and preaching. . . .

[The first Distinction opens with chapters on mattins, on the daily
chapter meeting, on keeping women out of convents, on the manner of
saying hours, on refreshment, on fasting.]

VII. On lunch
At a suitable time before lunch or dinner the bell is to be struck a few

[1] The reference is to the Rule of St Augustine (see p. 92) which, like most
medieval monastic or religious Rules, quotes Acts, 4:32. The bulk of the Prologue, and much of what follows, is taken from the customs of the Premonstratensian canons, word for word. Details are noted in Scheeben's edition, and
Vicaire (1965), pp. 162ff., gives the borrowings in italics. The Prologue and the
core of the chapters on mattins, chapter meetings, refreshment, fasting, lunch
(quoted below), other food, collation, compline, sick brothers, novices, postulants, clothes (quoted), shaving, and the bulk of the chapters on faults are
derived from the Premonstratensian constitutions; those on keeping out
women, on the manner of saying hours, some of the instruction to novices, the
sections of XIV–XV quoted below on probation, and the sections on profession and silence are original. Two brief sections on sick brothers were
added in 1236 (see p. 193, n. 1 below).

blows by the sacrist, so that the brothers are not late in coming to the refectory. Then the gong is struck, if the food is ready, but not if it is still being prepared. When they have washed their hands, the prior is to strike the hand-bell in the refectory, and the brothers are then to go in; after they are assembled, the brother who is reciting the versicles shall say 'Benedicite' and the convent concludes the blessing, and eats its meal. Those who are serving the meal shall begin with the most junior, and then go on up to the prior's table. . . .

[Chapters follow on the dishes to be served, on the collation – evening reading and drink – and compline; on beds; on the sick; on blood-letting; on the master of the novices; on receiving recruits, which ends thus.]

XIV. . . .

3. Let none be received under eighteen years of age.[1]

4. In every convent let three suitable brothers be chosen by common consent of the chapter to examine the candidates in character and learning with care, and report on the examination to the prior and chapter, and whether in their judgement they should be received.[2]

XV. On the period of probation

1. We have decreed that the period of probation should be six months or more, as the superior thinks right, so that the postulant may make trial of the Order's austerity and the brothers test his character, save if any older and wiser recruit wishes to renounce the period of probation and offer himself without delay to make profession.

2. Before profession novices shall free themselves from their debts and lay all that they have at the prior's feet, so as to free themselves of all possessions.

3. To none shall sure possession of books be granted, nor shall any be indignant if books are taken from them, whoever takes them or whoever receives custody of them.

[Next follow chapters on the ceremony of profession, on silence, and on giving scandal to a fellow-brother.]

XIX. On clothes

Let our brothers wear clothes of uncarded wool, where this can be obtained; or rough and poor at least, where it cannot; and this should be especially observed in their cloaks. Even the sick may not wear linen next the skin, and linen bandages shall be removed altogether

[1] The Premonstratensians set a lower limit of fifteen.
[2] This seems to be the meaning of a passage not perfectly clear.

from our infirmaries.[1] No brother should have more than three tunics with a sheepskin wrap for winter, or four tunics and no wrap, since the tunic may always be worn hooded. Fur wraps or hoods of any animal's skin our brothers may not wear. A tunic is long enough if it reaches the ankle; cloak and wrap should be shorter. Our breeches are long enough if they cover the knee. Boots we will have and shoes as may be necessary and opportunity permits. We shall not have gaiters or gloves.

[Then chapters on shaving, on faults light, grave, and graver, on the treatment of an apostate, and on the gravest fault.]

Here beings the second Distinction[2]

1. On the provincial chapter

1. We have decreed that every year, in each of the provincial chapters of Spain, Provence, France, Lombardy, the Romagna, Hungary, Germany and England,[3] four of the wiser and more suitable brothers shall be chosen by the provincial chapter by inquiry of the prior provincial and the prior and subprior of the convent where the chapter is held (or by two of them if the third is absent), in the following manner: the three (or two, if one is missing) shall inquire the wishes of each of the brothers separately, by brief discussion within the convent under the eyes of the rest, and they shall note down faithfully and promulgate their findings in writing, immediately and on the spot, before the brothers depart or speak together, and those brothers shall be accepted as diffinitors on whom the majority of the provincial chapter have agreed. If the votes are equal, then by a similar inquiry one brother shall be chosen by the chapter and the brothers he chooses shall be accepted as diffinitors. If there is still a division, another shall be chosen in the same way, and so forth, until a clear majority can be counted. The provincial chapter we reckon to comprise the priors of convents, each with a companion chosen by their own chapter, and the preachers general. The preachers general are those who have been approved as such by the

---

[1] This sentence was added in 1236.

[2] The majority of the extracts from the second Distinction belong to Jordan of Saxony's early chapters, 1222–5. The earliest stratum is of Dominic's time, mostly of 1220: XIII, 2 (where the General Chapter is to be held), XX, XXVI, 1–2, XXVIII, 1, XXIX, XXXI, 2, and the first few words of XXXV, 1 – 'Our brothers shall have modest and humble houses'. Later additions of 1228–36 are: VI, VIII, XIV. These details are shown in different types in Vicaire (1965) (French translation).

[3] These were the eight major provinces, formed in or before 1221, and reasonably accessible to Paris and Bologna; for the four other provinces, making up the total of twelve, see V, 2.

General Chapter or the provincial prior and diffinitors of the provincial chapter. . . . [There follow brief sections on accusation and punishment in provincial chapter.]

II.   On the diffinitors of the provincial chapter
These diffinitors will discuss every topic and bring it to a conclusion in collaboration with the provincial prior. If in their decisions they are equally divided, the opinion of those shall prevail with whom the provincial prior agrees; otherwise the majority shall prevail.

III.   On the powers of the diffinitors
These four diffinitors shall hear and correct any misdeed of the provincial prior which he has confessed or announced in the provincial chapter before the brothers; and they shall enjoin penance on him. If (which Heaven forbid!) he prove obdurate, they shall suspend him from office until the next General Chapter, and the prior of the convent where the chapter is being held shall be set to act in his stead; and they shall report his offence to the General Chapter in writing, under the common seal.

[IV.   Deals with the provincial prior's deputy and the place where the provincial chapter is to be held.]

V.   On the election of the diffinitor of the General Chapter
   1. We have also decreed that in two years out of every three one of the more suitable brothers shall be elected in each of the same eight provinces to be diffinitor of the General Chapter. The provincial prior and diffinitors shall assign him a fitting companion so that, if he dies meanwhile or is otherwise prevented from coming to the General Chapter, his companion shall be as of right accepted for diffinitor in his place.
   2. We have decreed that the four provinces of Jerusalem, Greece, Poland and Denmark shall have diffinitors every year in all general chapters.[1]
   3. In the third year of every three the provincial priors of the twelve provinces shall celebrate the General Chapter.
   4. We have also decreed that the diffinitors of the provincial chapter shall give their prior a companion when he goes to the General Chapter.

VI.   On avoiding prejudice
   1. We have decreed and by virtue of the Holy Ghost and of obedience

---

[1] The discrepancy which appears in this section, especially between cc. 2 and 3, is an example of the ambiguities which do occasionally mar the clarity of these constitutions (see p. 98).

and under sentence of excommunication strictly forbid that the provincial priors make bold to stir anything prejudicial to the diffinitors, or the diffinitors to the priors, by virtue of their work as diffinitors. If any try to do so, we forbid on the same terms that any brother presumes to obey them.

2. To avoid an excessive number of constitutions, we forbid that any be decreed henceforth, unless it has been approved by two chapters running, and then in the third immediately following it can be confirmed or struck out, whether by the provincial priors or by the other diffinitors, wherever that third chapter may be held.

VII.   On the diffinitors of the General Chapter

1. These twelve diffinitors for two out of the three years, and the twelve provincial priors the third year, shall determine, establish and discuss all matters with the Master of the Order.

2. If the Master happens to be absent for any reason, the diffinitors shall proceed in their task none the less. If they are equally divided, the opinion of those shall prevail with whom the Master of the Order agrees; if unequally divided, the opinion of the majority shall be accepted. But if they are equal when the Master's vote has been cast, then one of them shall be elected by the procedure decreed above for the election of provincial diffinitors [d. 2, c. I].

3. If any of them are for any reason prevented from coming to the general chapter, those who are present shall deal with all the business with the Master of the Order. If they are not all of one mind, the procedure given above shall be followed.

VIII.   On the power of the diffinitors

These diffinitors shall have full power to correct any misdeed of the Master of the Order, or to remove him from office altogether, and their sentence in this as in other matters shall be accepted inviolably; from their sentence none may lawfully appeal, and if an appeal is made it shall be reckoned frivolous and null. We absolutely prohibit under pain of excommunication any appeal to be made in our Order; for we have not come to strive, but rather to correct abuses.

IX.   On correcting a misdeed of the Master

1. The diffinitors shall correct and amend any misdeed of the Master after discussion among themselves. . . .

2. When the Master has died or been removed from office the priors of these provinces[1] shall receive full power in all matters until a Master

[1] I.e. of all twelve.

shall be elected, and all the brothers must obey them as they would the Master. . . .

X.   On the election of the Master of the Order

1. The provincial priors of these eight provinces, each with two brothers chosen in the provincial chapter, on whom the rest have devolved the right of electing the Master, shall come to the General Chapter, with the four provincial priors of the additional provinces of Jerusalem, Greece, Poland and Denmark, each with a single companion chosen for the purpose. They shall meet on the Monday after Pentecost and be firmly enclosed in a single conclave by the conventual priors of that province and the brothers present in the convent, where the election is to be made, in such manner that none shall by any means be able to leave it, nor shall any food, by any means, be given them, until the Master of the Order has been elected according to the legal form. . . .[1]

XI.   On the form of the election

This is the form of election: when the electors have been enclosed, if the election proceeds by inquiry or scrutiny the three provincial priors who have worn the habit of our Order longest shall inquire the wishes of all severally and one by one for a space, in the same house under the eyes of all. If grace inspires to a common mind by unanimous agreement, that brother shall be accepted as Master of the Order. If the votes are divided, he shall be Master by force of such an election and of this constitution. . . .[2]

[The rest of the chapter and XII deal with procedural details and sanctions, and other matters concerning the General Chapter.]

XIII.   On the Master's death

1. If the Master happens to die before Michaelmas, the conventual or provincial prior who is nearest the place where he dies, shall hasten to report to the convent at Paris or Bologna, whichever is nearer, and the one which first receives the report must announce it to the rest of the Order, thus: the convent of Paris must as quickly as it can tell the provinces of Spain, Provence, England, Germany, that of Bologna the provinces of Hungary, Romagna and the others it can reach. If he dies after Michaelmas, the Master's death must also be announced so that

---

[1] The enclosure of the electors may well have influenced the development of the papal conclave, first tried out in 1241.

[2] Owing to a change made in the chapter of 1236, the original conclusion of this section is not known.

no General Chapter be held that year, but in the year following it shall be celebrated where it was due the year before.[1]

2. The General Chapter shall be held alternate years at Paris and at Bologna.

XIV.   On avoiding defamation of the Order

By virtue of the Holy Ghost and of obedience we firmly command that no one dare knowingly publish to those outside the Order the cause of a Master's deposition, or his misdeed or correction, or those of a provincial prior, or any chapter's secret or any dissensions by the diffinitors or brothers, from which our Order would be disturbed or put in disrepute. If any contravene this deliberately, he shall be treated as excommunicate, schismatic and a wrecker of our Order, and he shall be wholly separated from intercourse with all brothers and subject to the penalty of a graver fault, until he makes satisfaction. In the same terms we command that none dare work by word or deed in any way to divide our Order; but if any does he shall fall under the same penalty.

[The next chapters deal with the election of provincial priors and their power, with procedure at General Chapter, visitors and their election.]

XX.   Of those fitted for preaching

After this [at General Chapter(?)] there shall be presented those who are thought by some brothers fitted to preach, and who have had licence and command from their own prior, but not yet received the office of preaching from their higher superior or chapter. They shall all be carefully examined one by one by suitable brothers, appointed to deal with this and other inquiries of the chapter, and the brothers with whom they have lived shall be carefully questioned on the grace of preaching which God has granted them, on their zeal, religious life, fervour of charity, purpose and intention; and when they have given their evidence, the brothers appointed will, with the consent and advice of the higher superior, approve whatever they judge the better course: that these brothers should continue still in study, or serve apprenticeship in preaching with older brothers, or are fitted and useful to exercise the office of preaching on their own.

[Next, chapters on questions, or problems concerning observance,

---

[1] I.e. if he dies after Michaelmas, a chapter will be held the next Whitsun solely to elect the new Master General; the following year the next ordinary chapter will be held at Paris or Bologna, whichever is next in turn.

preaching, etc., on celebration of anniversaries, on founding a new convent, on the election of conventual priors, on the subprior.]

XXVI.   That possessions be not received
1. On no account may possessions or rents be received.
2. None of our brothers shall dare insist or request for benefits [or benefices] for his own relations.

[XXVII forbids the brothers to procure chaplaincies, etc., to nuns, or churches to which cure of souls is attached, etc.]

XXVIII.   On the master of the students
1. Special care is to be taken of the students, and so they shall have a brother appointed, without whose licence they shall not engage in copying nor hear lectures. He shall correct whatever in their study seems to need correction, and if it is beyond his strength he shall lay it before the superior. They shall not study the books of pagans and philosophers, except that they may glance over them for an hour; they shall not learn profane sciences nor even the arts which are called liberal, unless for a time the Master of the Order or the General Chapter wishes to dispense otherwise for some brothers; but both young students and others shall read only books of theology.
2. We have decreed that each province must provide for its brothers sent to study to work on three books of theology at least, and the brothers sent to study the *Historia Scholastica* and *Sentences*[1] shall study with particular care both text and glosses.

XXIX.   On the dispensation of students
The superior shall make dispensation for those who are studying, so that an office or other distraction does not easily prevent or hinder them from study. A suitable place shall be appointed, by the judgement of the master of the students, where after disputation or vespers or at some other time when they are free they may meet in his presence to propound problems and questions. When one brother is asking a question or expounding a problem, let the others be silent so as not to hinder the speaker; and if any in a bad way, or a confused way, or loudly or captiously questions, objects or replies and so causes offence, let him be rebuked by whoever is at that moment in charge. Let cells be assigned not to all students but to those for whom their master reckons them expedient. If any is found not profiting from study, his cell shall

---

[1] Two twelfth-century theological classics, the paraphrase of biblical history by Petrus Comestor and the *Sentences* of Peter the Lombard.

be given to another and he set to other duties. They shall be able in their cells to read, write, pray, sleep and even work through the night if they wish, for study's sake.

[XXX concerns proceeding to the doctor's degree and other details of study.]

XXXI. On the preachers

1. We have decreed that no brother be made a preacher general before he has studied theology for three years.

2. After they have studied for one year those from whose preaching no scandal is feared can be admitted to practise it. Those who have shown themselves well prepared to go out preaching shall have companions given them by the prior to suit their character and sustain their good name. They shall receive his blessing and go out wherever they can act well as men who desire their own and others' salvation, and conduct themselves according to their Order, as men of the Gospel, following their Saviour's footsteps, speaking with God, or of God[1] among themselves or with their neighbours, and avoiding involvement in any suspect company. When they go to perform this office of preaching or travel for another purpose they shall neither receive nor carry gold, silver, money and gifts, save only food and clothing, necessary covering and books. Let all who have been appointed to preach or study have no duty or responsibility for managing temporal goods, so that they are able better and more effectively to fulfil the spiritual service enjoined on them; save when there is no one else to attend to their needs, since one should spend a certain time attending to the wants of the present day. They shall take no part in pleas and legal cases except on the business of the faith.

[XXXII–IV concern bishops' licence to preach, avoiding scandal, and conduct while travelling.]

XXXV. On buildings

1. Our brothers shall have modest and humble houses, so that the walls of houses without an upper room shall not exceed twelve feet in height, and of those with an upper room twenty, and the church is not more than thirty feet high; and they are not to have stone vaults except perhaps over choir and sacristy. Any who acts contrary to this shall be subject to the penalty for a graver fault.

[1] See Doc. 18, c. 37, at p. 181, n. 1.

2. In each convent three of the wiser brothers shall be chosen, without whose advice no buildings shall be built.

[XXXVI deals with a number of stray points, XXXVII with the life of the lay brothers, XXXVIII briefly confirms the Dominican liturgical office.]

23. From the Chronicle of Burchard, Prior of Ursberg

(Ed. O. Holder-Egger and B. von Simson (2nd edn, Hannover-Leipzig, 1916: *MGH in usum scholarum*), pp. 107–8; also in Lemmens, *Testimonia Minora* (see no. 7), pp. 17–18.) Burchard was a German Premonstratensian canon, prior of Ursberg in the diocese of Augsburg, who at the end of his chronicle speaks out strongly for the Emperor, Frederick II, against Pope Gregory IX, the friend of Francis and Dominic; so he had no *parti pris* for the Curia and its supporters. His account of the sects gives a valuable impression of how they and the new Orders appeared to a contemporary a little remote from the centres of their activities. His book was finished *c.* 1230 and he probably died soon after. The passage is set under the year 1213, but was probably written in the 1220s.

[1213] About that time, as the world was drawing to its end, two religious orders, the Friars Minor and the Preachers, arose in the Church, whose youth, like the eagle's, was renewed. These two were confirmed by the Holy See. Perhaps the reason they were approved was because of two sects which originated in Italy some time ago and have continued until now, some members of which call themselves Humiliati and some Poor Men of Lyon. Pope Lucius[1] in the past listed them among the heretics, as superstitious dogmas and observances were found in them. They also said things derogatory to the Church of God and the priesthood in their secret sermons, which they frequently held in hidden meeting-places. We saw at that time[2] some of their number, who are called Poor Men of Lyon, with one of their masters, Bernard, I think, at the Holy See, and these petitioned that their sect might be confirmed and privileged by the Holy See. In truth, by their own account, they undertook the way of life of the apostles, wishing to possess nothing and to have no settled home, travelling about through the villages and towns. But the lord Pope [Innocent III] took exception to them as there were some superstitious elements in their way of life: they cut off their shoes above their feet and walked as it were barefoot;

[1] Lucius III, 1184, included 'those who call themselves falsely Humiliati or Poor Men of Lyon' in his condemnation: see pp. 78–9.
[2] *C.* 1210; on Bernard Prim, see p. 86.

also, while they wore a kind of hood as if they were members of a religious order, they did not shave the hair of their head other than in the way laymen do. This also seemed reprehensible in them, that men and women walked together along the road and often lodged in the same house, and it was said of them that they sometimes slept together in bed; yet they asserted that all they did was derived from the apostles. However the lord Pope confirmed certain others, who arose in place of these. They called themselves Poor Minors. They spurned the superstitions and shameful practices I have mentioned, but actually walked with bare feet both summer and winter, and accepted no money or anything else whatsoever except food, and sometimes necessary clothing when it was offered to them unsolicited; for they would not ask anything of anyone. But later, considering that, notwithstanding their very great humility, the name was a boastful one, and that, as many bore the name of poverty in error, it would be vanity to glory in this before God, these men preferred to be called Friars Minor rather than Poor Minors, being obedient to the Holy See in all things.

Others, the Preachers that is, are believed to have come in place of the Humiliati. The Humiliati, indeed, having no authority or licence from the hierarchy, put the sickle in a harvest not their own,[1] preaching to the people and frequently taking it upon themselves to direct their lives, hearing confessions and disparaging the ministrations of the priests. Wishing to correct all this, the lord Pope instituted and confirmed the Order of Preachers. The former certainly, ignorant and uneducated though they were, applied themselves to manual work and to preaching, receiving the necessities of life from their adherents. The latter applied themselves constantly to study and the reading of Holy Scripture, working at the transcription of books and diligently attending the lectures of their masters, that with bow and arrows and all the shields of mighty men[2] they might stand fast and engage in the defence of holy mother Church, and go up into the breaches and make themselves a wall for the house of Israel.[3] Thus they strengthen faith, encourage and strengthen good and virtuous conduct, teach and commend the rulings of the Church, correct and reprove the vices and failings of men. Above all, these men obey in all things the Holy See, from whom they draw especial authority.

[1] Cf. Mark, 4:29.
[2] Cf. Song of Solomon, 4:4.
[3] Cf. Ezekiel, 13:5.

24. From the Letters of Jacques de Vitry, Bishop of Acre

(See *Lettres de Jacques de Vitry*, ed. R. B. C. Huygens (Leiden, 1960), intro. and Epistolae I, VI, pp. 75–6, 131–3; also in L. Lemmens, *Testimonia Minora* (see no. 7), pp. 79–80; G. Golubovich, *Biblioteca bio-bibliografica della Terra Santa e dell'oriente francescano*, Vol. I (Quaracchi, 1906), pp. 2–8 (but Lemmens and Golubovich print a different text: see p. 204, n. 2.) Jacques de Vitry was an able and devoted French secular clerk, who became bishop of Acre in 1216 (1216–28), and later Cardinal-bishop of Frascati (1229–40). He may have met Francis when he was at the Curia at Perugia in 1216 for his consecration by Pope Honorius III to the frontier see of Acre, and certainly met him when Francis was visiting the Fifth Crusade and the Sultan in 1219–20. He is a vivid witness to the impact of the saint and of his Order in early days.

A.

[Huygens, op. cit., pp. 75–6. Written from Genoa in October 1216, just after his consecration, waiting for a ship to take him to Acre. See Huygens, op. cit. p. 52.]

I found one comfort in those regions [i.e. in Perugia]. Many there were, men and women, rich and worldly, who have left all for Christ, fled the world, and were now called Friars Minor and Minor Sisters. They are held in great respect by Pope and cardinals. They pay no attention to worldly matters, however, but with fervent desire and earnest zeal labour every day to rescue perishing souls from the vanities of the world and take them with them into their community. Already by God's grace they have secured a large harvest and won many – so that he who hears them may say, 'Come! – and let the curtain pull the curtain.'[1] They live according to the pattern of the primitive Church, of whose members it was written: 'The multitude of the believers were of one heart and one mind.'[2] By day they go into cities and villages, winning whom they may by helping where they can; by night they return to their hermitage or the lonely places in which they pass their time in contemplation. The women live together in various hostels

[1] Or 'Let the kettle mind itself' – evidently a proverbial saying, whose origin is not known. [2] Acts, 4:32 (see Doc. 22, p. 191, n. 1).

near the cities, receive no gifts, but live by the work of their hands. They are much grieved and distressed because they are honoured by clergy and laymen more than they wish. The men of the Order meet once a year at a place determined with much profit, to rejoice and make merry in the Lord; with the advice of good men they make and publish their holy regulations and have them confirmed by the Pope.[1] After this for the whole year they are dispersed through Lombardy and Tuscany, Apulia and Sicily. Brother Nicholas, the Pope's *provincialis*, a holy and religious man, had lately left the Curia and fled to them, but because the Pope had particular need of him, he has been called back. I believe that in reproof of prelates who are dumb dogs who cannot bark, the Lord wishes to save many souls before the world's end by this kind of simple, poor man.

B.

[Huygens, op. cit., pp. 131–3: a postscript to Epistola VI missing in some MSS. Written from Damietta in Spring 1220: Huygens, op. cit., p. 54.]

... Reiner, prior of St Michael [Acre], has given himself to the Order of Friars Minor; this Order is growing mightily through the whole world, since it precisely imitates the pattern of the primitive Church and the life of the apostles in every detail. But it seems to us very dangerous in that not only perfect souls, but young men and far from perfect, who ought to be enclosed and proved for some time under conventual discipline are sent out two by two through the whole world.[2] Their Master, who established that Order, when he came to our army, was afire with the zeal of faith, and not afraid to go to the army of our enemies. When he had preached the word of the Lord for some days to the Saracens, he profited little, yet the Sultan, the King of Egypt, sent and asked him secretly to pray to the Lord for him, that he should be divinely inspired to follow the religion which pleased God the more. Colin the Englishman, our clerk, has joined the same Order, and two others of our company, Master Michael and Matthew, to whom I had committed the care of the church of Holy Cross; I am only just holding on to the precentor and Henry and others. . . .

[1] This is not quite right: see pp. 123; *EFG*, Chap. 9.

[2] This whole passage is a kind of postscript, evidently authentic (as Professor Huygens argues), but not present in all surviving manuscripts. In some it appears in a different version, perhaps due to revision after Francis's fame had grown and spread: this whole sentence, stressing the danger of the Order's basic principle, is omitted, and the next sentence starts: 'The Master of the friars is called brother Francis, and he is so lovable that he is revered by all men'. These differences illustrate how hazardous can be the interpretation of even the most authentic contemporary letters, unless we can be sure that their texts were not later revised.

25. From Jordan of Giano, *Chronica Fratris Jordani*

(Ed. H. Boehmer (Paris, 1908), pp. 1–53.) This account, composed in 1262 by an Italian friar who helped to plant the Order in Germany, is one of the best of the early Franciscan chronicles, simple, yet given to delightful irony – especially in the autobiographical passages (cc. 18, 59 – see p. 109).

Prologue

Brother Jordan of Giano in the valley of Spoleto to the Friars Minor living throughout Germany: may you in this life persevere in all good, and in the future be with Christ in eternal glory.

At different times I have related something of the conduct and life of the first friars sent into Germany, and since many of the friars listening have been edified, I have frequently been asked and by many to write down what I have told, and other things that I can recall to memory, and to note the years in which brothers were sent to Germany and in which years this and that happened. Because therefore, as the Bible says: 'stubbornness is as the sin of witchcraft, and disobedience is as iniquity and idolatry',[1] I have agreed to satisfy the brothers' pious wish, more especially as brother Baldwin of Brandenburg has urged me to do so, and both of his own free will and on the order of brother Bartholomew, then minister of Saxony, he has offered to do the writing.

So, in the year 1262, after the chapter held on the Third Sunday after Easter at Halberstadt, we remained behind in the place where the chapter had met; and I talked and Baldwin wrote, so as to satisfy the brothers' desire as I had agreed. I only wish that I may do it well. . . . On the actual dates, if anywhere I have made a mistake through forgetfulness, as I am now old and feeble, I crave the reader's indulgence, asking that wherever he may find me mistaken he will charitably correct and emend. . . .[2]

1. A.D. 1207 Francis, a merchant by trade, was pricked to the heart with remorse and felt the breath of the Holy Spirit and began to do penance, wearing the dress of a hermit. . . .

---

[1] I Samuel (I Kings), 15:23.
[2] Where Jordan's statements can be checked, they appear extremely accurate. See Boehmer's introduction, pp. lxxff.; *EFG*, pp. 20–7.

2. A.D. 1209, the third year of his conversion, after he had heard in the Gospel what Christ said to his disciples when he sent them out to preach, Francis at once discarded his staff and wallet and shoes. He changed his dress, assuming the one the brothers now wear, and became an imitator of evangelical poverty and a sedulous preacher of the Gospel.

3. A.D. 1219, the tenth year of his conversion, at a chapter held at St Mary of the Portiuncula, brother Francis sent brothers into France, Germany, Hungary, Spain and to other provinces of Italy that the brothers had not yet penetrated.

4. The brothers who went into France, being asked whether they were Albigenses, replied that they were, not understanding what was meant by Albigenses and not knowing that such people were heretics. Thus they were reckoned to be heretics. The bishop, however, and the Masters of Paris read their Rule, and seeing that it was based on the Gospel and catholic they consulted Pope Honorius on the matter. He made it clear in his letter that their Rule had genuine authority, since it had been confirmed by the Holy See,[1] and that the brothers were favoured sons of the Roman Church and true catholics. So they were freed from the suspicion of heresy.

5. John of Penna with about sixty or more brothers was sent to Germany. When they entered German territory and were asked in a language they did not understand whether they desired hospitality, or food, or something of the kind, they answered 'Ja' and found that they were kindly received. Seeing that this word 'Ja' procured them such good treatment they decided they ought to use it in reply to every question. Thus it happened that they were asked whether they were heretics and whether they had come expressly to infect Germany as they had perverted Lombardy, and they replied 'Ja'. Some of them were beaten, some imprisoned, some were stripped and led naked into the ring to be made a spectacle and to be mocked at by men. So the brothers saw that they could not achieve any success in Germany and returned to Italy. In the light of their experiences Germany was reputed so cruel by the brothers that none would dare to return there unless inspired by the desire for martyrdom. . . .

7. Of the brothers who went into Spain, five were crowned with martyrdom [in Morocco], though whether these five were sent out at that same chapter, or at the preceding one, when brother Elias and his companions were sent overseas, I am not sure.

8. When the record of the lives of these martyred friars was brought

---

[1] Their way of life was confirmed for the benefit of the French province in Honorius III's bull *Pro dilectis filiis* of 29 May 1220; Sbaralea, I, 5, Honorius III, No. 4; Eubel, *Epitome*, No. 4.

to St Francis he heard that he was receiving credit in it, and saw that his brothers were taking pride in their sufferings. St Francis himself had the greatest contempt and scorn for praise and glory.[1] He rejected the book and forbade it to be read, saying: 'Let each man glory in his own sufferings and not in another's' . . . .

[10. St Francis went to preach to the Sultan.]

11. St Francis crossed the sea with blessed Peter Cathanii, a jurist learned in the law, and left two vicars, brother Matthew of Narni and brother Gregory of Naples. He set Matthew at St Mary of the Portiuncula, to stay there and receive recruits to the Order; and instructed Gregory to tour Italy and comfort the brothers. Now according to the first Rule the friars fasted every Wednesday and Friday and by St Francis's permission on Monday and Saturday too, but on every day they might they ate flesh. But the vicars and some of the older brothers held a chapter, in which they decided that the friars should not make use of meat they had obtained on meat days, but only eat meat when freely offered by the faithful. They laid it down, furthermore, that they should fast on Mondays as well as the other two days, and on Mondays and Saturdays should not obtain milk foods but should abstain from them unless they were offered by the devout faithful.

12. One of the lay brothers was roused by the constitutions, since they had dared to add something to the holy father's Rule; and he took a copy of them with him and sailed without the vicars' leave. When he reached St Francis he first confessed his fault and asked his pardon for coming to him without leave; and he explained that he had been compelled to do so because the vicars Francis had left had dared to add new laws to his Rule. He added that the Order throughout the whole of Italy was upset both by the vicars and by other brothers presuming to try out new ideas. The constitutions were read when St Francis was sitting at table with meat dishes in front of him ready prepared for his meal; and he said to brother Peter: 'My lord Peter, what shall we do?' And he replied: 'Ha, lord Francis, what you will, since you have the authority.' Because brother Peter was educated and noble, St Francis in his humorous way honoured him by calling him lord, and in return he humiliated himself before his spiritual father and showed a like devout respect. And they showed the same reverence for one another overseas and in Italy. Finally St Francis said: 'Let us eat as the Gospel says whatever is put before us.'

[1] Cf. Francis's Sixth Admonition, *Opuscula*, pp. 9–10. The evidence of the admonition and Jordan here confirm each other. The words 'he was receiving' could be translated 'they were receiving' – the Latin is ambiguous.

[13. A prophetess told him to return; and Jordan gives an account of how brother Philip obtained privileges in the Curia for the poor Clares and brother John established what was virtually a new order.]

14. St Francis took with him brother Elias, brother Peter Cathanii and brother Cesarius, whom brother Elias minister of Syria had received . . . and other brothers, and returned to Italy. Once there, when he had fully grasped the causes of the troubles, he went, not to the trouble-makers, but to Pope Honorius. The humble father sat at the Pope's gate, not daring to beat noisily on the chamber door of so great a prince, but waiting long and patiently for him to come out of his own will. When he came, St Francis bowed before him reverently and said: 'Father Pope, God give you peace.' But he replied: 'God bless you, my son.' And St Francis: 'My lord, since you are a great lord and often occupied with much business, poor men often cannot approach you nor speak with you, as frequently as they have need. You have given me many Popes. Give me one, to whom I can speak when I have need, who may hear and discuss on your behalf my problems and my Order's.' 'Whom do you wish me to give you, my son?' the Pope replied. 'The lord bishop of Ostia'. And he granted his request. So when St Francis had explained the grounds of his trouble to the bishop of Ostia, his Pope, he instantly recalled brother Philip's letter and brother John and his followers were expelled from the Curia with contumely.

15. And so the trouble-makers, with God's help, were suddenly quietened and he reformed the Order according to his own decisions. . . . [Brother Cesarius is appointed by Francis to help him deck out the Rule with the words of the Gospel, and Francis holds a General Chapter at the Portiuncula.]

16. A.D. 1221 . . . 17. When the chapter was over St Francis remembered that the spread of the Order had not reached Germany. As he was a sick man by this time, brother Elias[1] gave out whatever he wished to say to the chapter. St Francis was sitting at Elias's feet and plucked his tunic. Elias lent down and listened to what he wanted, and then, rising, said: 'Brothers, the brother says this. . . . Because those who had been sent to Germany earlier had been badly treated he would not compel any to go . . . but if there were any who would like to go, they were to rise and stand over to one side.' About ninety friars, inflamed with the desire for martyrdom, arose, offering themselves for death, and, as they had been ordered, they stood apart, awaiting the decision

---

[1] On Elias, Francis's vicar – or, as the saint himself preferred, Minister General – in Francis's last years, and subsequently Minister General from 1232 till his deposition in 1239, see *EFG*.

as to who, and how many, and when and in what manner they should go.

18. There was at that time in the chapter a brother who was in the habit of beseeching God in his prayers that his faith might not be corrupted by the heretics of Lombardy nor turned by the ferocity of the Germans and that from each of these perils the Lord in his mercy would deign to deliver him. When he saw many brothers rise prepared to go to Germany he reckoned that they would at once be martyred by the Germans. Regretting that he had not known by name the friars sent to Spain and martyred there and wanting to insure that the same did not happen in this case, he rose and went to them, going to each in turn and asking: 'Who are you and where are you from?' He thought it would be splendid to be able to say, if they happened to be martyred: 'him I knew, and him I knew.' Among them was a brother called Palmerius, a deacon, who was afterwards made guardian of Magdeburg. He came from Monte Gargano in Apulia and was a jolly, playful man. When that inquisitive brother had come to him and asked him: 'Who are you and what is your name?' and he had replied: 'I am Palmerius', he caught hold of him and said: 'And you yourself are one of us and will come with us' wishing to take him with them to the Germans – though he had besought God so many times that he would send him anywhere he liked but not to them. Shuddering at the very name of the Germans he replied: 'I am not one of you. I came to you wanting to know who you were, not with any intention of going with you.' But with a laugh Palmerius succeeded in detaining him; and he pulled him, resisting and expostulating, to the ground and forced him to sit with him among the others. While this was going on and that inquisitive friar was thus detained, he was assigned to another province. . . . Those ninety friars were still awaiting a decision and a German friar, Cesarius, a native of Speyer, was made minister of Germany with the power to choose from among those ninety whom he wished. When he found that inquisitive brother among the group his companions advised Cesarius that he should take him with him. As he did not want to go to the Germans and constantly repeated: 'I am not one of you, because I did not get up with the intention of going with you', he was taken to brother Elias. The brothers of the province to which he had been assigned, hearing this, and knowing that he was not strong and that the country to which he was going was cold, sought to retain him. Brother Cesarius sought by all means to take him with him. Brother Elias broke off the dispute, saying: 'I order you, brother, on holy obedience, to decide finally whether you want to go or not.' Thus constrained by obedience, he was in doubt what to do. He feared to choose, being conscious that in choosing he would seem to prefer his own will. He was afraid to go

as the Germans were cruel, and if he was called upon to suffer his endurance might be destroyed and his soul endangered. Perplexed, and not finding counsel in himself, he went to a brother who had sustained many trials – he had been deprived even of his breeches fifteen times in Hungary[1] – and asked his advice. 'My dear brother, this is what I have been ordered, and I fear to choose and I do not know what to do.' He said: 'Go to brother Elias and say: "Brother, I have no wish to go or to stay, but whichever you command me, that will I do." In this way you will be freed from this perplexity.' That is what he did. Brother Elias ordered him, on holy obedience, to hasten with brother Cesarius to Germany. This man is brother Jordan of Giano, who is writing this for you, who in this manner came to Germany. He escaped the ferocity of the Germans that terrified him and with brother Cesarius and the other friars originally established the Order of Minors in Germany. . . .

21. . . . Beyond Brixen they climbed up into the mountains[2] and came to Sterzing after lunch. As men did not offer bread to them and the brothers did not know [enough German] to beg, they hoped that later in the day they would find a place where human kindness would refresh them, and so came to Mittenwald. There in great penury, after two mouthfuls of bread and seven turnips, they tempered or rather challenged the pain of their miserable hunger and thirst with a joyous heart. . . . In the morning they rose famished and empty and resumed their journey. When they had gone half a mile their eyes began to close, their legs to give way, their knees to tremble from fasting and their whole bodies to collapse. In the extremity of their hunger they gathered all kinds of berries from the thorns and various trees and shrubs they found by the way. Because it was Friday they feared to break their fast, but they felt somewhat heartened at carrying the fruits of various trees and bushes so that if they were forced by extreme necessity they had something they could eat. In this way, now resting, now going slowly forward, they came with difficulty to Matrei. There God, to whom the poor has committed himself,[3] was moved to provide for his poor. As they entered the town they met two generous men who bought for them two pennyworth of bread. But what is that among so many ?[4] Because it was then the season for turnips, they begged turnips, that when the bread ran out they could supplement it with turnips.

[1] There is an account of the first mission to Hungary in Jordan of Giano, pp. 6–7.

[2] They went through the Brenner Pass. Mittenwald (below) must be a slip, since the only possible places of the name are on a later stage of the route.

[3] Cf. Psalm 9 (10):14.

[4] John, 6:9. They followed the old Roman route from the Brenner Pass to Augsburg.

22. After the meal, filled rather than restored, they went on their way and, passing by villages and towns and monasteries, arrived at Augsburg. There they were most kindly received by the bishop, and by his nephew, who was a canon of the cathedral and *vicedominus*. . . .

26. In 1222 brother Cesarius . . . held his first provincial chapter in Worms.

. . . 27. The brothers who were in Salzburg had not come to this chapter and Cesarius sent two friars to them with a letter telling them to come to him if they so wished. They, however, set the highest value on living under obedience, so that they did not wish to do anything of their own volition. Not a little disturbed at this condition in the letter, that they were to come if they wished, they said: 'We had better go and ask him why he has written to us in this way, as we do not wish anything other than what he wishes.' On their way they came to a town where they hoped to eat, and begging in couples through the streets they received the reply in German: '*God berad*', which means: 'May God help you', or rather, 'May God provide for you'. One of them, seeing that with this reply they received nothing, thought and even said: 'This "*God berad*" will be the death of us today.' Hastening on ahead, this brother, who had been begging in German, began to beg in Latin. The Germans replied: 'We do not understand Latin. Speak to us in German.' The brother, mispronouncing it said: '*Nicht diudisch!*' which means: 'Understand that I know no German.' Then he added in German: '*Brot durch Got.*' They said: 'It is wonderful that you speak German when you say you do not know any', and they added: '*Got berat*'. The brother, exulting in spirit and smiling and pretending he did not understand what they said, sat down on a bench. The man and his wife looked at each other, amused at his impudence, and gave him bread, eggs and milk. Seeing that this play-acting could be useful in relieving their necessity he went in this fashion to twelve houses and begged enough for the seven of them. . . .

41. In 1225 . . . 43. On the advice of Henry, rector of St Bartholomew, Gunther, the *vicedominus*, and other burghers of Erfurt, the friars moved to the church of the Holy Spirit, which had formerly belonged to a house of Augustinian nuns but was then deserted and stayed there for fully six years. The man whom the burghers had assigned to the friars as procurator asked brother Jordan if he would like the building in the shape of a cloister. As he had never seen a cloister in the Order, he replied: 'I do not know what a cloister may be. Just build us a house near the water so that it will be convenient for us to go down to it to wash our feet.' And so it was done. . . .

50. On 4 October, 1226, the blessed father Francis, the first founder of the Order of Friars Minor, died at St Mary of the Portiuncula. He

had wanted to be buried in this church, but the people of the region
and the citizens of Assisi, fearing that the Perugians might carry him
off by violence, on account of the miracles which God thought fit to
work through him both in life and after death, transferred him to the
church of St George, near the walls of Assisi, and laid him there with
honour. It was in this church that Francis had first learned to read and,
later, he first preached.[1] When St Francis died, his vicar, brother Elias,
sent letters throughout the entire Order to comfort the brothers who
were grieved over the death of their great father. He announced to each
and all that he blessed them all on behalf of St Francis, as Francis
himself had commanded, and absolved them all from their sins. He
told them moreover about the stigmata and other miracles which the
Most High had condescended to perform for St Francis after his death;
and also ordered the ministers and custodians of the Order to assemble
to elect a Minister General. . . .[2]

57. A.D. 1230 . . . 58. Brother Jordan was deputed to go with a
companion to the Minister General to ask him to appoint a minister and
a lector for Saxony. . . .

59. When he was returning to Germany brother Jordan called on
brother Thomas of Celano,[3] who was delighted to see him and gave
him some relics of St Francis. When Jordan reached Würzburg he sent
word to the brothers of his custody that if they needed to contact him
they were to meet him in Eisenach as he was going that way. Delighted,
the brothers gathered at the convent there and gave orders to the porter
that when Jordan arrived he was not to admit him but was first to let
them know. When Jordan came to the door and knocked he was not
admitted, but the porter hurried to the friars with the news that he
was at the door. They instructed him not to let him in by the door, but
through the church. The friars, exulting in spirit, went into the choir
and entered the nave in procession, two by two, bearing crosses and
censer and palm branches and lighted candles in their hands. When
they were all drawn up in line they opened the doors of the church to
admit Jordan, welcoming him with joy and gladness, and singing the
antiphon: 'This is he who loves his brothers.' Astonished at this novel
reception, Jordan held up his hand for them to be quiet, but they
finished with joy what they had begun. As Jordan in amazement
wondered at this, it came into his mind that he had with him relics of
St Francis, which in his astonishment he had forgotten. When the
chant was finished he said, rejoicing in spirit: 'Rejoice, brothers, for I

[1] Now in the precinct of Sta Chiara.
[2] A surviving copy of this letter, addressed to the provincial minister of
France, is printed by E. Lempp, *Frère Elie de Cortone* (Paris, 1901), pp. 70–1.
[3] The biographer of St Francis.

know that it is not me for myself, but our blessed father Francis in me, that you are praising. I have his relics with me and without my saying anything his presence roused your spirits to his praise.' Taking the relics from his breast, he placed them on the altar. Jordan had seen St Francis while he was alive and so had the impression that he was somehow human; but from then onwards he held him in greater reverence and honour, as he saw that God had inflamed the hearts of the brothers through his Holy Spirit, not wishing the relics to be concealed. . . .

26. From Matthew Paris, *Chronica Maiora*

Matthew Paris was the most remarkable and prolific of the monk-historians of St Albans of the thirteenth century; a man of many talents, historian, hagiographer, draughtsman, artist and calligrapher; not an accurate historian, for he cared more for airing his prejudices than for historical accuracy, but a marvellous index to the prejudices and attitudes of well-informed Englishmen of the mid-thirteenth century – so long as we do not make the mistake of supposing that all his contemporaries had views so strongly held and eccentrically expressed as his. This passage was probably written in the late 1230s, and shows how quickly the new Order of Friars Minor had aroused the jealousy of a member of one of the old Benedictine houses. On Matthew, see R. Vaughan, *Matthew Paris* (Cambridge, 1958); this passage is from *Chronica Maiora*, ed. H. R. Luard (Rolls Series, London, 1876), Vol. 3, pp. 332–4; I have used the translation by J. A. Giles, *Matthew Paris's English History*, Vol. 1 (edn. of 1889), pp. 5–6, slightly corrected.

The insolence of the Minors

At this time some of the Friars Minor, as well as some of the Order of Preachers, unmindful of their profession and the restrictions of their order, impudently entered the territories of some noble monasteries, under pretence of fulfilling their duties of preaching, as if intending to depart after preaching the next day. Under pretence of sickness or on some other pretext, however, they remained, and, constructing an altar of wood, they placed on it a consecrated stone altar, which they had brought with them, and clandestinely and in a low voice performed mass, and even received the confessions of many of the parishioners, to the prejudice of the priests. And they said that they had obtained authority from the Pope to receive from those of the faith the confessions which they were ashamed to make to their own priests, or scorned to make, because the priests had committed the same offence, or were afraid to do so because the priest was drunk; and to such they, the Minors, gave absolution after having enjoined penance on them. In the meantime they sent a proctor to the Roman court with all speed, to plead their cause against the religious men, in whose territory they were staying, and obtained permission to remain there with some other benefit in addition. And if by chance they were not satisfied with this, they broke forth in insults and threats, reviling every order except their own, and asserting that all the rest were amongst those doomed to damnation, and that they would not spare the soles of their feet till they had exhausted the wealth of their opposers, however great it might be. The religious men therefore gave way to them in many points, yielding to avoid scandal and offending those in power. For they were the counsellors and messengers of the nobles, and even secretaries of the Pope, and therefore obtained much secular favour. Some, however, finding themselves opposed at the court of Rome, were restrained by opposition, and went away in confusion; for the supreme pontiff with a scowling look said to them, 'What means this, my brethren? To what lengths are you going? Have you not professed voluntary poverty, and that you would traverse villages and towns and distant places, as the case required, barefooted and unostentatiously, in order to preach the word of God in all humility? And do you now presume to usurp these estates to yourselves against the will of the lords of these fees? Your religion appears to be in a great measure dying away, and your doctrine to be confuted.' On hearing this they went away and began to conduct themselves more moderately, though they had formerly talked so boastingly, and refused to be guided by the will of others, although they were in houses not their own. . . .

Where names occur both in text and notes, only page numbers are normally given; where in notes only, 'n.' is given. 'Bro.' = brother; O.F.M. = Order of Friars Minor (Franciscan); O.P. = Order of Friars Preachers (Dominican).